FOOD SECURITY SYSTEM OF INDIA

About the Author

DR. K.C.S. ACHARYA (*b.* 1930), received his early education at Bharatpur (Rajasthan). In 1949 he joined Allahabad University where, after a meritorious academic career, he successfully competed in the All-India competition for the Indian Administrative Service which he joined in 1954 in the cadre of Madhya Pradesh. In the Service he has worked at various levels starting from the grass-root Tehsil level to the District and Divisional levels, interspersed with Secretariat assignments both in the State as well as in the Central Government. In the State Government he held important charge at the policy and decision making level in the Revenue, Irrigation, Power, Food and Tribal Development Departments and gained rich experience. In 1978 he moved to the Central Government and is at present holding the office of the Additional Secretary to the Government of India in the Ministry of Agriculture. Throughout his career, Dr. Acharya has been a development minded civil servant.

In his official capacity he has travelled widely and has represented India at a number of international conferences.

FOOD SECURITY SYSTEM OF INDIA

EVOLUTION OF THE BUFFER STOCKING POLICY AND ITS EVALUATION

K.C.S. ACHARYA

CONCEPT PUBLISHING COMPANY PVT. LTD.
NEW DELHI-110059

This book is based on the dissertation which was approved by the Bhopal Univerity for the award of the Ph.D degree in 1981.

ISBN: 978-93-5594-555-6

First Edition 1983

Published and Printed by

Concept
Since 1974

Concept Publishing Company Pvt. Ltd.
A/15-16, Commercial Block, Mohan Garden,
New Delhi-110059 (India)
T: 91-11-41101460
E: publishing@conceptpub.com, *W*: www.conceptpub.com

TO

MR. H.S. KAMATH

FORMERLY OF THE INDIAN CIVIL SERVICE
AND CHIEF SECRETARY TO GOVERNMENT, MADHYA PRADESH
IN WHOM I FOUND A
PERFECT EXAMPLE OF 'KARMA YOGI'
AN EPITOME OF THE
FINEST HUMAN VIRTUES

AND

A LIVING EMBODIMENT OF THAT RARE HERITAGE—

"THE C.P. TRADITION"

WHO AS A MEMBER OF THE 1943 FOODGRAINS POLICY COMMITTEE
IS ONE OF THE FOUNDING ARCHITECTS OF THE
COUNTRY'S FOOD POLICY,
THIS WORK IS
DEDICATED

BY

THE AUTHOR

Foreword

FOOD is basic to human existence, and has therefore always received the foremost attention of mankind, through development of land and agricultural practices. But systematic food management as a conscious effort on the part of the Governments—in the national and international fields—got a fillip only after the Second World War. Food security has now been internationally accepted as the primary goal of the world. In India, food management-policy and application, assumed importance after the great Bengal Famine of 1943, and took shape during the post-war years. Over the years, food policy has been evolved by the Government not only to foster and sustain production in the context of meeting the needs of increasing population, but also to manage situations of substantial surplus production. The food policy and management have been envisaged as an integrated approach with main emphasis on three interrelated aspects, viz. ensuring minimum remunerative support price for the producer, field-oriented agricultural research and infra-structure development, and foodgrains buffer stock policy coupled with well spread out public distribution system. While the basic strategy of food policy evolved by the Government of India over the years, has proved successful, food management which in its wide connotation covers production, storage, consumption and nutrition, remains a dynamic concept being tactically adapted to changing situations from time to time.

Dr. K.C.S. Acharya, a distinguished member of the Indian Administrative Service, has gained rich experience not only in the field in all its practical aspects during his service in the districts of Madhya Pradesh but also at the policy level during his work in the Food Departments in the State and the Centre. He has imbibed the balanced and sensitive approach, required of a Food Administrator. He is steeped in the experience of the forerunners in this field, at the same time having a sight for the future. He has taken up this deep and penetrating study in his spare time as "love's labour" as mentioned by him, because of his abiding interest in this subject and he deserves credit and thanks for his endeavour. I have no doubt that the study which has deservedly earned him a doctorate degree will prove of immense value to all interested in this fascinating subject, and serve as not only an inspiration to other members of the Administrative Service, but also a valuable reference point and guide for all students of the subject.

(B. C. Gangopadhyay)
Secretary to Government of India

Department of Food
New Delhi-110001

17 May 1983

Preface

FOOD administration in India has had its origin in situations of acute shortages. The dreadful Bengal Famine of 1942-43, accompanied by aggravating circumstances engendered by World War II led to the creation of the Food Department (December 1942) at the Centre. Soon followed a whole corpus of control orders, covering procurement, distribution, and movement of foodgrains (and also some essential commodities like salt and *gur*) which were applied, with appropriate modifications and adaptations to suit local conditions throughout India, including the princely states. In July 1943 the Central Government appointed the Foodgrains Policy Committee presided over by Mr. H.D. Vigor, OBE, which, for the first time in the history of Indian administration, prepared a scientific and cogently reasoned charter for food administration.

So much for the origin. But it would be erroneous to imagine that food administration is relevant to situations of scarcities and famines alone. Today, food administration is as much a dimension of surpluses as it was of scarcities in the forties and fifties. The problems thrown up by the Green Revolution that overtook this country in the sixties demand in a much more exacting manner a policy frame and a system of food management than did the scarcities and famines. The sea change in the scenario of Indian Food economy from the times of famines of the horrifying magnitude of 1630 or 1866, the metamorphosis of the elements which determined the parameters of Food Policy and administration then and now, the relentless pressure of new forces on Indian agriculture and the pricing phenomena, national as well as international, the steady emergence of ever increasing surpluses in agricultural production—all these have changed the relativity of forces impinging on the food economy in a manner and to the extent that food administration has become essential in both deficit as well as surplus times.

The relevance of food, as a discipline of study and inquiry, is never diminished. In times of scarcity, it occupies all attention and a position of pre-eminence in the day to day administration. Everything else is relegated to the back seat ; all other programmes are slowed down and resources diverted to meet the situation. In the years of bountiful crops, as was the case in the second half of the seventies, it again attracts attention, though in a different context. Falling prices evoke a howl of protest from the producers and no government can afford to see the producers of this vital commodity being 'priced out' of business. Secondly, increasing off-loading of stocks onto the market creates problems of market regulation, storage, procurement and finance. The successive bumper harvests in Punjab and Haryana have brought into sharper focus the acute problem of storage ; even the producers have no place to store the grain they have laboured to grow. Thirdly, movement of surplus stocks to areas where they are needed or to intermediate stations where they could be stored for some time is a problem of such complexity that we have yet to hit upon an ideal movement-cum-storage schedule. And finally, the problems of safe storage and maintenance of stocks in good health have their own dimensions.

'Food' and 'famine' are the positive and negative fields of one single universe, called 'agriculture'. In fact the two are intertwined in the most intimate manner, retaining, at the same time, their mutually exclusive character. Famine, which means a situation of diminution in food supplies has occupied a very prominent place in our history and in many parts of the country a lot of tradition and folklore is woven around them. Famine—we now prefer to use the word scarcity—is not something outside the ordinary experience of the peoples of this country ; it exists in the psyche of the people, as a spectre in the background, always visible alike to peasants, labourers and artisans, and which comes forward from time to time to wreck the social and economic life of one region or the other.

Many an administrative policy of the government has been determined on the experience of these famines. The Land Revenue Administration Policy which concerns more than 80 per cent of the population of this country and is thus of the widest relevance, has been exclusively fashioned on the experience of and the lessons learnt from the famines of the past two to three centuries. The Grow More Food Campaign was the direct outcome of the Bengal Famine of 1942-43. Scarcity relief programmes are designed specifically to meet these crises. A number of development programmes of the Agriculture Department are tailored to meet the threat of scarcity conditions in the long run. The Drought Prone Area Programme directs the focus on the areas which are vulnerable to scarcities and prescribes a number of activities calculated to improve the agricultural economy of those areas. The main thrust of the various programmes for small and marginal farmers is to build up their economic strength so that they can face the adverse conditions with confidence.

The buffer stocking policy of the Government of India is one more outcome of the experience of shortages and scarcities. The shape that this policy has taken and the manner in which it has grown and has been perfected is truly a saga of a Nation's most traumatic experience. While dealing with the administration of this policy in my official position, I had to delve into its various aspects—conceptual, empirical and administrative. I was drawn into an exercise partaking historical analysis so as to acquire a perspective of the factors that led to the emergence of this policy. Almost simultaneously, because of a continuous run of four successive good harvests in the second half of the seventies, with the exception of 1979, faint suggestions were made from certain quarters that to hold on to such huge stocks (in June 1979, they were 21.50 million tonnes representing an investment of over rupees three thousand two hundred and thirty crores) as buffer is not all that necessary and that alternate means should be devised to ensure the same insurance against scarcities at lower costs. It was argued that holding of such enormous stocks creates many problems, and involves huge costs and losses in the shape of deterioration of the grain.

At the same time, an important development emerged on the international scene. The Food and Agriculture Organization of the United Nations started devoting its attention to an exercise of working out a plan of nationally held buffer stocks for World Food Security. Earlier in 1974 the epoch making World Food Conference had been convened by the FAO. The Indian experience figured in it prominently. India was a member of the various working groups and preparatory committees and while examining the international model back at home, our system naturally came in for a critical analysis. It was also mooted that failing a global food security system, possibilities of regional cooperation be explored.

Questions of this nature led me to undertake an evaluation of this policy—to what extent has it been efficacious in achieving the objectives set for it and at what costs ? In which directions should it develop in future and what shape should it assume ? The labours of these studies are contained in the chapters following.

In the course of his official career in the civil service, such as has been my lot, an officer is sometimes called upon to face situations created by scarcities. He is then required to organise relief on a large scale and it is his sacred duty to save every life at whatever cost. In such situations, mere preparation of schemes or proposals is not enough ; what is required is resolute and sustained action in the face of the most trying conditions ; when everybody seems to lose patience, he has to retain his. I have had a unique opportunity of handling three such situations, and when I look back in retrospect I cannot but feel how rich, how rewarding and how satisfying has been the experience.

There is a class of administrators called the 'old food hand' who have a brotherhood of their own and about whom something can be said with just pride. Food administrators are cast in a different mould, for in this field of public administration it is not the placid, and 'out of the book' job that one does : nothing is routine here and nothing brooks delay. In this country conditions vary so widely that one has to summon all one's ingenuity to deal with them. In the first instance, there are highly surplus areas like Punjab, Haryana, western U.P., and pockets of irrigated commands in Andhra Pradesh, Rajasthan, Madhya Pradesh, Tamil Nadu and Bihar. Then there are chronic deficit and not-so-deficit areas like West Bengal, Kerala, Maharashtra, Gujarat and Karnataka. Thirdly, in the case of hill areas in the North and the ever sensitive areas in the East, logistics problems are the determining factors, plentiful production notwithstanding. And finally, the extreme vulnerability of up-lands situated in Central India and the Deccan Plateau to the deficiencies in rainfall is a problem that recurs almost regularly twice in five years. All these demand a highly versatile and sharply perceptive mind and an imagination matured in the practical affairs of mankind to deal with the kaleidoscopic problems of food administration at the national level. The food administrator has to have his reflexes right, his reactions prompt, and his reasoning pragmatic and down to earth. This is the brotherhood of food administrators, and the 'old food hand' are the masters.

This work has been love's labour. In fact the moments I could snatch from the routine of everyday life and devote to these musings, taking recourse to the company of books and libraries and trying to capture the charm of intellectual pursuits, provided me with that refreshing pastime which the human mind, of necessity, craves for. As I proceeded, I found that the vastness of a subject like food would, howsoever I may try to avoid, take me into alleys and side-tracks for comprehending the true nature and ramifications of the topic I had set out to study. That would have made this treatise unmanageable and, therefore, at all times, I tried to keep my focus trained on the specialized topic of this study. Nevertheless, I found that there are a number of areas intimately linked with the subject worthy of independent study and investigation. These are only evidential of the underlying generalised unity in human affairs and have been indicated at the appropriate places. I hope scholars of applied economics will delve into these areas and illumine them with their searching labours.

This work is based on the Indian experience, but the subject is of global importance. In human affairs contemporary experiences in different climes on a subject like food security should be of great relevance. The strides Indian agriculture has made during the last quarter of a century and the food security system that has been evolved in the country are, by wide agreement, regarded as success stories. In this background, the author feels that this monograph should evoke interest in other countries as well, more especially in the Asian and African regions where problems of food security are more or less of the same hue.

New Delhi
September, 1983

K.C.S. Acharya

Acknowledgement

I would like to recount here some personal remembrances. When I took over the charge of the Food and Civil Supplies Department in my cadre State (M.P.) in somewhat difficult times, the late Mr. R. P. Noronha was my mentor. He had received initiation in this department of administration under Mr. H.S. Kamath in the forties. Mr. Kamath had set up the Department from scratch and had built it up in every minute detail. The four volumes of the C.P. & Berar Food Manual and scores of files containing those classic minutes recorded by him which now form part of the State Archives still testify to his penetrating insight into a subject which has its motivation in millions of individuals. The life long association of these two very able administrators with the affairs of Madhya Pradesh made the Food Department one of the efficiently run Departments, so that when I joined it in March 1974, I inherited a tradition of sound and down-to-earth administration. The lessons in food administration that I learnt during my association with Mr. Noronha have stood me in good stead ever since. I owe a deep debt to Mr. Noronha which I cannot acknowledge too eloquently.

When in July 1978, I took over the assignment in the Government of India, I was privileged to serve for some time under Mr. R. Balasubramanian, Secretary, Department of Food. And when I approached him seeking his permission to undertake this study, he gave me his very generous support and encouragement. He was succeeded, a little later, by an equally illustrious officer—Mr. B.C. Gangopadhyay, who gave me every encouragement to complete this study. Both these civil servants belong to that class of 'old food hand' about whom I have spoken a little earlier. They have taken the country through very severe scarcities. Their understanding of the food problems of the various states in the country, their grasp on the intricacies of food administration, and the imperturbable temperament they possess are the very ideals for the food administrators to emulate.

No less is my gratitude to Dr. Ravi Prakash and Dr. Baij Nath Sharma, Vice-Chancellors of the Bhopal University who, readily granted my request for enrolment as a research scholar, and encouraged me in every possible way. Dr. Syed Ashfaq Ali was my guide and I owe much to him. He is a man of letters and has been a teacher all his life.

To my colleagues in the Department of Food also, I have a debt to acknowledge. Messrs K. Balakrishnan, K.L. Khanna, Amarjit Singh and R.N. Mallik, and G. Namasivayam of the FCI, and Dr. G. R. Saini of the Department of Agriculture—to mention only a few, helped me a lot in compiling the statistical material. Special mention should here be made of Mr. Virender Kumar, Librarian of the Central Secretariat Library, who was helpful in getting me the references—old and current—at very short notice. My special thanks are due to Mr. P.S. Seshadri, editorial staff member, Indian Institute of Management, Ahmedabad who took pains in going through the manuscript and suggested numerous improvements. To the patient and untiring labours of my personal staff, Mr. O.N. Malhotra and Mr. J.L Saini, I have every reason to be grateful. They typed the manuscript a couple of times and gave it the final shape.

Contents

PART THREE : WORLD DIMENSIONS OF FOOD SECURITY

ERRATA

page	*line*	*for*	*read*
1	15	'pot'	'put'
1	24	'rath'	'rate'
16	17	'itimes ncluding'	'times including'
45	2	'a strike'	'strike a'
62	19	'incresing'	'increasing'
83	11	'manimum'	'minimum'
84	7	'rates'	'rates,'
85	33	'on'	'in'
87	4	'thereof'	'therefor'
103	35	'betweeu'	'between'
112	26	'aberrvations'	'aberrations'
147	25	'mintaining'	'maintaining'
152	1 (below the table)	'deposed'	'depend'
152	5 (below the table)	'ralated'	'related'
273	25	'board'	'broad'

1

Food Security—What it Means

MEANING

THE TERM 'food security' has come into use only recently. The World Food Conference convened by FAO in 1974 drew the attention of the world community, for the first time, to the urgent need of devising ways and means for assuring food security to the hungry millions of the world. It was recognised that assurance of the world food security is the common responsibility of the entire international community. The conference gave the call that no child, woman, and man should go to bed hungry and no human being's physical and mental capabilities should be stunted by malnutrition.

There is considerable imbalance between the demand and supply of food in developing countries, and the call for 'food security' aims at removing this gap through both the short term and the long term measures. Nearly 3.3 billion of the human race, constituting more than 70 per cent of the world population, live in the developing countries. These countries, pot together, produce only 45 per cent of the world's cereal production. This imbalance between food and population compels the developing countries to get access to the surplus of the developed countries through commercial purchases, bilateral arrangements or through multilateral aid. The imperatives of food security arise from the fact that access by the developing countries to the surplus food is becoming progressively more difficult owing to a variety of reasons. During the last one decade (1970-81), whereas the food production of developed countries has been going up at an annual growth rath of 3.2 per cent, in the developing countries it has been going up only at 1.8 per cent, while the rate of growth in population has been 0.8 per cent and 2.4 per cent respectively. During the same period the total cereal import by the developing countries has gone up from 38 million tonnes to 91 million tonnes—in monetary terms from 3.4 billion dollars to 20.1 billion dollars. In contradistinction, the level of food aid to developing countries fell from 12.7 million tonnes (30 per cent of the total food imports) to 9 million tonnes (9 per cent of the total food imports). And to complete the picture, the world food stocks increased from 244 million tonnes in 1976-77 to 275 million tonnes during 1981-82. Food Security means not only availability of food for direct consumption—which indeed is the very heart of it—but has other implications as well. Availability of foodgrains will have little relevance if people do not possess purchasing power to buy them for their consumption. This compulsion casts a responsibility on the government to devise ways and means by which, in the first instance, food is available within the country and, in the second, people have the means to buy it. This, in turn would inevitably bring in the policy conspectus of employment generation schemes dovetailed with development programmes on a fairly continuing basis.

It has a special significance for groups such as old and infirm people, expectant mothers and young children. These groups are vulnerable in the sense that their capacity for physical exertion is severely limited, yet they are in most urgent need of food as well as nutrition. In this context, the concept of food security implies implementing policies for supplementing food and nutritional requirements of these groups.

Thirdly, nutrition is an essential aspect, because food as such is not enough ; food of right quality and content providing the necessary nutrition is what is really required, for keeping the body in proper health. In this aspect all food items, including milk, fruits, vegetables, and processed and fortified foods, etc., are included. Productivity is directly related to the health of the people and this gives nutrition the paramount place in the philosophy of food security.

Fourthly, the food security concept cannot be restricted to the boundaries of a country alone ; it is a global concept. Hunger and privation in any part of the world are totally incompatible with the food security concept of the modern world. No region of the world is totally free from scarcities and failure of crops ; but on the world-wide basis the surplus of one region would go a long way in meeting the deficit of others. In chronic deficit countries, however, domestic production may not be adequate to sustain the necessary reserves and in their case the stocks could be built through imports alone. Such food deficit countries are generally short of foreign exchange to finance the import bill and they will need the assistance of the surplus countries as also of the international financial institutions for building up their reserve and the infrastructure needed for it. It is in this sense that the concept of food security is global.

Fifthly, distribution—efficient and of the right type—is an integral part of any food security system. Availability of stocks with government will be of little use if they cannot be supplied to the people who need them and at the right time. Indeed there have been instances when absence of a proper distribution system (which includes stock building too) led to large scale famine despite availability of stocks. It would be no exaggeration to say that the distribution system takes care of a very large part of the food security concept. It is the art of managing scarcities and shortages which is the central feature of food security system of a country.

Food security, in the final analysis, depends on a stable and secure production base. In this wider context, it would include all avenues allied to agriculture, viz., horticulture, animal husbandry, dairy, poultry, fishery, etc. Nature is bountiful and has given enough resources to sustain food production necessary for a community. Land and water, appropriate cropping systems, scientific package of inputs and practices—all these are at the command of humanity to assure it of food security. Harnessing of water resources with a view to securing agriculture from drought ; command area development programmes so as to optimize the benefits from land, water and other inputs ; disease and pest control ; and organizing the allied and subsidiary occupations—all these judiciously planned and harnessed would ultimately constitute food security.

SHIFT IN EMPHASIS

Food security would have different connotations—though not different meanings—in times of plenty and in conditions of shortages and scarcities. The fundamental features of the concept briefly outlined here would hold good at all times, but the emphasis, the priorities, and the approach would be different. In times of plenty, nutrition, balanced diet, setting apart a reserve as an insurance against a probable lean year and planning for future would be the problems that would receive attention. But in times of scarcity, the situation is one of grave emergency, comparable to war, when everything else is relegated to the background and the problem of feeding the people receives the first and foremost attention. The only priority is that of mustering foodgrain stocks and reaching them the places where they are needed. The sole emphasis is on saving human life and, therefore, the concept of food security really boils down to a detailed and continuous exercise, at innumerable levels, in procuring stocks and moving them to the needy areas. The strains of times require an elaborate exercise of procurement and distribution in minutiae, and the implementation involves dovetailing of the employment programme with the food supply arrangements. Every consumable foodstuff—is procured and supplied under the relief programmes. Sometimes, quantitative restrictions have to be enforced in order to equitably ration out the available supplies and thereby prevent waste.

What is central to the concept of food security is the management of food economy in a manner that society does not have to depend on external assistance to meet the normal cyclical shortages that occur in the agricultural economy. In situations of exceptional misfortune or when the calamity persists for more than one year, it would be obvious that resources would be too slender to combat the misfortune and assistance from friendly countries would be essential. This mutual give and take is obligatory if the lessons of the human civilization are not to be ignored. Nevertheless, it is equally clear that help from outside countries and participation in collective food security would be possible only when the philosophy of food security is adopted by every country. For no principle or doctrine not practised at home could be worked collectively by the nations and this fundamental rule applies to food security with as much relevance as to any other department of human action. The concept of food security, therefore, is one of universal validity, to be adopted and practised by all countries and to be reinforced by mutual interaction—whether in times of plenty or in times of shortages.

The present work, however, is not addressed to the larger dimensions of the philosophy of food security. Problems of food security on global basis would cover a much larger ground and because of the peculiar circumstances attending upon the different countries and their pulls in different directions, the subject would require an altogether different treatment than what has been attempted here. The Indian experience which led to the evolution of the present policy-frame is the burden of this treatise. The evolution of the distribution system in India as a part of famine relief is indeed very ancient. The present policy has evolved over centuries and the two together—the buffer stocking and the distribution system—constitute a compact theme for study.

FOOD-POPULATION RELATIONSHIP

Operationally, the food security system boils down to food-population relationship. The manner in which this equation worked itself out since the time man appeared on the scene constitutes the theme of human civilization. The evolution of civilizations in the settlements on the river banks and valleys, the great movements and migration of population—sometimes even across the continents—from stark and inhospitable areas to places which could sustain the population, were all guided by this basic condition for human survival.

Two kinds of reserves are included in the general concept of food security—tangible reserves such as physical stocks of grains and intangible reserves represented in the shape of unused arable land and improvements in agricultural production by breakthrough in technology. The larger goal of food security in the present era when population is continually increasing, can be achieved only by judiciously combining and harnessing both the reserves.

The post-war world saw attempts to provide a tangible food security. Programmes of technical assistance to the agriculture of under-developed and developing countries were initiated on a substantial scale. Taking note of the grim fact that about two-thirds of the world population lives outside the food security, the World Food Conference called for international cooperation in holding reserves and the President of the World Food Council aptly observed : "The cost of not developing a dependable food security system could be the lives of the millions."

Ever since the commencement of the Five Year Plans up to the end of the Fourth Five Year Plan, barring certain periods of drought and floods and constraints in the supply of power and fertilizers, agricultural production in India has always outstripped population. It would be seen from Table 1.1 that the production of foodgrains has registered substantial increases—from 50.8 million tonnes in 1950-51 to 133.1 million tonnes in 1981-82, while population went up from 363 million to 704 million. At the same time, the number of people below the poverty line increased from 220 million

TABLE 1.1 : **Growth in population and increase in food production—India**

	Mid-year population as on July 1 (in millions)	Foodgrains production (in million tonnes)	Per capita availability (in kg/year)	Percentage increase in production (as compared with that in 1951)		
				Population		Per capita availability
1950-51	363	50.8	144.1	—	—	—
1960-61	442	82.3	171.1	21.8	62.0	18.7
1970-71	551	108.4	171.1	51.8	113.4	18.7
1973-74	590	104.7	164.7	62.5	106.1	14.3
1975-76	617	121.0	165.5	70.0	138.2	14.9
1976-77	631	111.2	157.6	73.8	118.9	9.4
1977-78	645	126.4	170.9	77.7	148.8	18.6
1978-79	659	131.9	173.2	81.5	159.6	20.2
1979-80	674	109.7	150.4	85.7	115.9	4.4
1980-81	689*	129.6	165.6	89.9	155.1	14.9
1981-82	704*	133.1	165.7	93.9	162.0	15.0

*Provisional

Note : Figures in respect of per capita availability are derived after making an allowance for seed, feed and wastage @ 12.5 per cent. They are, however, not strictly representative of the actual level of consumption in the country as they do not take into account any change in stocks with traders, producers and consumers.

on the eve of the Fifth Plan to 290 million at the beginning of Sixth Plan (1980-81)—an increase of the order of nearly one-third.

In terms of percentages, the increase in foodgrain production during this period was 162 per cent and in the case of population, 93.94 per cent. In other words, the average yearly percentage increase in agricultural production was little less than double of the increase in population. However, a comparison of the compound rates of growth in the two, presents a different picture :

Period	Percentage Annual Compound growth rates in	
	Population	Production
1950-51 to 1959-60	1.91	3.68
1960-61 to 1969-70	2.22	1.71
(1960-61 to 1969-70**)	—	(2.16)
1970-71 to 1979-80	2.25	2.08
(1970-71 to 1979-80*)	—	(2.98)
Between 1979-80* and 81-82		2.16

* Based on expected Index for 1979-80 which was worked out on the basis of base level figures given by the Planning Commission in the Sixth Five Year Plan.

** Worked out by adopting adjusted index numbers for the years 1965-66 and 1966-67 (which were drought years).

It is obvious that on the country-wide basis the rate of growth in foodgrain production has been marginally above the rate of growth in population. But averaging out a figure for the country as a whole is likely to give misleading conclusions. Let us have a look at some states :

State	Per cent rate of growth during 1971-81 in	
	Population	Production
Assam	3.0	1.0
Bihar	2.0	0.6
H.P.	2.1	1.3
J & K	2.6	2.4
Karnataka	2.4	2.2
Kerala	1.8	0.02
M.P.	2.3	0.8
Orissa	1.5	0.9
Rajasthan	2.9	1.7
West Bengal	2.1	0.93

The figures are too eloquent to need any comment.

PER CAPITA AVAILABILITY

We may examine this phenomenon from another angle—variation in per capita availability of food. This, apart from the supply factor, is materially affected on the demand side by two entirely unrelated factors—growth in population and income level. The impact of numbers is obvious. Increase in incomes leads to an increase in demand for food ; food contents themselves are diversified leading to improvement in the nutritional standards. Tomas Frejka, talking of this phenomenon, says :

> Higher incomes are associated not only with a larger quantity of food consumption but also with a more varied and—as most nutritionists would agree—with an improved nutritional quality of food consumption. The Indian data illustrate that if it were possible to increase the income of the "Lower poor" to the level of the "Poor", this would mean not only a substantial increase in the consumption of foodgrain but an even larger increase in the consumption of other foods and thus an improved quality of nutrition.*

The per capita availability of foodgrains which was 144.1 kg in 1950-51 went up to 173.2 kg in 1978-79, showing thereby an increase of 21.2 per cent, but the average per year was less than one per cent. This figure declined to 150.4 kg in the drought year 1979-80 and thereafter has remained stationary at 165.7 kg.

Here then the correct picture comes to light. Despite a spectacular rise in production, the increase in per capita availability has been less than one per cent during all these years and has deteriorated recently. In a number of states the food production is lagging behind the growth in population. The Indian phenomenon truly represents a case of concealed hunger, even though the country claims to be self-sufficient in food. Notwithstanding the symptoms of expanding production and modest exports in recent years, the basic character of the Indian food economy as one precariously balanced, which is upset by even one year of drought, has persisted.

For ensuring food security, therefore, building up of food reserve is indispensable.

---

* Tomas Frejka "Thoughts on Food—How Definitions Matter." *Populi,* Vol. 5, Number 3, 1978.

The buffer stocking policy of the Government of India is based on this basic principle of food-population relationship. The level of population, the per capita income and the minimum per capita requirements were among the key parameters fed into the data and treated by statistical techniques and an appropriate level of buffer and operational stocks determined. Under this policy, a minimum buffer stock of 12 million tonnes of foodgrains is required to be maintained. This is to be over and above the operational stocks which are needed for the maintenance of the public distribution system. The size of these stocks ranges between the lowest figure of 3.5 to 3.8 million tonnes on April 1 to the highest figure of 8.2 to 8.8 million tonnes on July 1 of the year.

As will be shown elsewhere, food reserves were built up right from the Second World War years. The size, however, varied and fluctuated widely ; on a couple of occasions the situation grew so serious that imports had to be arranged and it was like living from ship to mouth. It was only from the early seventies that the country built up appreciable reserves of foodgrains both from imports as well as internal procurement. The total year-end stocks which were of the order of 8.0 million tonnes in 1975 rose to 18.8 million tonnes in 1976. Imports were stopped and in the subsequent three years the stocks remained around the level of 17 million tonnes. The peak was reached in July 1979 when the total stocks with public agencies were of the order of 21.50 million tonnes. But more of it later.

2

Methodology

In the first part of this study relating to the evolution of the concept of foodgrain reserve in the food policy of India, the historical method of analysis has been adopted. This method is of special significance to the subject matter of this study. First, it gives a perspective, for human affairs evolve gradually and, in terms of the philosophy of social development, rationally. There is a plan, an order, an inner logic in the evolution of human institutions. In one of the epilogues to *War and Peace*, Leo Tolstoy says : "Some connexion undoubtedly exists between all who live contemporaneously, and so it is possible to find some connexion between the intellectual activity of men and their historical movements, just as such a connexion may be found between the movements of humanity and commerce, handicraft, gardening or anything else." There is a cosmic unity, a continuity and a causal relationship in them throughout. To understand this logic and relationship and to discover the continuity is to acquire perspective.

Secondly, it enables us to discover the underlying causes or prime movers of a fact. Unlike the historians of the old school who believed in the divine will and divine hand in the destinies of nations, the modern historians ask themselves—why did a particular event happen ? What force made the people of those times act in a particular manner ? How did that force emerge and how did it work itself out—and proceed to analyse them component by component and then discover the common thread that runs through them. This is possible only in the historical method of analysis.

Thirdly, it brings out the relativity between the cause and effect and how the one affects the other. In other words, it means that this method enables us to understand better the relativity of factors that constitute a historical situation, a historical fact, a historical phenomenon. What is their interrelation, what is their inner mechanism and what process of internal change governs them—these we understand better when we adopt the historical method.

Applying these high principles to the subject of our enquiry—how one famine was different from the other, what were their causes and where did they lie, what effects did they produce and on which sections of society, what was the nature of those consequences and how temporary or permanent they were, what lessons did they throw up and what action did they induce—these probes and enquiries would guide our endeavours in this methodology.

Fourthly, it helps in making projections for future. This is a logical corollary of the first premise and thus we make the full circle in the causation of human affairs.

There is a further advantage in this method over others, in that it is a combination of both deductive as well as the inductive method of analysis. In this method, we know what facts led to what policy deductions and how that policy actually worked. What was the relevance of the policy to events and facts and what changes, in turn, were made in it as a result of experience and why—all this wisdom is at our command under this method.

In the first part, my job has been one of a chronicler, who has tried to cull from historical accounts of all description, facts relevant to the subject of this study. I have also attempted to weave a thread of continuity through all this narration, deducing, where possible, general conclusions and tracing their connection or relation with developments that preceded them or were later in point of time. As stated in the foregoing paragraphs, in historical method there is very often relationism both backwards as well as forwards. Philosophers of history have confirmed that sometimes an age is premonitive of coming times, and at others history repeats itself. This law of historical events is true in the case of this chronicle of an aspect of food history also, and this grand view of the pageant called history is to be had only in the historical method herein adopted.

In the second part of this work, namely evaluation of the buffer stocking policy, comparative analysis method has been adopted. No public policy which lends itself to statistical analysis can be and should be evaluated except in a comparative sense. What does it cost to work out the present buffer policy and what would be the costs of alternatives ; what benefits have accrued from the policy and to whom ; can the costs be reduced and if so with what risks—these are some of the questions that have been examined in this part of the study.

In the third and final part some thoughts have been expressed on the relevance of our system to the policy that is evolving under the aegis of the U.N. (in the FAO) for world food security. We are being inevitably drawn into the crucible of World Food Security problem, and as and when a model acceptable to a large majority of the nations is evolved, we may have to adjust our policy suitably. But that is yet to happen and we can leave it at that.

PART ONE

EVOLUTION

3

Famines in Historical Perspective

PART A

STRANGE as it may seem, the food policy in India, viewed in its historical perspective, has been very largely fashioned by the famines and scarcities that afflicted this country through the centuries. When the large mass of humanity engaged in the primary pursuit of growing food, as it has always been, was thrown to the cruel vagaries of weather, the administration—whether the Imperial Mauryas or the medieval Moghuls or the liberal and mercantile English—could not afford to remain a passive onlooker. To alleviate the hardship and to provide succour to the suffering population—became their direct concern and the administrative machinery of the government was pressed into relief operations.

TRIGGERS

The famines worked as the triggers for the evolution of India's food policy through their pervasive character and with numerous dimensions. The first and the most direct dimension was human suffering and loss of life. To save human life was the first concern. The second, and one which manifested itself in a longer time-frame, was the impairment of peoples' health due to starvation, malnutrition and disease. This resulted in depressing the economy throughout for a number of years following the famine, so that the ugly face of the famine haunted the area it visited longer than its actual duration. The third dimension which was more relevant to the kingdoms in ancient and medieval times, was the diminution in the revenue of the king's treasury. This in turn affected his capacity to maintain his army and thus his entire kingdom was threatened. In the vital interests of his kingdom, therefore, were the compulsions to fight the famine and save people from the scourge of hunger, privation and pestilence. The earliest kings realised the importance of peaceful and undisturbed pursuit of the avocation of agriculture. They realized that on sound agriculture and steady food supplies depended the security of their empire. In ancient Hindu polity, the philosophy of *Dharma* applied to wars as well and hence in the Code of War of the Hindu kings, ravaging of crops and killing of agriculturists was prohibited. Megasthenes, the envoy of Seleukos accredited to the court of Chandragupta Maurya has testified to this fact.

IN EARLY TIMES

Sir Harcourt Butler has written at one place : "Famine lies broad written across the pages of Indian history." Famines are spoken of even in the ancient Vedic literature, and in the remote ages when the Jataka stories were composed. The Jatakas are of great value because they stretch from the pre-Christian era to the Mauryan period and contain a general picture of social and economic conditions of those itimes ncluding descriptions of famines. There are faint glimmerings of relief policy too. In the *Gahapati Jataka*, it is said that the villagers obtained oxen on loan from the *bhojaka* (administrator) on condition of paying for it in kind from the next harvest. In the *Kalpadruma Advana*, the high men of Sravasti collectively undertook to feed the famine stricken.

The association of sovereign responsibility with public calamities had a firm and universal hold on popular mind, so that it was high tribute to a king's administrative ability and a token of divine favour on him to affirm that in his reign there was no famine. The forts stocked with wealth and foodgrains served a double purpose of defence of the realm against mortals as well as against gods.

In later literature, namely after the Jatakas, we see a gradual evolution of an elaborate system of precautions against famine and for grappling with the food problems, some of which are remarkable for their modernity. The imperial Mauryas under whom India received her first unity—both cultural and political—laid down elaborate instructions for the higher officers with respect to the measures for dealing with famine and other natural calamities. Kautilya has mentioned them in detail in his *Arthasastra.* "In the first place, it was ordained that half of the stores in the State warehouses should always be kept in reserve for times of famine." When famine occurred the state distributed relief from this reserve, provided seed grain for the next harvest and started public works to keep the people remuneratively employed. He further says that when famine visits the country, half of the annual revenues in kind should be reserved for famine relief. If the state granaries fail to suffice, the ordinary laws of property should be promptly suspended, and the government should force the rich to yield up their hoards of grain and levy heavy taxes on them. Relief should be sought from friendly neighbouring states as well.

Authentic evidence is available to show that regulation of prices and preventive as well as relief measures against famine emerged during Ashoka's reign as an important branch of Hindu polity. *Arthaśastra* contains copious references to the effect that the surest guarantee against famine commended to every ruler as the first lesson of statecraft was an enlightened revenue policy. Loans of provisions and gratuitous relief were distributed by royal, private or corporate endeavour.

A fragmentary and mutilated terracotta inscription found in Mahasthan (Bogra district in Bangladesh) records the order of a Maurya prince to the *Mahamatya* (Governor) of Pundranagare (in the eastern part of the country) directing the latter to help the famine-stricken with loans in cash (*gandaka*) and corn (*dhanya*) which they are to repay in better times to the royal treasury. The Sohgaure Plate—another early Maurya document discovered in the Gorakhpur district records an order to the *Mahamatya* of Sravasti to the effect that certain store-houses (*kotha galani*) at Triveni, Mathura, Cancu, Modema and Bhadra are to be opened to cultivators in seasons of distress.*

* The Chinese also had a somewhat similar system of storing grain on state account for meeting the distress in famine times. They had a system which they called the "Ever-Normal Granary". A law was passed which provided that when the crops went beyond a certain size and prices below a certain point, the government were empowered to buy grain and put it into the Government-owned warehouses. Here it stayed untii a year came when the crop went below a certain point. The stored grain was then sold to the public. Gary H. Koer, Selman Kay and E. Dull, "Food and Social Policy", Proceedings of the 1976 Mid-Western Food and Social Policy Conference (edited in 1978) p. 224.

IN MEDIEVAL AND MOGHUL TIMES

The subsequent history contains extensive references to the famines occurring in the country. Kalhan's Rajtarangini contains graphic description of famines and measures adopted by the kings to provide relief to the people. In the medieval times and later during the Moghul rule, history is replete with instances of famines sweeping through the country and the government of the day fighting them. Sher Shah Suri (1486—1545) was the first Muslim ruler to put the revenue administration on a rational and sound footing. Having regard to the regularity and severity of famines that plagued the country in those days, he established a famine relief store to which each peasant had to contribute grain at the rate of 200 *Bahloli Tankas* in weight per *bigha*. The grain thus collected was preserved in local government stores and was distributed among the people through cheap grain shops when famine conditions prevailed.

The first famine in Akbar's reign almost coincided with his accession to the throne (1555-56). We learn from Abul Fazl that it was Akbar's policy to make arrangements for relieving the distress stricken people. It 1595 he appointed Sheikh Farid as a Special Officer to supervise relief measures. During Shahjahan's reign there was a great famine in 1625 when "a good Emperor distributed food but he was unable to prevent man eating man." There was another famine in 1630 and 1631 when the monsoon failed almost completely over the tract comprising Gujarat and Ahmednagar with portions of Bijapur and Golconda, and before the end of the year the local stock of food was exhausted. It is recorded by historians that supplies were available elsewhere, but it was impossible to bring them to the heart of the affected region, because transport animals need food and water along their routes, while the country was bare of grass, and the streams and ponds were dry. The emperor directed the officials of Burhanpur, Ahmedabad and Surat to establish soup kitchens or alms houses for the benefit of the poor. It was further ordered that so long as His Majesty remained at Burhanpur and Golconda Rs. 5000 should be distributed among the deserving poor every Monday, "that day being distinguished above all others as the day of the Emperor's accession to the throne. . . Thus on twenty Mondays rupees one lakh was given away in charity. His Majesty ordered the officials to distribute Rs. 50,000 among the famine stricken of Ahmedabad. . . Under the directions of the Queen of the generous Emperor, taxes amounting to nearly Rs. 70 lakhs were remitted, amounting to an 11th part of the whole revenues."

History goes on to record a number of famines that occurred during the 17th century and the measures adopted by the Moghul emperors to provide relief to the people. During Aurangzeb's times alms houses were opened, taxes were remitted and those already collected were used for the purchase of corn which was distributed among the poor. He spent large sums of money conveying grains by land as well as by water into the interior of the provinces. The grain was purchased at any price with the public money and it was re-sold at a very moderate rate. (Here was the embryo of the present policy of subsidization from the public exchequer).

UNDER BRITISH RULE

During the 18th century when the British had gained a foothold in the country, we have more accurate accounts of the famines that plagued this country. The famine which devastated the Karnataka lasted from 1780 to 1783. Sir W.W. Hunter has recorded that this famine was almost man-made because it followed the ravages of Haider Ali's army. The Madras Government raised public subscription and the institution of *monegal choultry* came up for the first time for providing relief to the poor. In 1783-84, when Warren Hastings was the Governor-General, Northern India, including Bihar, suffered from a prolonged drought. It was at that time that the construction of granaries (*golas* in the local terminology) was advocated and one such structure still stands today in Patna. In 1790 and 1792, Madras again suffered under the calamity of famine and it was in this famine that, for the first time, the government provided employment to the starving people on the relief works.

In 1860-61 the entire north western provinces experienced terrible shortages of exceptional nature, and government were compelled to make a serious attempt to alleviate the suffering of the people. The record says that at the peak time nearly half a million persons were given relief.

The most notable famine during the early British rule was the Orissa famine of 1866, which shook the government to pay serious thought to the framing of a famine relief or food security policy. The drought visited Orissa first in 1865 which people somehow bore through. But to their great misfortune it continued during the second year also and went right into the third. This was a famine of unprecedented severity, extending into Bengal proper, Bihar, Madras and the eastern part of the Central Provinces. Among the relief measures taken, the most important ones were construction of railway lines and irrigation canals. John Lawrence was the Governor-General at that time and he had advocated the spread of the network of railway lines to carry the surplus of one province to meet the deficit of others. These suggestions had not met with favour in the earlier years, but their value was fully realised during the Orissa famine and were promptly sanctioned by the Secretary of State.

Another notable famine—that of 1869—affected western Rajputana and parts of northern India, and the extension of the scarcity towards the western and southern parts produced a considerable rise in prices in Bombay, the Central Provinces and Hyderabad. In 1874 again, Bihar and Eastern U.P. were affected by scarcity conditions, and large purchases of grain were made by the government and distributed amongst the sufferers. During the twenty year period—1876-1896—large parts of the country suffered from famines which visited upon them at some time or the other, causing widespread suffering.

During the five year period 1896-1900, two distinct famines visited practically the whole of India. The first one occurred in the latter part of 1896 and extended into 1897; and the second visited in the latter half of 1899 and continued, like the previous one, through the ensuing year. These famines bore a close resemblance to each other in that they were more or less equally intense and equally widespread.

Taking the account from 1770 till the close of the nineteenth century, within a period of 130 years of the rule of the East India Company and that of the British Crown, there is a record of 22 famines.

IN THE TWENTIETH CENTURY

The wheat and oilseeds harvest of 1908 was very poor owing to deficient and badly distributed rainfall. Neither were the autumn crops good. The *rabi* crops of 1909 showed an improvement on the previous year, though the winter rains were generally deficient and the untimely rain in April damaged a certain quantity of grain on the threshing floor. The spring crops of 1919 suffered through drought in western and parts of northern India. In 1914 the spring crops again suffered through drought in many districts in northern and western India, chiefly in the United Provinces, Rajputana and Sind. The winter rice crop was adversely affected by deficient rainfall during the months of September, October and November in Bengal, Bihar, Orissa and the United Provinces. The monsoon of 1915 was also not very favourable.

During the quinquennium 1916-20 and thereafter, the monsoon was, generally speaking, good all through, excepting small deficiencies in certain parts here and there. Sometimes damage was caused by excessive rainfall or adverse weather conditions such as frost and early hot winds. But the overall yields of foodgrains not only continued to be steady but also registered a very gradual increase and conditions were by and large comfortable.

The most horrifying famine occurred in undivided Bengal in 1942-43 in which nearly three million human beings lost their lives. A Royal Commission of Inquiry was set up in July 1944 to report on the causes of this famine and the remedial measures that should be adopted in the context of the World War. Earlier in July 1943 a Foodgrains Policy Committee had been set up as an expert group to suggest ways and means to manage the food economy, particularly keeping in mind the exigencies of war. This Committee submitted its report within two months which was adopted by the Famine Commission in their report submitted in 1945. The labour of these bodies resulted in the formulation of a detailed and comprehensive food policy which, with improvement, continues to be in force till today.

IN RECENT TIMES

Failure of the monsoon in almost the entire country during the two successive years of 1965 and 1966 caused acute shortage of foodgrains which were managed with heavy imports, as shown below :

(*million tonnes*)

Year	Wheat	Rice	Other grains	Total
1965	6.58	0.78	0.10	7.46
1966	7.78	0.79	1.79	10.36

The country had to pay heavily in foreign exchange for these imports—the landed cost worked out to nearly Rs. 814 crores for both the years. Expenditure on handling in ports and moving them inland was in addition.

After a run of four good years from 1968 to 1971 the monsoon of 1972 was erratic, both in its total fall as well as in distribution. Consequently both the *kharif* as well as *rabi* crops were badly affected which produced scarcity conditions over a large part of the country. This was also the phenomenon of a lean year being followed by another and 1973 saw a phenomenal rise in foodgrain prices and acute shortages throughout the country. These conditions persisted right through in 1974 also, sending prices sky-high, but thanks to the government stocks and emergent imports, the public distribution was kept going which did not permit the situation to worsen. The prices of wheat, rice and coarse grains, however, touched an all time high mark.

The second half of the seventies was remarkably bountiful, with the single exception of the year 1979. The country experienced a rare bonanza in agricultural production—the highest peak being recorded in 1978-79 when the total food production touched the level of 131.9 m. tonnes. But in 1979 occurred widespread failure of the south west monsoon in the shape of delay in the onset as well as continuous dry spells stretching over a period of 4-6 weeks during the months of July and August. September rains remained confined by and large to the coastal areas and the north and north western parts of the country received scanty rainfall. The north-east monsoon too was highly erratic thereby creating scarcity conditions in the southern peninsular states.

The 1982 monsoon also played truant and was indeed a freak one. Although the monsoon arrived in time, its progress was extremely tardy. It ultimately arrived in the north and north western parts of the country 3-4 weeks late, with the result that *kharif* crops, like paddy and coarse grains were severely damaged. August was the month of deluge which drowned and washed away the crops over large areas. Finally, the monsoon withdrew abruptly from the second week of September thereby exposing the crops to grave hazards.

SUMMING UP

What does this rapid survey of famines and their impact on the health of Indian agriculture tell? It leaves one and only one impression—how vital rainfall is to Indian agriculture. It was not an unfounded statement made by the 1926 Royal Commission on Agriculture, that Indian agriculture is a gamble in monsoon and nor was that British officer transported by his poetic fancy when, in his memoirs, he portrayed the life of the Indian peasant as one—

Whose life is a long drawn question
Between a crop and a crop.

Realising the vulnerability of Indian agriculture to the vagaries of rainfall, the British administrators embarked upon a country-wide programme of conserving water with a view to protecting the agriculture, to the extent possible. In the Punjab, Uttar Pradesh, Andhra Pradesh and Tamil Nadu (the old Madras Presidency), some of the irrigation systems today are more than 100 years old. (In fact the barrage across the Cauveri is more than 800 years old). The Son system in Bihar also falls in this category. But experience has shown that when monsoon fails, the efficiency of these works also falls substantially. The run off in the rivers gets considerably reduced and ultimately not only the area under irrigation shrinks but also the full supplies are not made available with the result that yield per acre even in the irrigated commands falls. In the years when the monsoon failed for the second year in succession, the present writer was a witness to almost total water famine conditions prevailing and the irrigation works proving of very little avail.

This is not to suggest that the irrigation works have been of no use at all. In fact, the produce in their command areas in the scarcities of the past two decades was the mainstay of the country. What is being pointed out is only this much, that when the calamity is total and widespread, human action can only mitigate or alleviate to a limited extent ; for the rest Nature reigns supreme.

PART B

RELATIVITY BETWEEN RAINFALL AND FAMINE

BEHAVIOUR OF THE MONSOON

On the atlas India looks like an inverted triangle projecting into the Indian Ocean. Practically all the rainfall in most of her vast area is received during the months of June to September. She is fortunate to get the monsoon from both the sides—the south-west and the south-east. In a good year, both monsoons spread and envelope the entire country and two crops are taken off the land. In a bad year, the monsoon is either weak or desultory and the central, the northern and north-western parts of the triangle do not receive enough rainfall to support even one crop.

The history of famines in India throws up certain basic features of this great calamity. In the first place, total failure of monsoon has rarely happened except in the worst recorded famine of 1899 when the deficiency in rainfall in the country-wide average was 27 per cent. In all the other famine years right up to 1966, the deficiency varied between 12 per cent (1941) and 24 per cent (1918). The relevant figures are summarised in the following table.

Since average figures in respect of a country of the size and diversity of India are likely to give misleading conclusions, it would be desirable to focus attention on the different meteorological sub-divisions of the country with detailed percentage variations. Tables 3.1 and 3.2 give this information.

ANALYSIS OF MONSOON

According to the norms adopted by the Indian Meteorological Department, a 25 per cent departure on all-India basis and 19 per cent for individual meteorological sub-divisions is treated as normal. When deficiency is recorded in ten or more sub-divisions, conditions of drought are considered to prevail in the country. Analysing the

TABLE 3.1 : **Monsoon rainfall deficiency over India during the worst drought years**

Drought year	% of the total geographical area affected	% of the total monsoon	Rainfall deficiency percentage			
			June	July	August	September
1918	69.9	−26	10	−49	− 9	−41
1899	68.5	−28	16	−35	−41	−41
1877	59.5	−33	−23	−42	−39	−18
1972	40.4	−24	−26	−35	−11	−24
1965	38.3	−17	−35	− 4	−22	−16
1920	37.9	−16	− 6	3	−33	−33
1905	37.2	−18	−43	−12	−19	− 2
1941	35.5	−14	− 3	−20	− 9	−21
1966	35.4	−16	2	−16	−23	−21
1951	35.1	−19	−17	−16	−13	−33
1979	34.8	−19	−15	−17	−17	−27
1974	34.0	−13	−32	− 5	− 5	−21
1904	33.6	−12	6	− 8	−19	−24
1901	29.9	−14	−30	−16	9	−28
1982	29.1	−12	−15	−21	13	−29
1907	29.1	− 7	0	−20	28	−42

Source : India Meteorological Department, New Delhi.

figures in Tables 3.1 and 3.2, certain interesting conclusions emerge :

(a) percentage deficiency shown in col. 3 (Table 3.1) does not give a correct idea about the failure of the monsoon and its severity, unless the distribution thereof over the four monsoon months is also studied. Hence cols. 4 to 7. The years when the overall deficiency was as moderate as 21 per cent or less, the real aggravating factor was either scanty rain in the beginning, i.e., June, or abrupt cessation in September, or both. In some cases, significant deficiency in July must have led to the complete withering of crops which subsequent rains could not revive ;

(b) in 1899 while the north-eastern area as well as Bihar and U.P. had more than average rainfall, the entire southern, central, and north and north-western India was deficient in rain. The deficiency in western Rajasthan was as high as 91 per cent which means that there was practically no rainfall, with Gujarat closely following. Down south in Kerala it was only 29 per cent. If, therefore, the 1899 famine was the most horrible and devastating famine, it was

TABLE 3.2 : **Percentage departures of monsoon rainfall over different**

S. No.	Sub-Division	1877	1883	1891	1899	1901	1904	1905	1907	1911
1.	North Assam	—21	—19	—29	6	— 4	— 6	2	0	12
2.	South Assam	— 9	—18	— 7	— 3	— 3	— 2	10	9	— 1
3.	Sub-Himalayan West Bengal	—20	4	—45	4	—18	—33	14	2	9
4.	Gangetic West Bengal	— 2	— 7	—13	11	— 5	0	5	— 9	— 8
5.	Orissa	—17	19	6	— 7	—27	6	—15	1	— 3
6.	Bihar Plateau	— 6	— 4	—12	0	—15	9	0	8	12
7.	Bihar Plains	—39	—10	—36	45	—26	— 2	23	— 9	15
8.	East U.P.	—64	—27	— 2	13	—16	6	—13	—40	1
9.	West U.P.	—73	—33	20	—10	— 6	8	—44	—39	—20
10.	Haryana	—59	—29	2	—51	—25	— 1	—49	—32	—15
11.	Punjab	—24	— 2	23	—53	—20	—40	—32	—22	—51
12.	Himachal Pradesh	—49	—29	—23	—30	—11	—17	—30	—53	—34
13.	J & K	63	—77	—67	—11	—14	—16	3	—20	—31
14.	West Rajasthan	—72	—33	—39	—91	—53	—51	—59	19	—63
15.	East Rajasthan	—66	—25	—16	—48	—36	16	—62	—27	—35
16.	West Madhya Pradesh	—43	— 3	27	—49	—10	—18	—23	—30	—23
17.	East Madhya Pradesh	—23	—13	8	—38	0	—12	—17	—11	4
18.	Gujarat	—67	—12	—10	—79	—36	—51	—17	9	—56
19.	Saurashtra & Kutch	—71	4	6	—76	—55	—58	—26	7	—72
20.	Konkan & Goa	—31	20	— 2	—49	1	—19	—31	5	—23
21.	Madhya Maharashtra	—32	17	— 4	—53	—10	—26	—33	11	—29
22.	Marathwada	—41	68	+15	—49	8	— 9	—28	—26	—11
23.	Vidarbha	—28	43	18	—62	2	—27	—10	— 7	—15
24.	Coastal Andhra Pradesh	—27	—25	—25	—31	—24	—33	—16	—14	—15
25.	Telangana	—46	34	—24	—37	—20	—21	—14	— 5	—22
26.	Rayalaseema	—12	2	—42	—38	—36	—51	—18	—31	—34
27.	Tamil Nadu	— 1	— 2	—42	—31	+10	—26	—24	—19	—21
28.	Coastal Karnataka	—23	6	—25	—41	— 5	3	—19	14	—21
29.	North Interior Karnataka	26	20	—27	—37	— 9	—11	—33	33	—21
30.	South Interior Karnataka	— 4	10	—25	—13	—11	—15	—31	23	— 5
31.	Kerala	— 1	— 7	—19	—34	— 3	6	—15	24	— 8

meteorological sub-divisions of the country during the worst drought years (1877-1982)

1918	1920	1939	1941	1951	1965	1966	1971	1972	1974	1979	1982
28	−5	−2	−7	−12	−3	6	−9	−3	61	−10	3
26	−11	−7	3	−18	15	36	−12	−21	14	5	−19
13	17	−2	−1	−3	33	−6	−7	−26	16	−13	−16
11	−8	23	23	−18	0	−27	39	−3	4	−11	−18
−13	1	1	8	−17	−15	−15	−2	−5	−34	−19	−8
−5	10	12	4	−21	−21	−32	39	−16	−7	−27	−30
21	−2	5	6	−29	−6	−46	15	−35	10	−15	−28
−35	−13	2	−18	−22	−35	−29	32	−56	−9	−50	2
−43	−14	−12	−36	−25	−24	−3	28	−16	−18	−46	−20
−57	−26	−36	−35	−45	−27	+8	+23	−20	−27	−46	−11
−49	−31	−41	−11	−26	−38	18	17	−28	−36	−38	−25
−53	−22	−12	−20	−17	−41	11	31	−45	−40	−47	−50
−40	−43	−23	−2	−44	−39	21	−26	−26	−6	−34	−37
−76	−28	−59	−19	−43	−23	−14	−9	−23	−39	−14	−36
−58	−16	−36	−26	−47	−36	−34	23	−32	−21	−40	−18
−40	−30	−4	−26	−27	−37	−29	16	−17	−12	−32	−2
−2	−22	5	−36	−15	−40	−27	4	−17	−36	−40	−8
−59	−32	−30	10	−49	−31	−16	−10	−43	−61	−21	−27
−72	4	−52	−9	−36	11	−21	13	−61	−55	71	−46
−45	−29	−4	−35	−7	2	−21	1	−38	10	−25	−7
−55	−24	−2	−10	−19	−2	−11	−9	−35	−5	9	−18
−50	−51	−26	−33	−13	15	−13	−24	−50	−34	13	−19
−33	−47	−18	−20	−6	−28	−14	−28	−30	−34	−5	−27
−21	−38	−20	−11	39	−4	7	−18	−26	−13	−28	−17
−30	−39	−31	−29	−4	8	−3	−39	−34	−25	−20	1
−40	−36	−18	−28	−22	2	17	−29	−31	+4	−12	−16
−50	0	−17	7	−2	−8	29	13	9	16	18	−26
−45	−13	−17	−22	−4	−9	−21	2	−26	14	−12	10
−41	−13	9	−9	5	11	−3	−17	−14	−6	7	−9
−44	3	−10	−2	−11	−18	−15	19	−7	4	28	−16
−47	26	−7	−2	−35	−30	−26	5	−25	3	−10	−12

Source : Indian Meteorological Department, New Delhi.

because nearly three quarters of the country's area was highly deficient in rainfall—the deficiency being well over 33 per cent except in Kerala. In eleven meteorological sub-divisions, the deficiency was over 50 per cent. The number of sub-divisions which recorded deficiency was more than double of the norm.

This famine must, therefore, necessarily stand in a class by itself, though in geographical terms it ranks second to 1918 ;

(c) the phenomenon of the 1899 famine did not repeat itself in subsequent recorded famine years. The closest to it was the year 1918 when an area larger than that in 1889 was deficient in rain, though the deficiency was slightly less in certain areas compared to the earlier famine. The overall average 24 per cent deficiency came quite close to the 1899 figure ;

(d) the 1972 drought stands out in recent times as the most serious one, though, in terms of the area affected, it ranks seventh in the descending order. The deficiency in northwestern India was 23 per cent while in the peninsular India it was 28 per cent. During this year, out of 35 meteorological sub-divisions, 21 had recorded deficiency of 19 per cent and above. In terms of distribution, this year must rank a close second to 1899 or perhaps more severe than that ;

(e) in 1974, 18 sub-divisions out of 35, accounting for 42.8 per cent of the country's area, were deficient but the average deficiency was much less than that in 1972. In terms of the norms the deficiency in rainfall in peninsular India was normal, while in northwestern India it was slightly more than normal ;

(f) in 1965, 14 sub-divisions suffered average to severe deficiency, the weighted average departure being 19 per cent. This year was the forerunner of another year of deficient monsoon, and their cumulative effect put them in the category of very serious famine years ;

(g) the most notable feature of the drought in 1979 was its longest dry spell which lasted for 35 days. 18 sub-divisions recorded deficiency which in itself was not as high as in the years 1899, 1918 and 1972. But the all-time record duration of the dry spell aggravated the drought conditions to such an extent that the loss in paddy production in eastern U.P. and the Chhattisgarh in M.P. was over 60 per cent ; and

(h) in 1982 again, though the number of deficient sub-divisions was only 11, the distribution of rainfall was highly erratic. The dry spell was almost the same as in 1979 and it abruptly withdrew in the first week of September. In terms of the area affected, this drought will rank an exceptional one.

TOLERANCE LIMITS

From field observations, the present writer has come to the conclusion that a deficiency in rainfall of the order of about 20 to 25 per cent can be tolerated by the crops, provided the remaining fall is well distributed over the monsoon months. A deficiency over 33 per cent, even with proper distribution of the remaining rainfall, would damage the crops and if the distribution is irregular, the situation would be all the more aggravated. As a matter of fact, proper distribution of rainfall is so crucial that, speaking conversely, even if the deficiency is less—say 15 or 20 per cent, the crops will wither if the time lag is unduly long.

This phenomenon is measured in terms of gap(s) between two rainfalls—falls adequate for the crops of the area in question. Actual quantity received is also relevant. But what really determines the failure of the monsoon is the time lag between two falls. The greater the time lag, the greater is the damage to the crops. History records the fact that the longest dry spell was during 1899 when, excepting for a brief rainy spell during September 13 to 16, the period from August 31 to the end of September was dry. 26 days elapsed between the two falls during August and September. What puts this year in a class by itself is the fact that southern India too, experienced at the same time almost a month long dry spell with but a six day wet spell. In other words, the entire Indian sub-continent suffered a prolonged dry spell in the month of September, which converted the year into one of the most terrible famines. This record was broken by the monsoon of 1979 when practically in the whole of north India, with the exception of casual and stray showers in small pockets here and there, the dry spell continued for nearly 35 days from the middle of August to the third week of September.

BASIC CHARACTERISTICS

To talk in terms of an all-India average of excess or deficient rainfall is misleading. The size of the country, the different agro-climatic zones, the proportion between the forest cover and the cultivated area—all these render the phenomenon of rainfall highly area-specific, and, even in those meteorological sub-divisions, one of varying character over seasons. In fact the right thing to do would be to study the meteorological data in respect of each agro-climatic zone—the areas growing coarse grains in the western belt comprising Rajasthan, Gujarat, and western parts of Madhya Pradesh, Maharashtra, and Karnataka ; crops grown on the high lands of central India, covering Madhya Pradesh, Maharashtra, and the Deccan Plateau in Andhra Pradesh ; the rice bowl in the east comprising Chhattisgarh, Orissa, and West Bengal ; the cultivation done in the coastal areas ; and finally the rich fertile plains of western U.P. Haryana, and Punjab. Such studies should cover a sufficiently long period of time and prepare area-wise profiles of the monsoon, delineating its relativity with the famine history of those areas. This study will essentially be of the phenomenon called the "run of rain" divided into a seven-day or ten-day period according to the cropping pattern and the agricultural conditions of a region. The period is determined on the basis of the rainfall requirements of the agriculture of the area and the behaviour of the rainfall will have to be studied in relation to that period. In other words, the distribution of rainfall over the monsoon months and its impact on the crops grown in that area should be studied to bring out the true relativity between the rainfall and the famines.

These would be appropriate subjects for a separate inquiry.

The second characteristic of the monsoon is its late setting and/or early cessation and withdrawal. These features of the monsoon are very material for *kharif* and *rabi* crops. If the monsoon sets in late, not only the sowing of *kharif* crops is delayed, but whatever sowings take place in irrigated areas also wither away. Prolonged continuation of dry conditions ultimately reduces the monsoon period with the result that the probability of receiving lesser rain in absolute terms is rendered quite high. Late setting of the monsoon therefore is a very adverse circumstance widely affecting the *kharif* crops.

Early withdrawal of monsoon means that no rainfall takes place after the middle of September. As it happens, these rains are absolutely vital for the ripening of the *kharif* crops—particularly ric eand sorghum (*jowar*)—which happen to be in the milking stage at that time. The consequence is that grain formation does not take place properly and the crop withers totally. This happened during the famine years of 1965 and 1966 when the rainfall during June and July was good enough but it started withdrawing from August, giving very meagre showers in that month and completely withdrawing from early September. Almost the same thing happened in 1899 when 'the monsoon broke late and feebly in June. One good fall was received in July after which there was no rainfall till the second week of August. The monsoon then reappeared and gave eleven inches in August, but soon after the beginning of September it finally ceased and no rain fell till the end of the year.'

Early withdrawal also leaves the soil without any moisture and incapable of growing *rabi* crops. The result is that the sowing of *rabi* crops which is normally done in October and the first-half of November, is delayed and since this is not the time for rain to fall in north India and in the peninsular region except Tamil Nadu, *rabi* crops are also seriously damaged.

From the above description, the basic lesson that the history of famines throws up is that it is not the failure of the monsoon in relation to *kharif* crops which brings in the famine ; it is the failure of late September rains as well as the subsequent winter showers leading to the failure of *rabi* crops which is responsible for the real famine. The reason is that the principal *kharif* coarse grains like maize, sorghum, and millets require a moderate rain for ensuring a normal yield. In the entire western belt running down from north to south and comprising Rajasthan, western Madhya Pradesh, Gujarat, Maharashtra and Karnataka, the experience has been that even a moderate rainfall of 20-22 inches properly distributed over the season is enough for giving a normal crop of the *kharif* coarse grains, including cotton and groundnuts. This is exactly what happened in this belt in 1974 when the rainfall was deficient for the rice crop but was properly distributed over the season with the result that the outturn of coarse grains was normal.

As explained earlier, this much quantity of rainfall is received in most of the years and Nature's dispensation in regard to the coarse grains is that they fail but rarely. It is only rice which is totally vulnerable to the failure of the late September and early October rains. These rains are also vital for the sowing of *rabi* crops and when they fail, both *kharif* (rice) and *rabi* (wheat and gram) crops are lost. But if rain falls in October and subsequently in winter months too, the *rabi* crops are revived, thereby averting the famine. These rains are beneficial to *kharif* areas as well, because if the main rice crop has been lost, the farmers raise minor millets with the help of these rains.

This is not to suggest that deficient rainfall during monsoon months has no effect on the food economy. Its direct result is an overall dimunition in the production of foodgrains and cash crops, with the result that a climate of shortages comes to prevail with all its attendant evils.

Lastly, in the history of famines, there are numerous instances when one famine year was followed by another lean year. Sometimes a lean year (as happened in 1941) preceded a full-blooded famine. In the overall analysis, in Indian agriculture the droughts and failure of crops move in a cycle of five years. One year is very good and one is very bad. Of the remaining three, two are average and one is again below average. Sometimes, this 'below average year' either follows the very bad year or falls in between the average years. It is remarkable how these circumstances have combined in diverse ways and manners and have impinged on the Indian agricultural economy during the past hundreds of years. Two consecutive lean years are really the most terrible aspect of the calamity, because it completely breaks the back of the farmer. His economy is ruined and the sustaining power is totally lost. At the same time, his cattle wealth is also lost to a great extent both in terms of numbers and their health and vigour. The damage to the agricultural economy in such a situation is crippling and it takes years for the economy to return to a state of normalcy.

4

Evolution of the Buffer Concept in the Food Policy—Up to 19th Century

LESSONS OF PAST FAMINES

EVOLUTION of a famine relief policy, with foodgrain reserve as its essential part, can be said to date from the great Orissa famine of 1865-66, 67. At that time the British administration no doubt had an experience of Indian droughts and famines for slightly over a hundred years, but organization of relief on a vast scale and involvement of the administration in pursuing a purposeful relief policy was uncommon.

IN THE SECOND-HALF OF THE EIGHTEENTH CENTURY

The great famine of 1770 which visited parts of lower Bengal gave rise to a special enquiry into plans for the alleviation of similar disasters. The authors of the Permanent Settlement had entertained hopes that one of the effects of the measure they were going to adopt in certain parts of the country—chiefly in Bengal (which included the present states of Bihar and Orissa and Bangladesh) and Madras Presidencies in land revenue administration would be to put the country and the people in a better position for enduring the calamities of droughts and famines. But their hopes were to be belied by the visitations of famines in 1782, 1792, and 1807 over Madras, in 1784 over Bengal, and in 1792 and 1803 over Bombay. The government, following the notions commonly held at the time, appears to have acted on the belief that remedies for combating the distress were to be found in prohibition on the export of grain, penalties on merchants who hoarded it or enhanced its price and other interferences with the course of trade.

IN THE FIRST-HALF OF THE NINETEENTH CENTURY

It was not till the famine of 1812 in Bombay and of 1824 in Madras that the government adopted the principle of non-interference with trade as a cardinal rule of policy. The famine of 1837, for the first time, induced the government to formulate the principles on which the administration of relief was to be based. It was accepted as the general rule with regard to relief that it was the duty of the government to offer employment to able bodied persons, while the responsibility to provide relief to the helpless and infirm fell on the community at large. This policy, in its essential outline, was followed all through and reaffirmed by the various commissions, notably the Orissa Famine Commission, which brought about an important modification in that the responsibility for the infirm and helpless was not exclusively left to private charity, but also attached to the government.

THE GREAT ORISSA FAMINE

The Orissa famine made its appearance in 1865 when the monsoon abruptly terminated resulting in a very lean crop. The winter crop was also affected, giving rise to scarcity all round. The distress was felt "along the whole Eastern coast of India from Madras upwards extending to some distance inland, visiting Mysore, the district of Madras above the Eastern ghats, Hyderabad, the whole country in the south-west of Bengal and Bihar. It was most intense along the coast in the district of Orissa". The record left by a British officer says that the people somehow bore the distress, but the suffering did not cease with 1866 ; on the other hand it persisted through that year and went right into the third. The rainfall of the following year (1866) was so late as to cause general alarm and excitement. And when it came, it was so heavy as to cause great floods in the river Mahanadi so that in the words of Sir John Lawrence, the Governor-General, "what the drought spared, the floods drowned". In 1867, hopes were entertained that the distress had come to a close and the relief works may be given up, but the distress persisted relentlessly and the relief operations had to be continued with greater vigour. Relief was given mainly in the form of cooked food and in relief-houses managed on the system introduced by Sir John Strachey. By great exertion and at enormous cost, the government acquired 40,000 tonnes of foodgrains by end of November 1866, of which not more than half could be disposed of gratuitously, or sold at lower rates, or distributed in wages to the starving population. The monsoon of 1867, followed by an unusually fine harvest, put an end to the famine in 1868.

PUBLIC WORKS AND THEIR FINANCING

The Orissa famine proved with lamentable distinctness that neither the government nor the local administration possessed an adequate knowledge of the facts or the means necessary to offer relief with promptness and efficiency. But by that strange yet infallible rule of human affairs which found immortal expression from the lips of Duke Senior in *As you Like It*—'Sweet are the uses of adversity', this misfortune gave an impulse to the policy which Sir John Lawrence had desired from the outset to pursue, namely that of hastening the construction of railways and irrigation canals. He argued that if the government were to assume the responsibility, never fully assumed before, for saving the lives of a large population threatened with death, there must be railways to carry the surplus grain from productive tracts to the deficit areas. There must also be canals to utilise the available waters for the irrigation of the land. There was, however, the difficulty of providing financial means for executing these works. For all works of public utility the principle then adopted was that funds should be furnished from ordinary revenue. This was justly applied to buildings—civil and military—and to roads upon which toll tax was levied ; but it was never properly applicable to canals which would yield returns in the shape of water rate and for which the ordinary revenues could never supply the funds. Nevertheless, a number of large canals were taken up for construction whose costs were defrayed from current revenues and when the funds fell short, they were raised by borrowings.

Lawrence believed that India would be justified in raising loans for the permanent improvement of the country. He laid down a new principle that the ordinary revenues should defray the interest on loans raised for meeting the capital cost, while the receipts of revenues were also to be credited to that account. But the capital expenditure was to be made out of loan funds to be treated as extraordinary source of finance and separate from the yearly budget. A careful forecast was made of the amount that would be required to be expended on these works of permanent improvement during a cycle of years and for which loans were to be raised. Thus Lawrence introduced this principle for the first time into Indian finances and it was established firmly by his successors. (This principle was given final shape by Lord Lytton in 1878-79 by establishing a Famine Insurance Fund which continued as a Central Fund right up to 1936 when, under the Government of India Act, 1935, it was transferred to the Provinces and made into a Provincial Fund).

THE BIHAR FAMINE AND GOVERNMENT PURCHASES

In his memoirs, *Men and Events of My Time in India*, Sir Richard Temple speaks of the failure of rains in the autumn of 1873 and the spectre of famine that loomed large over the whole of Bengal Presidency. The summer crop of rice of that year had been short in yield and the principal crop was failing because of drought. This disaster affected nearly 20 million people in the whole Presidency. Lord Northbrooke was the Governor-General at that time and he urgently considered the question whether the government should undertake the responsibility for counteracting the effects of this drought and for averting the famine. He decided in favour of governmental action, although such a task had not till then been accomplished in India on any substantial scale. He received full support from the Secretary of State in England and the announcement of the Governor-General's intention of taking steps to combat the threat of famine quietened the public mind to a great extent in Bengal. But the rememberance of the Orissa famine was fresh in the minds of the people and there was much alarm in the Presidency.

GOVERNMENT PURCHASES

It was during this famine that the government adopted another principle very different from those accepted on earlier occasions. It was considered that the operations of private trade could not be relied on and therefore, it would be necessary to accept the responsibility of providing the distressed districts with the whole quantity of food likely to be required. All the information available pointed to the conclusion that large imports would be necessary. Fortunately, the neighbouring province of Burma was blessed with a bountiful crop and had a surplus to spare. The question before the authorities was as to how much grain should be purchased on government account. They calculated that, if the rains of June-July were delayed or had failed, the distress would be aggravated and continue for the entire year 1874. After careful estimates, it was decided, with the approval of the Secretary of State, to import 4.80 lakh tonnes of rice. The greater part of this stock was purchased in Burma, transported by vessels to Calcutta, and distributed to the depots scattered over the famine area by government officers. Relief was administered mainly in the form of works of public utility and gratuitous assistance was confined to the infirm. About 3.40 lakh tonnes of grain were disposed of in relief operations, leaving more than one lakh tonnes of grain on the hands of the government which was constituted into a reserve.

THE MADRAS FAMINE

The great famine of 1876-78 which visited southern India was, in terms of area and population affected and the duration and intensity, a very grievous calamity experienced in British India. The government declared that the "task of saving life, irrespective of the costs, is one which it is beyond their power to undertake......but they will adopt measures to provide efficient assistance for the suffering people without incurring disastrous expenditure." "Everyone admits the evils of indiscriminate private charity, but the indiscriminate charity of a government is far worse" as it resulted in the demoralization of society and fostered indolence. The principle that all able-bodied persons must work for relief was finally and unequivocally laid down.

FIRST FORMULATIONS OF POLICY

As a result of the experiences gained during this period and from the various measures adopted to mitigate the suffering of the people, the Government of India under Lord Lytton formulated and codified, for the first time, in 1878 its policy in regard to famine relief. The main object was to sustain human life where, by reason of famine, starvation is likely to ensue. This object was not to be attained by means of indiscriminate charity which, they believed, "leads to a demoralization of society and pauperization of the people ; but by the exaction from all those who are able to work, of a task which they are able to perform in return for a wage, which, having regard to the price of food ruling at that time, shall be sufficient to sustain life." It was, however, stated that the weak, the sick, and the infirm were fit objects of charity for whom poor houses were to be established.

The government enjoined upon their officers a strict injunction to abstain from any interference with the ordinary course of trade in the buying and selling of grain. The authority to direct measures to be taken for the importation of food into any district from outside was reserved with the local government. The public officers could purchase grain only under the express permission of the local government for distribution amongst those who were authorised to receive free grain.

It was laid down that purchases of grain should, in the first instance, be made from local dealers ; but when food was to be supplied at sites far away from the supply sources and where government had opened public works, it was prescribed that an agreement with some respectable dealers may be entered into for supplying the quantity required. Advances could also be made on the proper security without interest, but on the understanding that grain will be supplied at a price not higher than that current in the neighbouring markets. The government recognised that the situation will differ from place to place and, therefore, the means to be adopted for ensuring supplies would also vary. Retail sale of grain was to be encouraged, as far as possible, through the dealers or their agents and only in the case of absolute necessity the government officers were to undertake the procurement and distribution of grain themselves.

REGULATION OF PRIVATE TRADE

The question whether government should directly intervene and control the operation of private trade in the supply of grain in famine times was further considered by the Famine Commission which submitted their report in 1880. The prohibition on exports of grain was from the very beginning looked on as the first weapon in the government armoury, and it was used in 1867 in Orissa famine and again in 1873 in the case of Bengal famine. But on the latter occasion the Governor-General Lord Northbrooke gave such convincing arguments against government interference with private trade that they were finally accepted and embodied in the minutes of the Secretary of State for India, who said that nothing could justify such a measure except a reasonable certainty that exports would so exhaust the resources of the country as a whole as to render them insufficient to supply the want of the distressed districts. But, the minute goes on to say, exceptional circumstances might justify or even require such an action. After examining all the material available and considering the matter in all its aspects, the views expressed by the Famine Commissioners (1880) were adopted :

> We have no doubt that the true principle for the government to adopt as a general rule of conduct in this matter is to leave the business of the supply and distribution of food to private trade, taking care that every possible facility is given for its free action, and that all obstacles, material or fiscal are, as far as practicable, removed.

As regards exceptional cases in which the government might be compelled to intervene which would be a departure from the general principle of abstension from interference with private trade, the Famine Commissioners enumerated four instances in which this could occur :

(a) when government has to provide food on its own relief works and for gratuitous distribution ;
(b) when a stimulant is required to trade in areas where it is sluggish ; for instance in districts lacking in means of transport and communication ;
(c) when in purely agricultural tracts where wages are paid in grain and not in money and the local demand is met from small purchases from local agriculturists, the agriculturists refuse to sell and the local traders are not in a position to import from outside ; and
(d) when the trade combines and refuses to sell or sells at unduly high prices.

In 1897 yet another Famine Commission found that it was the policy of the Government of India to adhere to the recommendations of the Famine Commissioners of 1880 and to abstain from intervention in private trade. With the object of encouraging private trade to properly manage food supplies, they recommended that the government adopt the following further measures :

(a) dissemination of full knowledge and facts about food production for general information ;
(b) guaranteed opening of public works in areas where distress was felt. The idea was to generate effective demand, i.e., the people must have money to purchase foodgrains ; and
(c) free action for private trade and removal of all obstacles—material or fiscal.

The Commission finally noted that the provincial governments endorsed this as the only right policy, though in certain instances (the famine in the Palamu district of Bihar ; Bhadrachalam taluk of Bombay ; and Mandla, Balaghat, and Chanda districts in C.P. and Berar in 1897), it was found that local supply of foodgrains was totally inadequate and the local officers had to arrange foodgrains for the people.

FAMINE INSURANCE FUND

To return to the policy decisions of 1878-79, another important decision taken by the Government of Lord Lytton was the creation of the Famine Insurance Fund. Over Rs. 14 crore had been spent by the government to combat the ravages of the famines during 1874-78, and a review of this heavy expenditure had revealed the fact that it had, in reality, been defrayed from loan funds, the ordinary revenue of the country just sufficing to meet the normal expenditure of the government. Since famines were regular at that time, the government came to the conclusion that it was financially unsound to depend on loans for meeting such charges. Instead, there should be a standing fund to be drawn upon in times of need for financing famine relief works which, in their nature, were works of permanent improvement of the country. The main idea behind this fund was to create new resources by which in normal years a surplus of revenue could be secured to meet the extraordinary charges thrown upon the state in times of famine. It accordingly decided to make a provision against the cost of periodical famines by earmarking, with the approval of the Secretary of State, £ 1 million. Additional funds were raised by means of a famine cess levied upon land and a licence tax imposed upon persons following particular professions. The licence taxes were later merged in the general income tax in 1886 and the last of the famine cesses were abolished in 1906-07.

The object of the Famine Insurance Fund and the method by which the proceeds of the new taxes were to be utilised are described in the report of a parliamentary committee appointed in 1879, presided over by Lord George Hamilton. The following is an extract from the Committee's Report :

> During the financial years 1877-78, 79 additional taxation was imposed in India in order to establish an annual Famine Insurance Fund of a crore and a half (in the currency of that time a million and a half sterling). That amount was fixed with reference to famine expenditure which during the last six years amounted to the enormous sum, exclusive of the loss of revenue, of 14 crore of rupees and of which a large proportion had been met by borrowing. The object of this Famine Insurance Fund was by increasing the revenue, to avoid constant additions to the debt of India which the prevention of periodical famine would entail by either applying that increase of income to works likely to avert famine and thus obviate famine expenditure, or by reducing annually the debt contracted for famine, so that if the famine expenditure should again become inevitable the reduction of debt made in years of prosperity would compensate for the liabilities incurred during scarcity.

Every province was required to maintain this fund with the Governor-General of India by assigning to it every year the stipulated sum of money from its revenues. The administration of the fund was on the following lines :

(a) of the annual provision of Rs. 150 lakh, the actual expenditure during the year on famine relief, which included a provision for the purchase of grain, was first met ;

(b) the surplus was partly utilised for the construction of protective irrigation works and railways and partly for granting loans to cultivators and others under the Agriculturists' Loans Act for relief purposes ; and

(c) the balance was applied to the avoidance of new debt or the reduction of old debt.

Looking upon this fund in retrospect, it is at once clear that, by 1978-79, the government had unequivocally recognised the need for an insurance against famines. Though no buffer stock of food-grains as such was created, setting apart of money in the Insurance *Fund for utilization for famine relief, which included a provision for* purchase of grains, was tantamount to making a provision for buffer in monetary terms.

REVIEW OF THE 'FUND'

The working of the Fund was reviewed by the Famine Commission of 1897 and they came to the conclusion that the actual expenditure during the past fifteen years on protective works amounted to more than half the share of the full grant allotable to such works under the scheme. In respect of such works therefore, they said, the intentions of the scheme as approved by the Secretary of State appeared to have been fully carried out on a series of years, if not annually, and the short appropriations affected only the head—"reduction of debt". The question whether the short appropriations had affected this head really or only nominally seemed to depend upon whether they were inevitable or had been avoided by measures of economy in the general administration of the finances. They further found that, in seven years out of fifteen, expenditure against the grant was limited to the actual outlay on famine relief as such as well as on protective works, and that there was no famine surplus applied to the avoidance or reduction of debt. They finally concluded that although the exigencies of finance or other considerations might have prevented the government from completely fulfilling the self-imposed application, the finances as a whole had been so administered as to practically fulfil the policy of insurance involved in the scheme. They noted that at the end of 1885-86 there was an aggregate surplus of over Rs. 1.31 crore which, by causing the reduction or avoidance of debt to the same amount, gave the government the necessary borrowing power to meet the cost of the great famine in the two following years.

THE SURPLUS—WHETHER TO BE STORED BY THE GOVERNMENT

The Famine Commission of 1880 which did a pioneering work towards evolving the government policy in regard to famines and famine relief sought to determine that net surplus of foodgrains that would be available in a year of normal outturn. They found that the normal outturn of food in British India exceeded 50 million tonnes, and after meeting the requirements on account of consumption, seed, cattle feed, and wastage, a surplus of 5 million tonnes could be expected. They concluded that in global terms the production was sufficient to meet the total requirements of the country and it was only the transport bottleneck which aggravated the situation in a famine year.

The Commission examined the question of grain stocks to be held by the government, and considered it inadvisable for the government to store grain for the following reasons :

(i) The probable cost appeared to them to be the most serious objection. It was estimated that if the population that may at any time require relief for a year may be taken at 7½ per cent of the affected population and further assuming the population of the famine stricken tract at 40 million, which was about one-fifth of the total population, a reserve of 5 lakh tonnes was required to be maintained. This quantity, they further argued, would be required for relief every year, whether it was stored or purchased on the occasion. If it was to be stored, its original cost would be enhanced by interest on the capital invested in the purchase, which would be two and three quarters times its first price, and if the costs of storing, renewal, and management which should certainly be taken at not less than the interest rate were added, the ultimate cost would be six and half times of the first cost. On the other hand, if grain were to be purchased when it was required, the probable cost could hardly exceed three times the price in a season of low prices, and on the average it would probably be cheaper than this. Consequently, far from there being a financial advantage in the storing, it would almost certainly be more than twice as costly as the purchase at the time the grain was wanted.

(ii) Any hope of reducing the cost by laying in the stock by degrees in the course of years of plenty was obviously incompatible with the essential condition that famine may occur in any year, and that the store must always be ready and always sufficient. Moreover, the expectation that by selling operations of the stock in years of high prices, but not of famine, a profit might be obtained and the ultimate cost of the transaction might be thus reduced, would be wholly inconsistent with the intention of keeping a reserve of food sufficient for all possible contingencies, and such a proceeding would be entirely beyond the proper scope of government action.

(iii) The suggestion was also open to serious doubt on grounds of economy. The Commissioner felt that the proposal could be defeated only on the assumption that there was a probability of crop failure on a country-wide basis or that the means of conveying the surplus of one region to meet the deficit of the other did not exist. It stated that both assumptions were not correct and that there was no such probability. It referred to the "experience of the various States in Europe which have passed from a condition of frequently recurring famine, such as that which now characterises India, to one in which, though high prices are at times inevitable, actual famine due to absence of food was unknown." It also referred to the experience of England where attempts to secure food supply by direct state interference always ended in failure and "the safety of the population and their freedom from extreme fluctuations from the price of flood were only assured from the time when such efforts were finally abandoned."

(iv) The Commission pointed out the dangers and difficulties consequent on the storage of grain by the government, especially in the manner in which the stocks would be utilised and which the government would regulate by releasing or withholding them. "The result, upon the dealers in grain, of the government suddenly opening the stocks when prices rose beyond certain limit, and upon the people when the stores were closed, the local trade having meanwhile been destroyed or its action paralysed, must, we think, be disastrous."

(v) It was feared that any system of the government storing grain, once brought home to the people, would have a great impact on their providential habits. "With the existence of public granary in every village, ready to be thrown open whenever distress occurred, would be a standing encouragement to improvidence and recklessness. The plan would a strike death blow at that healthy development of the internal trade of the country, now in an early stage, but steadily thriving under the encouragement given by the extension of railways and complete free trade, and it would raise a fatal barrier to the growth of those qualities of self-reliance in the community without which the country can never raise itself in the scale of civilization." Tutelage of state, they said, was no way to fight famine.

The Commission nevertheless recognised the necessity for providing storage capacity for the surplus grains of the year of plenty and expressed their confidence that this was already being done on a large scale. What was required was to encourage the practice within the limits that true economy required, not by the intervention of the state but by the growing intelligence of the people to do what was necessary to ensure the surplus being rendered available, whenever and wherever it was needed, by extended railway communication and through the agency of the internal trade of the country.

DISSENTING VIEW

Two members of the Commission, James Caird and H.E. Sullivan, expressed dissent with the majority report on the question of grain reserve to be held by the government. They felt that "under present conditions, it might be not only expedient, but absolutely necessary, for the state to make a provision in the manner condemned by our colleagues." They referred to certain localities in southern, western, and central India which were isolated and inaccessible and which were especially vulnerable to visitations of famine. For these areas they strongly suggested a plan of storage which they thought should be adopted initially on a limited scale leaving the extension of the operation to be decided by the success or failure of the experiment.

They plainly rejected the theoretical surplus of five million tonnes arrived at by the Commission. They said that the annual exports of wheat and rice from all over India were of the order of one million tonnes and not more. If the five million tonnes figure was to be accepted, then how was it that when the famine came, affecting not more than one-tenth of the population roughly, it was only by immense pressure on other parts of India and at a quadrupled price that the supplies could be obtained ? This was a clear proof, they argued, that the surplus of five million tonnes must be greatly overestimated.* As to the theory of famines being the disease of "infancy of a nation," the two members said that "India as a nation has long passed its infancy," and the task of the British Government was by "fostering diversity of occupation, to guard it against decline."

The minute of dissent goes on—the food of two-thirds of the people of India is grain and of one-third, rice. The annual surplus of rice, as shown by the export, is so great that a sufficient supply from the current crop can always be relied on to meet a partial rice famine. "But the export of foodgrain other than rice from India during the past ten years had been less than one day's consumption of the grain eating population. There would thus appear to be no sufficient annual surplus within the country to meet the demand of a severe grain famine, without drawing part of their ordinary food from the unaffected districts, thereby diminishing their supply, raising the price and thus extending the area and general pressure of the famine." This, they stated, has been the uniform effect of drawing supplies suddenly to the famine districts from other parts of India. Supplies from foreign countries are practically impossible to obtain and in a country where the annual surplus is so small, they concluded, the absolute need for keeping reserves for seasons of scarcity, particularly for places which are inaccessible, is almost imperative. The most effectual remedy for this would be the storage of grain in such localities in seasons of plenty.

They recommended that in accessible and outlying places, the government, should "through their resident officials, do for the safety of the poorer class what the wealthier now do for themselves." The people have different varieties of dry grain—generally speaking coarse grain and minor millets—grown in their areas, which are the specific food they are accustomed to. As these common grains are rarely an article of export, their storage, they argued, would in no

*They referred to the notional surplus of over five million tonnes calculated in para 156 of the 1880 Famine Commission Report and said that, since the writing of the report, the population had risen by 1.7 per cent per annum and the food requirements to 54.30 million tonnes. During the same period the area under foodgrains had registered an increase of only 8 per cent (166½ million acres to 185 million acres) and the outturn could be reckoned at 56 million tonnes. On these figures a surplus of only 1.70 million tonnes could be determined.

> ment to improvidence and recklessness. The plan would a strike death blow at that healthy development of the internal trade of the country, now in an early stage, but steadily thriving under the encouragement given by the extension of railways and complete free trade, and it would raise a fatal barrier to the growth of those qualities of self-reliance in the community without which the country can never raise itself in the scale of civilization." Tutelage of state, they said, was no way to fight famine.

The Commission nevertheless recognised the necessity for providing storage capacity for the surplus grains of the year of plenty and expressed their confidence that this was already being done on a large scale. What was required was to encourage the practice within the limits that true economy required, not by the intervention of the state but by the growing intelligence of the people to do what was necessary to ensure the surplus being rendered available, whenever and wherever it was needed, by extended railway, communication and through the agency of the internal trade of the country.

DISSENTING VIEW

Two members of the Commission, James Caird and H.E. Sullivan, expressed dissent with the majority report on the question of grain reserve to be held by the government. They felt that "under present conditions, it might be not only expedient, but absolutely necessary, for the state to make a provision in the manner condemned by our colleagues." They referred to certain localities in southern, western, and central India which were isolated and inaccessible and which were especially vulnerable to visitations of famine. For these areas they strongly suggested a plan of storage which they thought should be adopted initially on a limited scale leaving the extension of the operation to be decided by the success or failure of the experiment.

They plainly rejected the theoretical surplus of five million tonnes arrived at by the Commission. They said that the annual exports of wheat and rice from all over India were of the order of one million tonnes and not more. If the five million tonnes figure was to be accepted, then how was it that when the famine came, affecting not more than one-tenth of the population roughly, it was only by immense pressure on other parts of India and at a way interfere with the operation of foreign trade, and as the storage would be sub-divided in every village, it could be done without disturbance to the usual operations of husbandry.

Favouring government reserve of foodgrains, they said, in times of famine, not much reliance could be placed on private trade. Trade, as a rule acted cautiously, and was not influenced by sentiments. Thus trade remained inactive until the uncertainty had become reality, when the task of replenishing the exhausted stocks over an enormous area become one of such vast proportions that, without fast and dependable means of communication, the task could not be done. But in the meanwhile, famine became the master of the situation and trade supplies arrived too late to save the lives of the multitude. They argued that the stored provision of an adequate supply of food for the poorest class in every village would give time for trade to operate, and, by inspiring confidence among the people, would prevent wandering and disruption of local and family ties.

SCHEME OF PARTIAL STORAGE

They therefore, put forward a suggestion for partial storage, more as a means of saving life than of saving money. They suggested to proceed gradually, making one locality after another safe against famine after careful trials. They calculated that 0.66 million tonnes of grain would be required, in the first period of eleven years (for they estimated that a severe famine visited once in 11 years) to feed, for 54 years, 10 per cent of the population of one-fifth part of India—the population assumed to be difficult of access. Sixty thousand tonnes of this would be purchased annually in years of plenty. In the eleventh year, one-fifth of the stores would be required to meet a famine, and this quantity should be replenished in the first-two good seasons following the famine year. In the next period of eleven years the second-fifth of the stocks would be required for meeting the famine which would again be replenished in the manner indicated above. The third-fifth of the stock will be consumed in the famine following the third eleven year period, namely, between the twenty-second and thirty-third year and would again be replenished in the like manner. They calculated that the average annual cost of the stocks including maintenance would progressively decline and the entire expenditure would be £ 5.34 million, which would be much less than the amortised value of the £ 1.5 million famine insurance anxiety as to the ability of private trade to deliver food where it was needed. They referred to the examination of these and kindred issues by the 1880 Commission and observed that their approach and views continued to be valid. They, however, stressed the necessity of improving the means of transport by expanding the railway system.

5

Evolution of the Policy in Twentieth Century

PART A

IN THE FIRST-HALF OF THE TWENTIETH CENTURY

THE initial decades of the present century were, comparatively speaking, comfortable from the point of view of food supplies and excepting the years of 1918 and 1920, no major scarcity or famine visited the country till 1942-43. There were minor deficiencies in rainfall in various parts of the country, but the distress that is associated with a full scale drought or famine fortunately spared the country.

FAMINE INSURANCE FUND—A FURTHER REVIEW

The Famine Insurance Fund continued to be maintained by the central government and to be utilised for the purposes explained earlier. A critical review* of the composition and utilization of this fund was undertaken by the Government of India in 1926 and the expenditure on famine relief over a 20-year period—1896 to 1916—and on protective irrigation works over a more recent period of 10 years—1907 to 1917—was critically examined. It was found that the expenditure on famine relief had been considerably less than in the 15 years period examined by the 1897 Famine Commission and that considerable outlays from this fund were applied towards reduction of ordinary debt. A criticism was also voiced by certain provinces that, whereas they were required under a statute to make annual assignments to the fund, the proceeds thereof were at the disposal of the

*This material has been gathered from the records in the National Archives.

Government of India which were often being applied to strengthening the financial position of the Central Government. It was also complained that the rate of annual assignment prescribed was also excessive whereas, because of remarkable improvement in agriculture and irrigation, the incidence of famine relief was steadily going down.

The matter was discussed in detail in a conference of financial commissioners of the provinces and arising out of their deliberations and general consensus, the following recommendations were made to the Secretary of State for India :

(i) the 'Famine Insurance Fund' should now be called 'Famine Relief Fund' ;

(ii) the provinces would be making annual contributions to this fund at the rate prescribed in Rule 29 of the Devolution Rules. These contributions would stop on the credit balance of a province reaching the figure prescribed in this rule ;

(iii) the Governor-General would credit the provinces' account with interest calculated on the average of balances on the last day of each quarter ;

(iv) the fund shall continue to form part of the general balances of the Governor-General ;

(v) when the balance to the credit of a province exceeded the amount prescribed in the rules, the provincial government was free to withdraw the excess and utilise it for any of the following purposes :

  (a) protective irrigation works ;
  (b) grant of loans to the cultivators ;
  (c) repayment of loans contracted earlier ; and
  (d) famine relief.

A proviso was, however, added that should a provincial government consider a work or relief measure, not covered under the above categories, of such value and public utility as to be taken up out of these funds, they could do so with the approval of the Governor-General. Thus discretion was allowed to take up other works too, if they, in the opinion of the local government, would accord with the general principles of famine relief.

In May 1928, the Secretary of State for India approved the above proposals, with minor amendments, but with the stipulation that the modified scheme be treated as an experiment and a report be submitted to him on its working after expiration of five years.

The passing of the Government of India Act of 1935 introduced yet one more change, in that it did not contain any provision for the continuance of this fund as a statutory fund and as part of the central government funds. As a result of this constitutional change, the fund merged in the general finances of the provinces and became available for spending on ordinary services of the provinces. But the Central Legislative Council adopted a resolution on February 3 1936, saying that these balances should be conserved and they should continue to serve the purpose which they were serving till then. Finally, each province passed a Famine Relief Fund Act to which these balances were transferred and thus the fund which started as a central fund became a provincial fund. But the rules and principles of its operation were retained by and large as before.

THE GREAT BENGAL FAMINE

The Bengal famine of 1942-43 was in its intensity and extent, comparable to the great famines that ravaged this country in the second-half of the 19th century. The vastly improved network of roads and railways, no doubt helped in rushing supplies from all over the country but the effects of rising prices and short supplies were felt almost everywhere. Narration of the horrors of this famine and the lamentable loss of life and privations of people have been covered in innumerable works but a brief resume of the situation as it developed, culminating in the Great Famine and giving rise to numerous policy measures, including government purchases and holding of buffer stocks, will be given here.

The difficulties may be traced to Japan's entry into the Second World War in December 1941. The fall of Burma resulted in the cessation of rice imports from that country. The fear that India might be invaded also agitated the public mind. In October 1942, the districts of Midnapore, Barisal, Dinajpore, and 24-Parganas were swept by a severe cyclone, devastating both *aman* and *boro* crops. The harvest of the earlier year was also a poor one. The prices of rice started rising immediately after the cyclone and rose abnormally high in November and December 1942. The key to the situation was the Calcutta market. The remedy, the Bengal Government thought, lay, in the first instance, to check speculation and restore healthy conditions in the Calcutta market and, in the second, to maintain steady supplies from the hinterland. But how was this to be brought about ? Statutory price control had been tried earlier and had failed ; imposing restrictions on the trade not to buy or sell above the prescribed price would only worsen the condition. Experience had shown that the use of the "denial" stocks had helped to check the rise in prices. Proceeding on the basis of this experience, the first procurement scheme began in December 1942 with the district officers commencing buying operations through the local traders. A target of 7,400 tonnes had been fixed and each district was given a quota. The officers were also authorised to requisition stocks. They were however told in clear terms that the stocks were not intended for their own districts and that they would not be permitted to immobilise them for local purposes, except with previous sanction. However, not much was achieved under this arrangement.

CONTROL MEASURE—PROCUREMENT

As the war situation worsened, the provincial government was compelled to undertake procurement operations on a more extensive scale. A number of agents from private trade were selected and allotted areas in which they were to make purchases. The maximum price at which purchases were to be made was fixed and the district officers were directed to warn all traders in the buying areas that their licenses would be cancelled and their stocks requisitioned if they bought above the government buying rates. It was soon found that the warning did not suffice to protect the government agent against competitive buying with the result that the government could but procure only small quantities. Restrictions were immediately imposed in the buying areas (which were also the surplus areas) prohibiting export except under a permit. Speculative buying was also prohibited in the non-buying areas. Yet, all these measures did not help much.

In January 1943, the government appointed a foodgrains purchasing officer to supervise and control the activities of the buying agents and regulate the issues of export permits. This too did not result in the acquisition of substantial stocks.

A breakdown in the supplies for Calcutta appeared imminent and a vital decision on the policy had to be taken urgently. Two courses were open : (i) to intensify the policy of controlled procurement, hold prices rigidly, and pass over from reliance on voluntary sales to coercion for securing supplies at a fixed price. This, among other measures, meant seeking out stocks wherever they were—whether with the traders or producers—and to requisition them ; (ii) to allow prices to rise and to secure stocks by purchase in the open market as well as by imports from other provinces. Deciding in favour of the second option, the policy was declared on March 11 in the following terms :

> (i) To clear up misapprehensions which are still impeding the flow of paddy and rice into the markets, the Bengal government declare categorically that there is and will be no statutory maximum price for wholesale transactions in paddy and rice. Both cultivators and traders are free to bring their grain to the market without fear of having it taken from them at a price to which they do not agree. No trader who has declared his stock under the Foodgrains Control Order will be compelled to part with it below the prevailing market price,
>
> (ii) The Bengal government, in full accord with the government of India, adhere to the policy of buying as much rice and paddy as possible by free market operations in order to secure the best use of the resources of the province and their most equitable distribution,
>
> (iii) The clear abrogation of any vestige of price control in the primary wholesale market does not imply unrestricted profiteering. Government's own operations as buyer and seller coupled with the removal of the black market are in their opinion most likely to be successful in moderating prices at a reasonable level ; but to prevent buying at reckless prices by wealthy areas the embargoes prohibiting the movement of paddy and rice from one area in the province to another will remain in force. The government itself takes the responsibility for the movement of paddy or rice to deficit areas.

This decision of the provincial government was in accord with the policy of the government of India at that time and was indeed taken with the latter's approval. The immediate effect was an increase in the volume of supplies purchased by the government, in a short period of three weeks in March, the government purchases exceeded 17,000 tonnes, which were much more than the purchases made between December 1942 and February 1943.

Till 11 March 1943, the Government of Bengal and the Government of India were moving on the whole in the direction of increasing Government control on the entire food economy. But from this date onwards there was a striking change in the direction of the policy and a retreat from control began. Decontrol was the first step ; removal of barriers within Bengal was the next and introduction of free trade into the eastern region as a whole was the culmination of this decontrol policy which came into force by May 18, 1943.

CENTRALISED PURCHASES

The first scheme for centralised purchase of foodgrains was evolved by the central government in September 1942 ; it was also considered in detail at the sixth Price Control Conference held in that month. Two courses were open : unrestricted free trade and modified free trade. The plan of action approved at this conference was as follows :

(a) Exports of wheat from surplus provinces and states were to be regulated by a central government organization which should purchase the requirements of the armed forces, labour, and the deficit provinces and states up to a predetermined figure. The purchases were to be made through agencies selected in consultation with the provincial or state governments ;

(b) purchase operations were to be conducted in close collaboration with the price control authorities in the surplus provinces and states which were to render all possible assistance to the central organization ;

(c) in allocating supplies for civil distribution, priority was to be given to the requirements of fair price shops, consumer cooperatives, industrial areas, big cities, public utilities, and places where military works were under construction ;

(d) supplies were to be despatched only to consignees approved by the Director, Civil Supplies, or to the Director himself;

(e) in calculating the export quota for the surplus areas and import quotas for the consuming areas, the principle of "equality of sacrifice" was to be borne in mind. In other words, the scale of consumption as reduced by the overall inadequacy of supplies was to be uniformly applied to all provinces.

BASIC PLAN

This plan of action really represented the second approach—modified wheat trade—which, with some modifications and refinements, came to be known as the "basic plan". This concept was concerned with that aspect of the general problem of enforcement which involved a determination, first, of the magnitude of the aggregate surplus of foodgrains available in certain states ; and, second, with the magnitude of the aggregate deficit in others, and of the assistance which could be mustered from the surplus areas for the benefit of the deficit areas. Since production varied from time to time, readjustment of figures from time to time would be inevitably necessary and such revision of figures should not be taken to mean failure of the basic plan. The Committee, therefore recommended that, within any one calendar year, there should be two dates at which stock was to be taken of the situation. The first of these dates was to be in April and the other in November, they were harvest months when fairly reliable estimates of crop production would be available. During the intervening period the figures of the Basic Plan were to be kept continuously under review with the object of preparing as accurate an estimate as possible of the crop size.

This system was originally conceived for wheat but the conference recommended that it should be adopted for other staple foodgrains (rice, *jowar*, *bajra*, *ragi*, barley, gram, and maize). But whereas in the case of wheat the whole of India was regarded as one unit and the responsibility was laid on the centre for purchasing and allocating supplies, the conference favoured the division of India into different regions and the treatment of each region as a unit for the control of inter-provincial movement of goodgrains other than wheat. This was, perhaps, to be done through the regional price and supply boards set up to operate either through their own machinery or through the machinery of the provincial governments subject to the general direction of the central government.

FOODGRAIN ENQUIRY COMMITTEE

In July 1943, the Government of India set up the Foodgrains Enquiry Committee. The question of creating a central foodgrain reserve received a scientific, rational, and systematic treatment for the first time at the hands of this Committee. It considered the proposition primarily in the context of the war situation and the climate of defeatism and rumours that were pervading the atmosphere then. Hoarding and profiteering were rampant. They considered this subject from two angles "To break defeatism and to curb the monopolist who is prepared, for his own profit making motives, to hold government to ransom," the Committee observed that the instrumentality of a central reserve was the best guarantee for securing maximum flow of supplies from the cultivators to the consumers.

The Committee also considered this device in the context of making procurement a central government monopoly. The central government would become the sole owner of foodgrains and no one would be allowed to buy, sell, or deal in foodgrains except as part of the central government's procurement agency. All movement of foodgrains within the country would, by implication, be also on government account. It was argued before the Committee that the only completely satisfactory system of procurement and distribution of foodgrains was one in which, first, the whole of the surplus was at the disposal of the government and second, the entire population was rationed. Such a system alone would be, it was urged, a consistent and self-contained "full monopoly". In other words, it was a completely government controlled supply system worked through universal rationing. For obvious reasons, this idea was not seriously pursued.

VARIOUS METHODS OF PURCHASE/PROCUREMENT

The power of requisitioning was also suggested when the offer of supply was not maintained by voluntary sales. The Committee, however, made it clear that stocks should not be requisitioned from small cultivators who had a marginal surplus over and above their own needs. It suggested that requisitioning be limited to holdings with an acreage above a prescribed minimum. The protagonists of the monopoly procurement system, in force in Bombay and Madras, however, recommended it as a substitute for requisitioning. They argued that the compulsory sale of the levy quota in Bombay and of the assessed surplus in Madras and some of the states like Travancore-Cochin, Mysore and Kolhapur were as good as requisitioning. These were tested and reliable methods of building up government stocks and commended them to the government.

The Committee, after considerable deliberation, came to the conclusion that the scheme of full monopoly would not be practicable in deficit provinces like Bengal, Bihar, and parts of Orissa and

Assam. In areas which had an assured surplus, on the other hand, the scheme of full monopoly would not be necessary, provided the procurement machinery was adequate. In Central Provinces and Berar, a limited monopoly scheme was in force which gave the government a limited right of purchase over the marketable surplus. It finally concluded that, strictly from the stand-point of principle, complete government monopoly would be the only solution but which, in view of the more urgent compulsions of the war and the unpreparedness of the government for enforcing such a system, was impracticable. On the other hand, the central foodgrain reserve was indispensable. In order to achieve these varied objectives and to avoid unnecessary competition, it recommended that procurement should be entrusted to the provincial governments, with the overriding right of the central government to intervene and insist upon remedial measures should the procurement agency and arrangements prove unsatisfactory. It, therefore, left the choice of the means of procurement to the provinces and states.

The argument on the other extreme namely "Free Trade" was dismissed as utterly impracticable in the conditions prevailing in the country at that time and aggravated by the compulsions of World War.

CENTRAL RESERVE

The Committee built up the case for the central reserve thus. It examined the level of imports and exports for the country as a whole and noted that ever since the separation of Burma the country had imported more rice than wheat. Imports of wheat were comparatively less. Immediately before the war, rice imports were as high as 2.43 million tonnes. This, however, progressively came down as the war progressed and southeast Asia went into Japanese hands. The Committee reiterated that the food problem in India could not be solved merely by an absolute increase in the supply ; a very considerable degree of substitution of grains which were in short supply by those which were in greater availability would be necessary. The aggravation caused by the war had only highlighted this necessity.

The Committee also devoted considerable attention to the question of exports and imports in the light of the exigencies of the war. It noted that the declared policy of the government of India was not to allow exports of foodgrains which they considered to be the right and, indeed, the inevitable policy for the government to adopt in the circumstances then prevailing. It however emphasised that total stoppage of all foodgrain exports would inflict considerable inconvenience, and even hardship, on areas which traditionally depended, in part, for their supplies from India. For wider strategic reasons the Committee observed that it might not be desirable to restrict supplies to such areas. On the other hand, loss of imports would create its own complications. The position in certain deficit areas might be aggravated and seriously affect the sense of security generally.

The Committee stated unequivocally that for the duration of they war, India must stop being a net exporter of foodgrains until supplies were once again available from Burma. Export of rice was recommended to be prohibited altogether. It was possible, it said, that exports from the west coast to the Persian Gulf could be compensated by imports on the east coast, but prescribed that the government should not commit even to such compensatory transactions unless they were assured that for every tonne of foodgrain they were prepared to release, another tonne of foodgrain would be made available to them.

As regards imports, the Committee observed that foodgrain supply in certain deficit areas was closely bound up with the maintenance of imports which provided a safe and comfortable cushion to support public morale. Imports were important weapon in the hands of the government to combat profiteering and hoarding. The Committee came to the following conclusions :

(a) India required 0.5 million tonnes to build up a central foodgrain reserve not as an expedient or a substitute for vigorous efforts on the part of every provincial or state government, but as a supplement. The procurement and rationing programmes as well as the price problems, they said, needed this reserve to attain maximum efficiency. This was absolutely necessary to prevent a breakdown of the machinery of the procurement, rationing, and holding the price line ; and

(b) India required by way of imports for current consumption nearly one million tonnes of foodgrains. This was determined on the basis of the imports for the last five years.

PURPOSE OF THE RESERVE AND RULES OF OPERATION

Elaborating the concept of the foodgrain reserve, the Committee considered the creation of this reserve as "indispensable." It went on to say : "We believe that no one single factor would contribute more to the solution of the food situation in India than the knowledge that such a reserve existed and that it would be used ruthlessly and fearlessly as a counter weapon in any attempt to hold the country up to ransom." In order to build up this reserve and strengthen it, it made the following recommendations :

(a) the reserve should be at the exclusive and undisputed command of the central government ;
(b) the provincial governments should not weaken their procurement activity in the hope that help would be forthcoming from the centre ;
(c) the reserve should be over and above the quantum required for current consumption (this was the precursor to the concept of "operational stocks" adopted by the Technical Group in 1976) ;
(d) the reserve must be used to convince the speculators and profiteers that the government of India was in a position to break any ring which may be formed against it ; and
(e) the reserve should be "turned over" from time to time with a view to preventing deterioration.

The Committee went to the extent of saying that the actual quantity in the reserve must be kept a close secret, "but the fact of its existence should not be left in doubt." Finally, the sale of these stocks to private trade was forbidden.

THE FINAL APPROACH

The report of the Famine Enquiry Commission of 1945 may be quoted here as a postscript to this whole era during which the policy of foodgrain reserve emerged in a clear and unambiguous outline. It stated in categorical terms that the state should recognise its ultimate responsibility to provide enough food for all. "It is abundantly clear that a policy of *laissez faire* in the matter of food supply and nutrition can lead nowhere and would probably end in catastrophe. All the resources of government must be brought to bear in order to achieve the end in view." In putting forward this principle, they quoted recommendation (iii) of the U.N. Conference on Food and Agriculture to which Government of India was a signatory :

"That the Government and authorities here represented :

"(a) Immediately undertake the task of increasing the food resources and improving the diets of their people in accordance with the principles and objectives outlined in the findings of the Conference, and declare to their respective peoples and to other Governments and authorities here represented their intention of so doing."

TABLE 5.1 : **Availability and supply of foodgrains on government account**

(*in million tonnes*)

	1945	1946	1947	1948	1949	1950
Opening stocks	N.A.	N.A.	1.15	0.65	1.06	1.60
Procurement	3.94	4.05	4.14	2.69	4.44	4.69
Imports	0.86	2.28	2.37	2.88	3.76	2.15
Total availability	4.80	6.34	7.66	6.23	9.27	8.45
Total supplies on govt. account (including exports)	N.A.	N.A.	7.18	5.27*	7.82*	7.67

N.A. — Not available.

Import figures for the period 1945 to August 15, 1947, relate to undivided India and thereafter to the Indian Union.

*Includes exports of 65,000 tonnes in 1948 and 10,000 tonnes in 1949.

From Table 5.1 it becomes apparent that the policy of the government holding stocks for public distribution came into full implementation from the very beginning. The policy at this time was not to hold stocks, but to work out the basic plan and thus determine the 'deficit' and the 'surplus' of the provinces and princely states and require them to receive and hold the stocks accordingly. The suggestions of the Foodgrains Enquiry Committee to create a central reserve was no doubt accepted by the government but the exigencies and preoccupations of the war prevented it from acquiring these stocks. Moreover, in the circumstances then prevailing, the first priority was to feed the people and the stocks internally procured or imported were directly allocated to the provinces and the states for keeping the rationing system going.

The policy of building up a 'reserve' thus emerged in unambiguous relief, which received further improvement in subsequent years.

PART B

IN THE SECOND-HALF OF THE TWENTIETH CENTURY

FIRST POLICY STATEMENT

A major development in the independence era was the first ever elaboration of an All-India Policy on Agriculture. The spade work for the policy statement was done by a number of Expert Groups. A preliminary plan for economic development covering Agriculture was prepared by the Reconstruction Committee of the ICAR constituted in early 1943 finally leading to a Memorandum prepared in 1944 indicating the ways and means of optimising agricultural production. This was endorsed by the Policy Commitiee on Agriculture. The Famine Enquiry Commission, 1945 also made a series of recommendations in its final report for imporving agriculture. After careful consideration of the various suggestions and recommendations made by these Bodies, the Government of India issued a statement on "Agriculture and Food Policy in India" in January, 1946, which inter alia stated :

"The all-India policy is to promote the welfare of the people and to secure a progressive improvement in their standard of living. This includes the responsibility of providing enough food for all, sufficient in quantity and of requisite quality. For the achievement of this objective, high priority will be given to measures for incresing the food resources of the country to the fullest extent and in particular to measures designed to increase the output per acre and to diminish dependence on the vagaries of nature. Their aim will be not only to remove the threat of famine but also to increase the prosperity of the cultivator, raise levels of consumption and create a healthy and vigorous population." The ten objectives of policy set out in the statement included increase in production of foodgrains and protective foods; improvement in methods of agricultural production and marketing; stimulating production of raw materials for industry and exports; securing remunerative prices for the producer and fair wages to the agricultural labourer; ensuring fair distribution of the food produced, and promoting nutritional research and education.*

* Report of the National Commission on Agriculture, 1976, Part I—Review and Programmes, page 136-7.

THE 1947 COMMITTEE

The first committee to examine the foodgrains policy was set up in September 1947 under the chairmanship of Sir Purshottamdas Thakurdas. The terms of reference of this committee were :

(a) measures to increase domestic production;
(b) extent to which reliance can be placed on imports; and
(c) modifications necessary in the foodgrains policy so far pursued.

The Committee confirmed that there was a gap between the demand and the supply which was to be met with from imports. But they observed that the scale of imports was to be restricted, as far as possible, to quantities needed for the maintenance of the central reserve and meeting an emergency such as crop failure. The Committee said that the need for imports should be terminated after a period of not more than five years. It recommended a ceiling of 2 million tonnes to be imposed on total foodgrain imports during 1948.

The Committee briefly considered the question of creating the foodgrains reserve in the context of the food policy to be adopted during the next five years. Having regard to the increasing tendency of the countries throughout the world to restrict the movement of foodgrains on government to government basis, it recommended that in 1948 the central government should endeavour to build up a foodgrains reserve of 0.5 to 1 million tonnes. During the five-year period after 1948, the government should maintain throughout a reserve of 1 million tonnes. Since coarse grains like sorghum and maize were subject to rapid deterioration, the reserve was to be maintained mainly in wheat and rice over and above the current requirements (the present concept of "operational stocks") and the grain should be periodically turned over so as to minimise the losses occurring in storage.

The Committee further recommended that the government should examine the desirability of setting up an autonomous executive organization to handle imports. It should receive the grain, keep it in proper storage and dispose it off at prices determined by the government from time to time. It should also be entrusted with the task of holding, maintaining, and turning-over the central reserve.

FOODGRAINS INVESTIGATION COMMITTEE

In August, 1949, the Foodgrains Investigation Committee was set up. It was chiefly concerned with the evaluation of the controls as they had worked till then and a review of administrative arrangements in regard to the handling of foodgrains at the ports, their transport and storage and the incidence of distribution costs and matters of that nature. Since a policy of gradual decontrol had been introduced from January 1948, the Committee directed its labours to examine the details of operational mechanics of the food policy and in that context stressed the need of taking steps to create a sense of self sufficiency in the minds of the people so that the transition from control to decontrol may be free from panic. It recommended that steps be taken to build up buffer stocks with a view to relieving pressure on intensive and rigid procurement.

THIRUMALA RAO COMMITTEE

The Foodgrains Procurement Committee appointed in February 1950, under the Chairmanship of Shri M. Thirumala Rao, M.P., was required mainly to enquire into the systems of procurement and distribution with a view to minimising imports and to suggest measures to bring about uniformity in these systems in the country to the extent possible. They were also asked to recommend any changes necessary in the central government's organisation to supervise and coordinate procurement and distribution in the states. The matters relating to the creation and maintenance of the central foodgrains reserve, therefore, did not receive any elaborate consideration at the hands of this Committee.

FIRST FIVE YEAR PLAN (1951-52 TO 1955-56)

The Food policy in relation to the pricing of agricultural produce received a systematic and scientific statement for the first time in the first Five Year Plan. It was stated that a policy of price stabilization must have in view a certain maximum as well as a certain minimum. When the economy is subject to inflationary pressures, the authors of the Plan document said, the emphasis was to be on the maintenance of the maximum within reasonable limits. But when prices showed a downward trend, a system of controls with defined procurement prices could be used—and indeed should be used—to safeguard the interests of the producers to prevent prices from falling unduly. Judicious purchases by the government at defined prices was an excellent device for stabilising prices and for evening out, to some extent, inter-state disparities. State trading in a few essential commodities was recommended and in regard to the foodgrains, it was observed that trade in these commodities would divert to the public sector surpluses which might accrue.

On the efficacy of procurement as an instrument of food management, the planners stated that it should be adopted to aim at channelling into the hands of the official agency the surplus available in the states after the needs of the local populace were provided for. Whether it should be a monopoly procurement or some form of levy had to be determined in the light of the conditions prevailing in each state. The aggregate requirements of the central and state governments for meeting their commitments, since the restoration of controls towards the end of 1948, were computed between seven and eight million tonnes. The domestic procurement was around 3 to 5 million tonnes, the balance being made good by imports which varied between 0.7 and 4.8 million tonnes.

The Central Government had not yet started directly acquiring grain stocks on its own account. It continued with the system of the states holding the stocks which it was watchfully feeding by moving stocks from the surplus areas or by making allocations from imports. The year 1951 opened with a gloomy portent : stocks of foodgrains with the states were only a little over 0.70 million tonnes. The previous *kharif* crop had been extensively damaged by floods and by prolonged drought thereafter. The government resorted to urgent imports as well as reduction in the quantum of rationing with a view to improving the stock position. These measures proved quite effective as can be seen below :

Thus, the year 1952 opened with a better stock position. As a result of internal procurement and lessening of pressure on the public distribution system, the stock of foodgrains with the state governments in the middle of 1952 stood at the record figure of 3.31 million tonnes. The original target of 5.00 million tonnes of imports was also scaled down and finally only 3.93 million tonnes were actually imported. This general improvement in the food situation continued in 1953 which witnessed a record production since Independence. The opening stocks of foodgrains with the states and the centre

TABLE 5.2

(*in million tonnes*)

Opening stocks with states on January 1, 1951	0.74
Local procurement	3.83
Supplies to states from imports	4.80
Total availability	9.37
Offtake in states	7.99
Closing stocks with states on December 31, 1951	1.38 (derived) 1.33 (reported)

(1.9 million tonnes) were higher than the previous year's. This year also saw a low point in imports—only 2.00 million tonnes. These favourable factors operating in the food economy were largely responsible for the government deciding to implement the recommendation of the Foodgrains Enquiry Committee of 1943 relating to creation of the central reserve, apart from the stock held by the state governments. Approximately 0.53 million tonnes were held in the central reserve.

The year 1954 marked a turning point in the history of India's food position. Progressive relaxations in the war-time food controls initiated in the middle of 1952 gradually had led to the restoration of an almost free market by the middle of 1954. The production of cereals in 1953-54 was also the highest ever on record and exceeded the target envisaged in the First Five Year Plan by 3.6 million tonnes. Internal procurement was continued but the general availability was so good that it was discontinued from July. The imports touched an all time low, only 0.84 million tonnes. At the end of the year, the central reserve went up to 0.87 million tonnes.

The happy trends in the food situation continued to operate in 1955-56 with the agricultural production maintaining the upward trend and the imports sliding to lower and lower levels. During this year only 0.71 million tonnes of foodgrains were imported; the lowest quantity since the Second World War. There was no compulsion for resorting to internal procurement which had been discontinued in the previous year, and the availability in the open market was extremely satisfactory. The stock in the central reserve at the end of 1955, which was the terminal year of the First Five Year Plan, was of the order of 0.75 million tonnes.

Table 5.3 summarises foodgrain stock, imports, public distribution, and the reserve stocks with the states as well as the central government during the First plan period.

TABLE 5.3 : **Balance sheet of foodgrains**

(in million tonnes)

	1951	1952	1953	1954	1955
Opening stocks with states at beginning of year	0.74	1.33	1.95	1.47	1.67
Local procurement	3.83	3.48	2.09	1.43	0.13
Imports (supplies to states)	4.80	3.93	2.03	0.84	0.70
Total availability	9.37	8.74	6.07	3.74	2.51
Offtake in states	7.99	6.80	4.60	2.15	1.64
Closing stocks at the end of the year with states	1.33	1.53	0.94	1.67	0.17
Central sales during the year	—	—	0.19*	0.63*	1.18
Central reserve at the end of the year	—	0.42	0.53	0.87	0.75
Total (central and state stocks)	1.33	1.95	1.47	2.54	0.92

*Central sales of wheat to trade. Variations in the figures of derived stocks and actual stocks are on account of rounding of the figures and stocks in the pipeline.

SECOND FIVE YEAR PLAN (1956-57 TO 1960-61)

While deciding upon the approach to the Second Five Year Plan, it was felt that it would be desirable to avoid, as far as possible, control and rationing of the necessities of life like foodgrains. But in a situation of shortages when supplies fall short of demand and prices tend to rise, the only way out would be imports. It was, however, noted that not much reliance could be placed on imports which would also mean diversion of scarce resources. It was, therefore, recommended that the government should build buffer-stocks of foodgrains and operate on them so as to moderate price fluctuations. Domestic commodity resources, judiciously operated upon, it was observed, are an important device for price stabilization and, in so far as they are used to meet an adverse situation, they are a necessary safeguard against inflationary pressures implicit in a big developmental programme. The role of the buffer-stocks was particularly emphasised as a safeguard against the consequences of deficit financing which was gradually becoming a regular feature of plan finance.

It was argued that sufficiently large stocks of foodgrains would certainly counteract inflationary pressures that may emerge from time to time. No recommendation was, however, made with regard to the size of these stocks.

The comfortable trend both in the prices as well as in the stock position was suddenly halted in 1956-57. Whereas, in the previous years, the government was disposing off foodgrains held by them by auction or open tender to avoid possible loss in deterioration, the situation in this year compelled the government to conserve and build up stocks by imports. Distribution from fair price shops was also reintroduced. Long-term contracts for imports of foodgrains from the United States and Burma were entered into primarily with the idea of building up stocks. A total quantity of 1.44 million tonnes of wheat and rice was imported. Internal procurement, however, could not make much headway because the prices generally ruled high and the government was not able to purchase much at the official procurement prices. During the year about two million tonnes of foodgrains were released from government stocks for the public distribution system.

PL-480 AGREEMENT OF 1956

During 1954, when the memories of the war-time shortages were still fresh, the Ministry of Food and Agriculture had conducted an exercise to determine the net shortfall in food supplies and the means to make them good through sustained imports. It had come to the conclusion that, at least during the second plan period, shortfall in wheat would be around 8 to 10 million tonnes and in rice around 4 to 5 million tonnes. Accordingly, negotiations were initiated with the United States for importing foodgrains under PL-480 to meet this shortfall, as well as for building up the buffer stock. Eventually an agreement was signed in August 1956. Simultaneously, commercial purchases were also negotiated with other countries such as of rice from Burma and of wheat from Australia and Canada.

The manner and the extent to which imports were resorted to under PL-480 as well as on commercial basis from foreign countries till 1976 (for about 25 years) has been touched upon in the next chapter. But for the purposes of this chapter, it needs to be said that the system devised in 1954-55 and the mechanism settled with the United States under PL-480 were of the crucial importance for the buffer stocking policy.

ASOKA MEHTA COMMITTEE

In the first-half of 1957, the prices maintained a continuous rising trend despite higher production. This development gave considerable concern to the government which thought it proper to get the whole matter investigated through a high-powered committee. Accordingly, a Foodgrains Enquiry Committee was set up in June 1957 with Asoka Mehta as Chairman. The Committee briefly traced the history of the concept of reserve stocks and referred to the recommendations made by the Foodgrain Policy Committee of 1943. The endorsement of this proposal by the Famine Enquiry Commission of 1944 was recalled. The Committee next referred to the recommendations of the Agricultural Prices Enquiry Sub-Committee of 1947 to the effect that a reserve stock of the order of 15 lakh tonnes would be necessary, while some other members of that Committee felt that the size of the stock should be as large as 3 million tonnes. The Foodgrain Policy Committee of 1948 had also recommended that a reserve of one million tonnes should be built up immediately. Since the foreign exchange situation in the years following was not easy, the reserves could not be built up when, in February 1954, to everybody's relief, the food situation eased. The government considered the circumstances opportune and took swift action to maintain a central reserve of foodgrains of 15 lakh tonnes partly in rice and partly in wheat. In March 1954, an agreement was concluded with Burma to import 0.9 million tonnes of rice, partly for building up the reserve stock and partly for meeting the shortages in certain parts of the country.

The Committee considered this particular aspect of the food administration also. Since a general upward trend in prices had started because of the plan expenditure incurred during the First Five Year Plan, the Committee approached this question from the price-stability point of view. Its principal recommendation, therefore, was that a Price Stabilization Board be set up which would keep a constant watch over the price situation in respect of foodgrains and recommend, from time to time, measures for maintaining the general price level within reasonable limits. Since prices of foodgrains could be controlled only through controlling the demand and supply of foodgrains, the Committee further recommended undertaking timely and effective purchase and sale operations. For these operations, it suggested that a suitable organization be set up under the ministry with branches all over the country. The most important work of this organization should be to undertake what they termed buffer stock operations. They went on to explain these operations thus :

> The main idea of such operations is simple. Whenever prices tend to fall, even if such a fall is not general but is confined to a particular locality, this organization should step in and start purchasing at reasonable prices. Similarly, when prices tend to rise, this organization should sell at reasonable prices. The organization will, from time to time, have to fix limits of prices at which it would buy or sell, within the range of prices for its operations which will be fixed by government on the advice of the proposed Price Stabilization Board. If the organization starts operating from a position of strength, with sufficient stocks at its disposal and sufficient funds to invest, it will soon find itself in the position of a dominant trader in the economy and will be able to control the market effectively. It will then be able to counteract the market trend seeking to depress prices when the market is rising and support prices when the market is falling. This would thus go a long way to protect both the producer and the consumer against violent fluctuations in prices.

The Committee explained that operations by this organization would have beneficial effects on the food economy in general. By purchasing in surplus years, the stocks would be carried for future years of short crop while, in lean years, it will have resources to control the prices and thus even out fluctuations in both prices and supplies. It also made a number of suggestions as to how this organization should operate, after citing the manner in which similar organizations in Canada and Australia operated.

GOVERNMENT TAKEOVER OF WHOLESALE TRADE

The overall deficit in the net supplies available within the country which appeared in 1956 persisted right through the Second Plan period with the result that the government had to continue with heavy imports of cereals, mainly from the United States under PL-480. Internal procurement was meagre, whereas demands on the government stocks from all parts of the country were heavy. Shortly before 1958 came to a close (November 1958) the National Development Council decided that the government should take over the wholesale trade in foodgrains. A working group was constituted to work out the details. The scheme formulated by the working group involved steady expansion of purchases by the government with a view to establishing strategic control over the market. It also suggested progressive development of cooperatives so that the marketable surplus might be acquired through them. Till this network was fully developed, it suggested regulation of the wholesale trade by licensing the dealers with obligation to submit returns regarding purchases, sales, stockholding, etc.

The Government of India examined the report of the Working Group and decided that :

(a) state trading in foodgrains should be designed on a system under which the surplus foodgrains should be collected right from the villages through the service cooperatives federated into an apex Cooperative Marketing Federation ;
(b) the distribution should be through retailers and the consumer cooperatives ;
(c) in the interim period the wholesalers may be permitted to function as licenced dealers and make purchases on their own behalf at prescribed minimum prices. The government will have the right to acquire the whole or a part of the stocks from them at controlled prices ; the balance stock could be sold by the wholesalers to the retailers at prices not exceeding the controlled price ;
(d) in the initial stages only wheat and rice were to be covered under this scheme ; and
(e) an agency for making direct purchases of foodgrains from the producers should be set up with a view to ensuring minimum prices for the producers.

These decisions were applied in the 1958-59 season and the state purchase/procurement operations were extended from surplus areas to even deficit and marginally placed areas. The systems of procurement/purchase naturally differed from state to state but the adverse effects of this decision were felt almost immediately in the deficit and marginally placed states. The open market prices tended to rise appreciably above the maximum controlled prices and procurement of foodgrains from the wholesaler at controlled prices was found to be extremely difficult. Within one year, therefore, state trading in deficit states like Rajasthan was suspended. By September 1960, it was given up even in states like Punjab, U.P., and M.P.

The most important event which took place in 1960 was the conclusion of a long term agreement with the United States for import of wheat and rice under PL-480. This had a salutary effect on the market sentiment and the food position during 1960-61 remained generally satisfactory. Under this agreement, 16 million tonnes of wheat and one million tonnes of rice were contracted to be imported over a period of four years, which, besides meeting the current consumption requirements, would have enabled the government to build up a reserve stock of 5 million tonnes. Almost at the same time a decision was taken to build a reserve stock of 5 million tonnes. This agreement led to a psychology of dehoarding on the part of traders and producers and ultimately resulted in a sharp decline in the market prices in the latter part of 1960. The demand for foodgrains from the government stocks also dropped considerably. All these factors, coupled with steady imports from the United States, enabled the government to build up substantial reserves. Internal procurement yielded 0.73 million tonnes of rice and 0.54 million tonnes of wheat. Imports amounted to 5.14 million tonnes of which nearly 86 per cent were under PL-480—the remaining being commercial purchases. Total issues from the central stocks amounted to 4.47 million tonnes. The stocks in the central reserve at the end of this terminal year of the Second Five Year Plan were of the order of 1.94 million tonnes.

The position of procurement, imports, public distribution and the balance in reserve with Centre and the states during the Second Five Year Plan is summarized in Table 5.4.

TABLE 5.4

(*in '000 tonnes*)

Year	1956	1957	1958	1959	1960
Internal Procurement	37	295	526	1806	1275
Imports	1443	3646	3224	3868	5137
Total public distribution (both from central & state governments)	2082	3050	3980	5164	4937
*Closing stocks**					
With state governments	108	416	387	605	858
With Central Govt./ Central Pool	211	759	519	793	1943
Total	319	1175	906	1398	2801

*Stocks including total quantities in transit, docks and holds of steamers.

THIRD FIVE YEAR PLAN 1961-62 TO 1965-66

In the Third Plan, the emphasis on the maintenance of buffer stocks was in the context of stable foodgrain prices. It was noted that in a country like ours where substantial proportion of the family expenditure of a very large population is on foodgrains, reasonable stability of their prices is a matter of vital importance. The plan document said that government must always be in a position to regulate effectively the course of foodgrain prices. At the same time, the producer must also get a reasonable return. He should have the necessary incentive to invest on fertilizers, improved seeds and irrigation practices with a view to expanding production. The proposal for building up the central reserve was also being advocated in the context of anticipated increase in the agricultural production as a result of substantial investment in that sector in the Five Year Plans. The Plan expenditure in the agricultural sector during the First Five Year Plan was anticipated to boost the production by 7.6 million tonnes, whereas the target fixed for the Second Five Year Plan was 10 million tonnes of additional production. From this point of view also a policy to guarantee a certain minimum level of price was considered essential in the interests of agricultural production. The twin consideration of protecting the interests of the producers as well as of the consumers, therefore, were the broad outline of the food policy in the Third Five Year Plan.

The key to stabilising prices was recognised to be the buffer stocks and operating on them through continuous purchase and sale over the country-wide front. The level of stocks with government were recommended to be of the order of five million tonnes. In order to build up this reserve, the stocks were steadily augmented, keeping in view the problem of turning over of stocks and the availability of storage accommodation. In 1963-64, the level of buffer-stock was raised to 6 million tonnes—the grain-wise composition being 4 million tonnes of wheat and 2 million tonnes of rice. The stocks of wheat were to be built up from imports under PL-480 Agreement of May 1960, and those of rice mainly from internal procurement, because rice was a scarce commodity in the world market. But to the extent rice imports were feasible, they were also to be resorted to. In 1964-65 the position remained the same with regard to the building up of buffer stocks. The year 1965-66 was a year of country-wide scarcity, and though the decision in regard to the building up of the buffer stock was reaffirmed, the heavy drawals on the limited stocks (by middle of 1963, stocks with the centre and states were of the order of 2.46 million tonnes) during 1963-64 and 1964-65 depleted them very considerably. And since the year 1965-66 was a lean year, there was no hope of building up the buffer—the primary concern being to feed the people through the public distribution system.

The situation as it obtained during this quinquennium is summarized in Table 5.5.

TABLE 5.5

(in '000 tonnes)

Year	1961	1962	1963	1964	1965
Internal Procurement	541	479	750	1430	4031
Imports	3495	3640	4556	6266	7462
Total Public Distribution (both from Central & State Govt.)	3977	4365	5178	8665	10079
*Closing Stocks**					
With State Governments	330	395	319	486	973
With Central Govt./Central Pool	2306	1886	1940	530	1106
Total	2636	2281	2259	1016	2079

*Stocks including total quantities in transit, docks and holds of steamers.

VENKATAPPIAH COMMITTEE

In March 1966, the Foodgrains Policy Committee was set up under the chairmanship of Shri B. Venkatappiah. This Committee also endorsed the policy of maintaining a buffer stock as a powerful lever to exert a stabilising influence on the foodgrains market and on the intra-seasonal movement of prices. This Committee was examining various issues concerning the foodgrains policy referred to them at a time when a year of very severe famine had already gone by, and the scarcities were persisting in the second year in succession, thereby unleashing very serious problems of management of the food economy. They were, therefore, compelled to recommend that the minimum level of the buffer stock at the disposal of the central government should be four million tonnes and the stocks that the state governments may choose to hold should be over and above this level. They recognised the difficulty of building up such a huge buffer stock in one or two years, and observed that it was of such crucial importance that it should be given the highest priority in the formulation of the national food budget. They suggested that the level be reached at the most in four years' time. They added that to the extent imports were necessary to build up this buffer stock, they should be resorted to. At the same time internal procurement should also be maximised. The importance that they attached to this mechanism of buffer stock can be gauged from the fact that they stipulated that it should be drawn upon only with the approval of the Union Cabinet. Finally, they suggested that the buffer stock should be held and managed by the Food Corporation of India.

PLAN HOLIDAY

The three years—1966-67, 1967-68 and 1968-69 were the years of plan holiday. The precipitous fall in production of all foodgrains during 1965-66 and 1966-67 led to the liquidation of even the limited reserves built up from imports. But the crop prospects for 1967-68 were bright and a target of 3 million tonnes was fixed for the buffer by the end of October 1968. But this target could not be achieved because of delay in imports from abroad. The total stocks with the central and state agencies at the end of 1968 were of the order of 3.99 million tonnes, of which 2.8 million tonnes were treated as buffer and the rest as operational stocks. There was some accretion to these stocks during January-February 1969 so that total stocks at the end of February 1969 stood at a reassuring figure of 4.5. million tonnes.

FOURTH PLAN 1969-70 TO 1973-74

The framers of the Fourth Five Year Plan with the memory of the drought years of 1965 and 1966 vivid in their minds, recognised the importance of the buffer stocks as a means to stabilise the food economy of the country. They stated that a buffer stock was necessary not only to meet the shortfalls in production, resulting from bad years, but also to impart inter-seasonal stability to the price level. A buffer stock of adequate size was therefore, suggested to be a central feature of the food policy during the Fourth Plan.

On the question of its size, they referred to the two million tonnes level having been reached in 1968-69 and said that on consideration of a number of attending factors, they estimated a five million tonne level to be the reasonable size of the stocks which should be maintained by the Food Corporation of India. They went on to say that necessary provision was being made in the Plan partly by way of margin money for organising purchases and creating storage capacity and partly for having recourse to bank finances.

A series of good harvests in 1969-70, 1970-71 and 1971-72 helped build up the buffer stocks and at the end of 1971, they stood at 8.14 million tonnes. Thus the target fixed for the Fourth Plan was achieved ahead of the schedule. In fact this favourable development in the accretion to the stocks prompted the government to revise and update the level of stocks from 5 million tonnes to 7 million tonnes. But the very next year (1972-73) both the *kharif* and *rabi* crops suffered heavily, and the whole country was affected. Demands on the public distribution system suddenly multiplied and government were compelled to make heavy issues. The result was that by the end of 1972, the stocks with the government dwindled down to 3.44 million tonnes.

The position as it obtained during the Fourth Five Year Plan is summarized in Table 5.6.

TABLE 5.6

(*in '000 tonnes*)

Year	1969	1970	1971	1972	1973
Internal Procurement	6381	6714	8857	7665	8424
Imports	3872	3631	2054	445	3614
Total Public Distribution (both from Central & State Govts.)	9385	8841	7816	10487 +909*	11414
*Closing Stocks**					
With State Governments	1532	1670	1498	968	1175
With Central Government/ Central Pool	2921	3899	6639	2475	1959
Total	4453	5569	8137	3443	3134

*Stock including total quantities in transit, docks and holds of steamers.

Avenues which will push up the demand for foodgrains :

(a) export—either directly in the international market or by way of assistance to developing countries ;
(b) possibility of industrial uses ; and
(c) use of coarse grains as animal feed.

The Working Group suggested that the size of the buffer stock should be determined on the basis of the trend of production and annual fluctuations therein. They referred to the analysis of the 16-year figures for the period 1949-50 to 1964-65 done by the Working Group on the Fourth Five Year Plan which came to the conclusion that a buffer stock representing 7 per cent of the average production in that period would be adequate to meet situations of fluctuations in supply in two out of three years. And thus a buffer-stock of 7.00 million tonnes was considered desirable. The Working Group further noted that the proportion of irrigated area is likely to increase significantly during the Fifth Plan resulting in higher yield and the fluctuations in the production may not be of a very high order. But since to build up and to maintain a buffer stock of foodgrains is very costly, and cannot be enlarged indefinitely, they quoted the Agricultural Prices Commission which had observed in their Report on Kharif Policy for 1972-73 that the buffer stock policy "should supplement rather than supplant a direct attack on the problem of instability in the country's foodgrain economy through a re-orientation in the production strategy. The emphasis in the Fifth Plan should, therefore, be on conducting appropriate buffer stock operations to maintain price stability rather than to increase the size of buffer stock." The buffer stock target, in their opinion, represented the maximum level of stocks which should be maintained in good crop years which will surely be drawn down in lean years.

THE TECHNICAL GROUP

As to the actual size of the stock, they left the task to the Technical Group already appointed by the Government of India under the chairmanship of the Union Food Secretary, but stated at the same time, that the target of seven million tonnes should be the minimum to be maintained at all times. The operational stocks referred to earlier were to be over and above this target.

The Working Group also made certain observations on the buffer. They said that the proportion of rice and coarse grains should be progressively enlarged. They noted that since a major break-through in the rice production had not been achieved, as had been done in the case of wheat, it will be difficult to obtain large stocks of rice and hence the need for a continuous effort to augment these stocks by careful means. Finally, they briefly made an observation relating to the disposal of stocks, should a continuous run of good harvests yield bumper crops and swell the stocks in the government's

TABLE 5.7 Internal procurement, imports, public distribution and stocks of foodgrains (calendar year/all foodgrains)

(in million tonnes)

Year	Internal Procurement	Imports	Total Public Distribution (Both From Central & State Governments)	Reported Closing Stocks*		
				With State Governments	With Central Government/ Central Pool	Total
1	2	3	4	5	6	7
1950	4.69	2.16	7.68	0.74	—	0.74
1951	3.83	4.80	7.99	1.33	—	1.33
1952	3.48	3.93	6.00	1.53	8.42	1.95
1953	2.09	2.84	4.60	0.94	0.53	1.47
1954	1.43	0.84	2.15	0.80	0.87	1.67
1955	0.13	0.71	1.64	0.17	0.75	0.92
1956	0.04	1.44	2.08	0.11	0.21	0.32
1957	0.30	3.65	3.05	0.42	0.76	1.18
1958	0.53	3.22	3.98	0.39	0.52	0.91
1959	1.81	3.87	5.16	0.61	0.79	1.40
1960	1.28	5.14	4.94	8.86	1.94	2.80
1961	0.54	3.50	3.98	0.33	2.31	2.64
1962	0.48	3.64	4.37	0.40	1.88	2.28
1963	0.75	4.56	5.18	0.32	1.94	2.26
1964	1.43	6.27	8.67	0.49	0.53	1.02
1965	4.03	7.46	10.08	0.97	1.11	2.08
1966	4.01	10.36	14.09	1.33	0.88	2.21
1967	4.46	8.67	13.17	1.43	8.53	1.96
1968	6.81	5.69	10.22	1.98	2.81	3.99
1969	6.38	3.87	9.39	1.53	2.92	4.45

TABLE 5.7 (*Contd.*)

1	2	3	4	5	6	7
1970	6.71	3.63	8.84	1.67	3.90	5.57
1971	8.86	2.05	7.82	1.50	6.64	8.14
1972	7.67	0.45	10.49 **0.91	8.97	2.47	3.44
1973	8.42	3.61	11.41	1.17	1.96	3.13
1974	5.65	4.87	10.79	1.12	1.61	2.73
1975	9.56	7.41	11.25	2.65	5.64	8.29
1976	12.85	6.52	9.17	4.22	14.70	18.92
1977	9.96	0.56	11.73	3.50	13.85	17.35
1978(P)	11.09	—	10.18	3.23	13.93	17.16
1979	13.84	—	11.66	2.98	14.54	17.52
1980	11.17	0.05†	14.99	3.12	8.62	11.74
1981	12.94	0.86‡	13.01	3.22	8.28	11.50
1982(P)	15.35	2.09	14.78	3.05	9.63	12.68

*Stock including total quantities in transit, docks and holds of steamers.

**Quantity supplied to Bangladesh.

†Quantity received in repayment of wheat loan to Bangladesh.

‡Includes 0.08 million tonnes of rice received in repayment of loan to Bangladesh.

Note : The difference between the reported physical stocks and the derived stocks worked out on the basis of opening stock plus procurement and imports, minus public distribution is mainly on account of the fact that some of the procured stocks could not be taken in the stock returns sent by the various reporting agencies for the month of December, i.e., the closing month of the year.

possession. Liquidation of these stocks in such a situation would be a problem and to that end they recommended that, among others, the following outlets may be explored :

(a) increasing the supplies through the public distribution system ;
(b) encouraging industrial use of foodgrains ;
(c) promoting use of cereal as animal feeds ;
(d) regulated sales in the open market ; and
(e) exports by way of assistance to developing countries.

In Table 5.7 are shown the figures of stocks held by central as well as state governments as buffer stocks in fulfilment of the policy as it developed from time to time.

6

PL-480 Imports and Buffer Stocking

A NEW EXPERIMENT IN GRAIN TRADE

Food imports under PL-480 represent a unique development in international relations. The policy contained in this US law enacted in 1954, combined the philosophy of aid, mutual cooperation, self-help and trade in a judicious manner. These imports (see Table 6.5) at least on two prolonged occasions in the past 25 years (1957 to 1960 and again during 1964 to 1967) helped India tide over serious shortages in food supplies and enabled her to avert famine. On the third occasion when acute scarcity persisted for almost two years—1973 and 1974—the shortfall was met chiefly from non-PL-480 imports. At the end of this period the government stocks were heavily depleted and the imports which were contracted were received only in 1975 and 1976. Since these years were also of abundant harvests within the country, the imported stocks went straight into the buffer. Strangely enough, imports under PL-480 during these years were of a small order. Since then the country has been fortunately placed in a position where imports have been dispensed with—except during 1981-82 and 1982-83—and continues to hold heavy stocks that were built up from imports and replenished from internal procurement from year to year.

There is, however, a section of opinion which believes that PL-480 imports which gave us cheap and easy food, instilled a sense of relief and complaisance and thus lulled the country into a kind of a false security and diverted attention from more urgent and faster agricultural development. Protagonists of this opinion would like us to believe that the disastrous consequences of such a sense of security are visiting on us even today when after more than 30 years of independence, we have not become self-sufficient in foodgrains.

Not an insignificant cause of this state of affairs, they say, is the PL-480 imports.

SCHEME OF THE ACT

The Agricultural Trade Development and Assistance Act of 1954—more popularly known as the PL-480—came into effect in 1954. The main purpose of the Act was to authorise the U.S. administration to dispose of American "surplus" agricultural commodities by sale in local currencies.

The disposals were to be limited to "friendly" countries and its programmes were developed to bolster putative allies. The U.S. Congress generally supported the stand of the Department of Agriculture, and loans of PL-480 currencies for development purposes were made only after the Department of Agriculture was satisfied that no increased agricultural competition would result. A reserve was also to be established both to protect the domestic market from unstable supplies for commercial exports and the PL-480 programmes*. The Johnson years had seen a major shift in USDA attitudes towards food security systems. The emphasis had begun to shift from producer to consumer, from opposition towards technical assistance to championship of it, from the view of surpluses as a burden to the view of reserves as a trust for the world's peoples.

Most of the grain imports were under Title I of the act for which payment was made in rupees in India. A special account was maintained for this purpose and credited to the account of the United States government. The mechanism relating to foodgrain imports and mode of payment for them were as under :—

(a) in pursuance of each agreement the United States government issued purchase authorizations from time to time keeping in view the availability of the commodities and India's shipment plans ;
(b) on the issue of a purchase authorization, the India Supply Mission in Washington made purchases in the market ;
(c) after the purchase contracts were finalised, ships for carrying the grain were fixed ;

*Koer, Day, and Dull (eds) op. cit., pp. 229-30, 234.

(d) immediately after shipment, the suppliers were paid by the United States government, the cost of grain supplied by them ; and

(e) on receipt of advicc of payment, the United States government's rupee account in India was credited to the extent of the cost of the consignment.

ESSENTIAL CONDITIONS

Some of the conditions stipulated by the United States government were :

(a) the importing countries will import commercially a certain mainimum specified quantity of wheat (and rice where that was applicable) in the concerned U.S. fiscal years ;

(b) restrictions on export of commodities imported under the agreement or of commodities of foreign or domestic origin same as or like the commodities imported under the agreements ; and

(c) supply of information to the United States government on foodgrains received under the agreements and the fulfilment of commercial marketing requirements.

IMPORTS IN THE FIFTIES

The first agreement under PL-480 was concluded in August 1956. Although the food situation during 1954, 1955, and 1956 was quite easy, the Ministry of Food and Agriculture had started exploring possibilities of regular imports on a large scale to meet the deficit in food requirements. In May 1955, the Ministry initiated negotiations for the import of substantial quantities of wheat and rice from the United States under PL-480. The estimate was that the country would require 8 to 10 million tonnes of rice from abroad during the Second Plan period. The conclusion of negotiations, however, took some time. In May 1956, an agreement was signed with Burma for importing 2 million tonnes of rice during the next five years and in August 1956 an agreement was signed with the United States for importing 3.1 million tonnes of wheat and 0.19 million tonnes of rice under PL-480 in the next three years. While the Burmese purchase was on cash basis, purchase from the United States was on loan, repayable in 30 years.

One of the conditions imposed by the United States was that at least 50 per cent of the AID cargo be shipped in United States flag vessels despite the fact that freight rates were higher. The United States government however, bore the differential between the U.S. and non-U.S. flag freight rates. India's liability for freight being limited to the freight payable on similar non-US flag vessels. Till 1954 the U.S. government used to finance out of PL-480 funds even that part of freight which was India's liability. Consequently the freight on U.S. flag vessels, to the extent it was our liability, was paid for by us only in Indian rupees. From 1965 however the U.S. government required that the non-U.S. part of freight on U.S. flag vessels be met by us in foreign exchange. This position continued till 1967 when, as described in later paragraphs, the PL-480 underwent a radical modification.

DISPOSAL OF RUPEES

Most of the PL-480 imports during the period 1956-66 were paid for by us in rupees in the U.S. government account in India. The PL-480 legislation indicated broadly the uses to which such rupees could be applied. The exact stipulation in each agreement about the use of such funds has varied from agreement to agreement. However, broadly the rupees were to be used for (a) U.S. Embassy disbursements in India, (b) giving grants to India for financing mutually agreed projects and (c) for loans to India for agreed projects. A small proportion was also to be used for loans to private enterprise. The total position under the various agreements executed between 1956-1969 was roughly as under :—

Use	*Proportion*
U.S. Disbursements	13%
Grants	18%
Loans (to Government)	63%
Loans (to private enterprise)	6%

There has been considerable controversy in regard to the economic impact of the utilization of these 'counterpart' rupees. Some have held that the utilization of the rupees has had an inflationary impact because of the support these rupees provided in the government budget. A committee under the Chairmanship of Prof. A.M. Khusro went into this aspect of the question in 1968 and came to the conclusion that "it is difficult to establish inflationary tendencies arising out of these 'transactions' and that the impact of the PL-480 transaction on money supply and indeed on the general price level is neutral."

CHANGES IN THE SYSTEM

By an enactment entitled 'Food for Peace Act' carried out in November 1966, the PL-480 underwent a radical modification. The following changes were introduced in the act which came into effect on January, 1967 :

(a) the concept of 'surplus commodities' dominant in the old legislation was done away with. Supplies under the modified legislation could be of commodities which may not be 'surplus' ;
(b) supplies under the amended law were clearly made an instrument of US foreign policy ;
(c) emphasis was shifted from sale in 'local currency' to sale in dollars, it being provided that all local currency transactions were to be completed by December 31, 1971. The dollar payments, however, could be made under credit terms for 20 or 40 years ;
(d) countries trading with Cuba and North Vietnam were to be excluded from those entitled to receive supplies on concessional terms ;
(e) a new emphasis on 'self-help' was added ; and
(f) a provision was made for 'making identification' at the point of distribution of the commodities indicating their receipt on concessional terms through the generosity of the U.S. people, etc.

The agreements since 1967 have naturally been affected by these changes. In particular, there is a marked transition from rupee payment to dollar payment for the commodities imported. After the Food for Peace Act came into force, the first agreement signed on February 1967 required payment of the entire amount in local currency. It also contained a provision that the government of the importing country shall—

'take all possible measures to prevent the export of any commodity of either domestic or foreign origin which is the same as, or like, the commodities financed under this agreement during the export limitation period specified in the export limitation table in Part II (except as specifically approved by the Government of the United States of America).'

The agreements signed in June, September, and December, 1967 provided for payment of 20 per cent of the total (for all commodities) in convertible currency ; the agreements of April and December 1968 provided for payment of about 50 per cent in convertible currency. The net proportion in respect of foodgrains alone was as under :

Date of Agreement	Proportion of funds for commodities for rupee payment	Proportion of funds for commodities for $ payment (on credit terms)
20.2.67	100%	—
24.6.67, 12.9.67 & 30.12.67	78%	22%
23.12.68	53%	47%
25.4.69 & 13.10.69	40%	60%

Note: Generally speaking, the dollar payments were to be made on the 40-year credit terms including a grace period of 10 years.

It has been stated above that since 1965 our part of freight on U.S. flag vessels was being paid in foreign exchange. Since 1967, however, this freight though payable in foreign exchange, could be paid on credit like the commodity costs. The new provisions of the Act had given us this small advantage, as compared to the position in 1965, in respect of freight payment on American flag vessels.

Mention was made earlier that supplies under PL-480 should not disturb the commercial sales of the United States or the normal commercial patterns in international grain trade. Hence under each agreement, there lay on India an obligation for commercial imports to the extent specified in the agreement. That quantity was specified after mutual consultations and was based on commercial purchases in the past years. Sometimes, the US government also required that a specified proportion of the commercial imports should be from that country itself.

IMPORTS IN THE SIXTIES

After going through the most traumatic experience of the 1965 and 1966 famines, the government of India ordered in 1968 an exercise for determining the size of the buffer stock and the imports that would be necessary thereof. The agricultural production during 1964-65, 1965-66, and 1966-67 was 89 million tonnes, 72 million tonnes, and 75 million tonnes respectively, the latter two years being one of extreme scarcity. The government had started importing substantial quantities of wheat and some rice too, right from 1964 as shown below :

(in million tonnes)

	Wheat	*Rice*
1964	5.25	.33
1965	5.92	.28
1966	6.47	—

The production during 1967-68, which was the first good year after a serious drought, was estimated at 95 million tonnes. The size of the buffer stock which was considered practicable was fixed at 3 million tonnes. The public distribution in the previous three years had been of the following order :

(in million tonnes)

1965	10.9
1966	14.1
1967	12.9

and during 1968 it was estimated at 10.5 million tonnes.

Although the conceptual distinction between buffer and operational stocks was maintained, it was stated that they could not be kept physically separated and that the stocks would always remain dispersed all over the country. Imported stocks would also get mixed with the indigenous wheat stocks.

Procurement from the 1967-68 crop was estimated at 6 million tonnes. Adding up the requirements of public distribution and the projected figure of the buffer stock (3 million tonnes) and deducting from it the internal procurement, the import requirements during 1968 were estimated at 7.5 million tonnes.

These requirements were calculated from another angle as well. The gap between the consumption requirements (86.5 million tonnes) and the availability from internal sources (80.5 million tonnes after allowing for seed, feed and waste) came to 6 million tonnes of the buffer stock, thus giving a figure of 9 million tonnes. This was considered too high a figure. 7.5 million tonnes was considered sufficient which was finally adopted. But it was recognised that the per capita availability would be at the level of 1961-63 which would ignore the increased demand owing to increase in population and incomes that would have taken place in the intervening period of six years.

IN THE SEVENTIES

The total foodgrain production for 1970-71 was estimated around 105 million tonnes of which the net availability for consumption was put at 91.9 million tonnes. The Fourth Five Year Plan had fixed the target of the buffer stock at 5 million tonnes, which was required to be built up as quickly as possible. On January 1, 1971, the total stocks with the government were about 5.3 million tonnes, including the pipeline or operational stocks. (Operational stocks were assumed at 2 million tonnes and the buffer was taken at 3.3 million tonnes). To reach the target of the buffer, import of 1.7 million tonnes was considered necessary. Another 2 million tonnes were required for operational stocks, thus the total import was placed at 3.4 million tonnes. Of this, 1.57 million tonnes were covered under the PL-480 agreement signed in March 1971 ; 0.8 million tonnes were expected to be received as aid from Canada, Australia and others, as well as by way of commercial imports This left a balance of one million tonnes which was covered in the next PL-480 Agreement signed on April 1, 1971 (the quantity actually imported was 1.09 million tonnes).

No PL-480 imports were contracted during 1972-73, 1973-74, and 1974-75. In March 1975 an agreement was entered for the import of 0.8 million tonnes of wheat and wheat flour at a cost of $ 128 million. Another agreement was signed in May 1976 for the import of 0.4 million tonnes of wheat and wheat flour and 0.1 million tonnes of rice at a total cost of $ 83 million. Thereafter there were no imports under this arrangement. These imports were resorted to in the wake of a severe scarcity that persisted during 1973 and 1974.

IMPACT ON INDIA'S FOOD ECONOMY

Taking an overall view, it can be stated that PL-480 imports have occupied a very crucial position in the management of the food economy, as shown in Table 6.1.

TABLE 6.1 : **Percentage to total net Imports***

Year	Rice	Wheat
1956	—	13.3
1957	26.3	88.5
1958	—	70.7
1959	—	89.4
1960	36.7	92.5
1961	50.7	68.5
1962	48.3	83.1
1963	62.6	95.3
1964	51.4	90.5
1965	36.9	90.9
1966	—	82.6
1967	—	63.4
1968	—	77.6
1969	22.0	70.2
1970	—	72.0
1971	—	66.8

**Source* : B.R. Shenoy, PL-480 Aid and India's Food Problem.

Looking at these figures together with table 7.1 in chapter 7, one is struck with a remarkable correlation between PL-480 imports and the gap between production and requirements. In that Table, in all the years studied by the Technical Group, except 1971-72, a deficit in the availability of food supplies was found to exist. The PL-480 imports for these years perfectly fit into this picture of huge deficits as shown in Table 6.2. The co-efficient of correlation works out to +0.78 which represents a very high degree of correlation.

TABLE 6.2 : **Food deficit and PL-480 imports**

(*in million tonnes*)

Year	Gap between production and requirements	Imports under PL-480
1961	1.3	2.3
1962	1.7	2.9
1963	4.7	4.2
1964	5.5	5.6
1965	3.4	6.3
1966	15.0	8.2
1967	13.1	5.8
1968	1.9	4.1
1969	3.5	2.6
1970	3.0	2.5

ASSESSMENT OF BENEFITS

A comparative analysis of the imports under PL-480 and those on commercial account (Tables 6.6 and 6.7) reveals certain interesting facts. Whereas in the initial years right up to 1965 the f.o.b. costs of wheat imported under PL-480 were higher than those of the commercial imports, excepting 1959 and 1963 when they were slightly cheaper, in the decade 1966-76, the f.o.b. costs of PL-480 imports were lower than those of the commercial imports. In the case of rice, the f.o.b. costs were much higher in all the years. The freight expenses incurred on the PL-480 imports were, as a rule, substantially higher than those expended on the commercial imports, with the result that even when the f.o.b. costs were lower, the c.i.f. value was higher than those of the commercial imports excepting in 1966 and 1975. Fifty per cent of the imports were to be carried necessarily in vessels flying the U.S. flag and it appears that the freight rates of these vessels were abnormally high. The advantage (whatever it was) of cheap grain was, thus, more than offset by high freight rates.

In the overall costing, the c.i.f. values of wheat and rice imported under PL-480 were much higher than those of the commercial imports. Perhaps the only thing that can be said in retrospect in support of the PL-480 imports is that they were assured and were available to India on a long term basis and were planned to meet the recurring deficit in the total availability of the food supplies. The technical assistance that came from the United States for faster development of Indian agriculture, the visit by a high powered delegation in 1959 consisting of thirteen top U.S. agricultural scientists led by the greatest agricultural statesman of U.S.A. Sherman Johnson, and the role played by the Ford Foundation in evolving a long term strategy for the development of Indian agriculture through the intensive agricultural development programme, and the widespread popularization of high-yielding varieties, particularly in wheat, are some of the benefits that attended upon the Indian agriculture in the wake of these imports.

The costs of both the imports, namely, PL-480 as well as others, have been compared with the internal support prices in Tables 6.3 and 6.4.

TABLE 6.3 : **Wheat**

(Rupees per tonne)

Year	Landed cost of imported stocks		Indigenous	
	PL-480	Commercial	Procurement Price	Issue Price
1956	388	352	—	375.10
1957	418	385	—	375.10
1958	374	340	—	375.10
1959	354	336	—	375.10
1960	356	302	—	375.10
1961	360	320	—	375.10
1962	371	325	—	375.10
1963	375	331	—	375.10
1964	406	352	—	375.10
1965	375	285	530-650	480.00
1966	482	513	540-650	700.00
1967	629	554	540-950	700-950
1968	608	549	650-810	780.00
1969	608	570	660-760	780.00
1970	559	563	700-760	780-840
1971	630	520	710-760	780.00
1972	—	504	710-760	780.00
1973	—	913	710-820	780-960
1974	—	946	1050.00	1250.00
1975	1393	1441	1050.00	1250.00
1976	1561	1494	1050.00	1250.00

TABLE 6.4 : **Rice**

(*Rupees per tonne*)

Year	Landed cost of imported stocks		Indigenous	
	PL-480	Commercial	Procurement Price	Issue Price.
1956	—	505	—	429-536
1957	807	484	—	429-804
1958	—	468	—	429-804
1959	—	475	—	429-804
1960	641	460	—	429-804
1961	643	472	—	429-804
1962	700	483	—	429-804
1963	740	506	—	429-804
1964	695	536	582-717	429-804
1965	702	535	633-762	520-1000
1966	—	911	658-908	580-810
1967	—	1105	700-952	800-960
1968	—	1227	727-960	1000.00
1969	1469	1028	742-960	1000.00
1970	—	765	743-952	1000.00
1971	—	660	743-952	1000.00
1972	—	644	830-952	1000.00
1973	—	—	980-1190	1250.00
1974	—	—	1158-1250	1350.00
1975	—	2053	1170-1270	1350.00
1976	3141	1920	1170-1260	1350.00

In the case of wheat, the procurement price in all the years till 1972 has been more than the landed cost of the imported stocks—both PL-480 as well as commercial. In those days wheat was procured in four grades, and different prices were fixed for different varieties. In the foregoing table, the range of issue prices has been shown compared to which the cost of imported stocks was lower. The imported stocks during 1975 and 1976 were almost twice as costly as they were in the latter half of the sixties. In those years the procurement price was lower than the landed costs of the imported stocks.

Issue prices are fixed with a host of considerations and it is not always possible to fix them at a level so as to realise all costs. While they appear to be higher than the costs of the imported stocks, excepting in the years 1975 and 1976, that is not always the case with respect to the internal procurement prices. The reason, as explained in earlier chapters, is that the supplies being intended for the vulnerable sections of society, the issue prices of government stocks have to be subsidised to a certain extent.

TABLE 6.5 : **Statement showing import of foodgrain under PL-480**

(*million tonnes*)

Year	Wheat	Milo	Corn	Rice	Total foodgrains
1956	0.15	—	—	—	0.15
1957	2.51	—	—	0.20	2.71
1958	1.90	0.09	0.03	—	2.20
1959	3.18	0.01	0.01	—	3.20
1960	4.04	0.03	0.02	0.26	4.35
1961	2.12	0.02	—	0.19	2.33
1962	2.70	—	—	0.19	2.89
1963	3.90	—	—	0.30	4.20
1964	5.25	—	—	0.33	5.58
1965	5.93	0.10	—	0.29	6.32
1966	6.48	1.73	0.01	—	8.22
1967	4.02	1.82	—	—	5.84
1968	3.61	0.47	0.02	—	4.10
1969	2.16	0.30	—	0.10	2.56
1970	2.45	—	—	—	2.45
1971	1.21	—	—	—	1.21
1972	—	—	—	—	—
1973	—	—	—	—	—
1974	—	—	—	—	—
1975	0.79	—	—	—	0.79
1976	0.41	—	—	0.10	0.51
1977	—	—	—	—	—
1978	—	—	—	—	—

In the case of rice the comparison is slightly difficult. The procurement prices were fixed for different varieties of rice and the difference was generally substantial. Whereas the PL-480 imports were costlier compared to the price of the lowest variety of rice, they was cheaper in relation to the superior varieties. This was true of the commercial imports till 1972, excepting for a period of three years from 1966 to 1969 when they were even costlier compared to our superior varieties. Imports during 1975 and 1976 were abnormally costlier compared to the internal procurement prices. The remarks made in regard to the issue prices of wheat also generally apply to the issue prices of rice.

TABLE 6.6 : **Statement showing per tonne f.o.b. cost, freight and c.i.f. value of wheat and rice imported under PL-480 during the period 1956 to 1976**

PL-480 IMPORTS (*in Rupees*)

	Wheat			Rice		
	f.o.b. Cost	Freight	c.i.f. Value	f.o.b. Cost	Freight	c.i.f. Value
1956	269	119	388	—	—	—
1957	301	117	418	633	174	807
1958	297	77	374	—	—	—
1959	290	69	354	—	—	—
1960	283	73	356	541	100	641
1961	287	73	360	548	95	643
1962	295	76	371	599	101	700
1963	297	78	375	630	110	740
1964	316	90	406	576	119	695
1965	288	87	375	584	118	702
1966	368	114	482	—	—	—
1967	474	155	629	—	—	—
1968	450	158	608	—	—	—
1969	453	155	608	1271	198	1469
1970	394	165	559	—	—	—
1971	461	169	630	—	—	—
1972	—	—	—	—	—	—
1973	—	—	—	—	—	—
1974	—	—	—	—	—	—
1975	1109	284	1393	—	—	—
1976	1244	317	1561	2499	642	3141
1977	—	—	—	—	—	—
1978	—	—	—	—	—	—

END OF THE ERA

In the history of PL-480 imports, 1971-72 could be treated as the terminal year. For the next three years, there were no imports and the quantities contracted for during 1975 and 1976 were, in the overall context, marginal and for meeting the emergent requirements of the acute shortages prevailing at that time. By this time, the Government of India had gained experience of the working of the rupee funds at the disposal of US government. They came to the conclusion that the continued existence of these funds would create a situation in which their utilization, together with interest, would continue

TABLE 6.7 : **Statement showing per tonne f.o.b. cost, freight and c.i.f. value of wheat and rice imported on commercial account during period 1956 to 1978.**

COMMERCIAL IMPORTS (*in Rupees*)

Year	Wheat			Rice		
	f.o.b. Cost	Freight	c.i.f. Value	f.o.b. Cost	Freight	c.i.f. Value
1956	260	92	352	444	61	505
1957	297	88	385	426	58	484
1958	294	46	340	426	42	468
1959	297	39	336	434	41	475
1960	264	38	302	421	39	460
1961	282	38	320	431	41	472
1962	290	35	325	439	44	483
1963	313	18	331	463	43	506
1964	311	41	352	497	39	536
1965	233	52	285	496	39	535
1966	422	91	513	645	266	911
1967	489	65	554	1046	59	1105
1968	461	88	549	1174	53	1227
1969	487	83	570	962	66	1028
1970	435	128	563	652	111	763
1971	439	81	520	582	78	660
1972	436	68	504	566	78	644
1973	746	167	913	—	—	—
1974	643	303	946	—	—	—
1975	1215	226	1441	1930	123	2053
1976	1281	213	1494	1848	72	1920
1977	1212	192	1404	1806	—	1806
1978	—	—	—	—	—	—

in perpetuity. According to some projections made at the current level of US expenditure, the deposits of the United States would have increased to over Rs. 30,000 million by A.D. 2012. The Government of India, therefore, initiated discussions with the US government for the disposition of these colossal funds which in its opinion were coming in the way of healthy economic relations between the two countries. Eventually, an agreement was signed on February 18, 1974 under which the US Government made a grant of a very substantial part of these funds to the Government of India for attribution, over a period of five years, to a number of development projects identified and included in the Five Year Plans. The US Government retained a small proportion of these funds for its use permitted under the existing agreements.

7

The Final Shape

A RESUME

We have already referred to the recommendation of the Foodgrain Policy Committee that the size of the buffer stock was to be at least 4 million tonnes. The Working Group on Food Policy for the Fourth Plan (1969-70 to 1973-74) further examined this question on the basis of a study of the fluctuations in production during the years 1949-50 to 1964-65. The Group estimated that for dealing with situations of shortfall in production in two out of every three years, a buffer stock of about seven million tonnes would be required. Considering the relevant factors such as cost of operations, problems of storage and handling and magnitude of fluctuations in production, the government decided, in March 1969, to build up a buffer stock of only 5 million tonnes (including rice) during the Fourth Five Year Plan period.

The following two years proved to be good and the bumper harvests in 1970-71 and 1971-72 contributed handsomely to the procurement drive. By June 1972, the government was holding 8.8 million tonnes of foodgrains in stock. Accordingly the target of 5 million tonnes was later sought to be raised to seven million tonnes for the Fourth Plan period in the context of rising stocks, and the level having already exceeded the target.

PLANNING COMMISSION CONSIDERS THE MATTER

The bulging stocks meant locking up of ever-increasing sums of public funds and other costs, for which clearance from the Ministry of Finance and the Planning Commission was required. In a high level discussion that took place in the Planning Commission in November

1971, a number of important issues such as the likely inflationary pressure of investing huge funds in the buffer stock, guarding against attempts at over-insurance, financing of the buffer stock through non-traditional methods (payment through coupons which could be exchanged for agricultural inputs), building up of requisite storage capacity, place of coarse grains in the buffer stock, etc., were raised.

These questions were examined by the Food Department afresh and the matter finally came up before the Planning Commission in May 1972. In this meeting it was suggested that the foodgrain stocks with the Food Corporation of India should be conceptually classified into three categories—buffer, operational, and surplus. As regards the buffer stock, a longer time perspective was adopted and, considering the likely size of the crop and fluctuations in production, it was suggested that a buffer stock of about 10 million tonnes (which was about 10 per cent of the production in the base period* 1968-69) should be achieved, if situations of excess or shortfall in production were to be met in 19 out of 20 years. However, it was recognised that the constraints of storage, finance, and turnover would impose a limit on its size. Finally, a buffer stock of about seven million tonnes was considered more realistic. (This was to be over and above the operational stocks required for meeting the normal requirements of the public distribution system.)

In regard to the operational stocks, the formula based on two months offtake in the case of wheat, six months offtake in the case of rice, and seven months offtake in respect of coarse grains was adopted for determining the levels at which these stocks were to be maintained at a particular time of the year. The formula was based on proximity to the harvest season and was to be reckoned with as on April 1 and stock levels worked out accordingly. The surplus stocks were to be disposed of by sale in the open market at current market prices.

The following decisions were also taken in this May 1972 meeting :

(a) the optimum size of the buffer stock may be fixed at seven million tonnes *ex post facto*, as against five million tonnes adopted earlier for the Fourth Plan. The Fourth Plan

* Production in the base year, 1968-69 was taken as 102 million tonnes. It was assumed that the additional 52 million tonnes expected in the Fourth Plan period will be due to development programmes concentrated on irrigated areas and that this will not be subject to wide year-to-year fluctuations.

outlay for the buffer stock should be raised from Rs. 255 crore to Rs. 500 crore which would be financed to the extent of Rs. 125 crore from the budget and the balance of Rs. 375 crore from the institutional sources ;

(b) the total stocks with the Food Corporation of India should be conceptually divided into : operational stocks, buffer stocks, and surplus stocks ;

(c) in procuring foodgrains, either on central or state government account, the agency concerned should take utmost care in maintaining standard and quality. The grain of fair average quality or at the most permissible within the margins of specification may be accepted. The FCI will have to act more as a commercial organisation in handling procurement operations, giving particular attention to the quality of grain purchased than as a mere collector of surplus grain stocks. If in certain unusual circumstances, purchase of grains below specified quality have to be done, it would be treated as separate purchases on account of the state governments concerned. Strict adherence to quality in procurement may enable cutting down the costs on distribution and procurement ;

(d) a suitable price policy should be evolved whereby the unloading of stocks by the FCI starts as soon as the prices display rising and disturbing trends. This implies a regular exercise and watch over price trends and an active marketing policy to be pursued by the FCI for an effective impact on the market ;

(e) the possibilities of disposal of coarse grains into animal feed may be looked into and details worked out by the Department of Agriculture and the Food Corporation of India ; and

(f) for the disposal of a part of surplus food stocks with the FCI by way of payment of wages under the employment schemes in drought prone areas as well as in rural works programmes, the Ministry of Agriculture may finalise a scheme and circulate it to the states.

As would be seen from the subsequent narration, these decisions were taken in the context of a comfortable food situation during 1971-72 which yielded a bumper crop and also because the public agencies carried sufficient stocks. They do not reflect the anxiety born of urgency of feeding people in scarcity conditions.

A.P.C. REPORT

In their report on price policy for *kharif* cereals for the 1972-73 season, the APC reviewed the stocks position and observed that for neutralizing, even though in part, the incidence of instability in supplies as well as in prices of foodgrains, a buffer stock was indispensable. But it felt that substantial costs were incurred and it would not be feasible to go on enlarging the buffer stock indefinitely In its view the buffer stock policy "ought to supplement rather than supplant a direct attack on the problem of instability through a reorientation in the production strategy." Referring to the benefits from extending irrigation systems both in production as well as in securing stability of prices, the Commission observed that it would be more economic, at the margin, to invest in irrigation works than in larger and larger buffer stocks to secure the same stability. It advocated a re-orientation of production strategy for food grains by shifting the season to *rabi* from *kharif.*

GOVERNMENT DECISION

While the Food Department agreed with the general approach and arguments advanced by the Commission, it came to a different conclusion on the specific question of downward revision of the size of the buffer stock. The Department stated that the original Fourth Plan target was five million tonnes which was achieved a couple of years ahead of the schedule. It was at its instance that the target was revised to seven million tonnes and the subsequent events had shown that this was a wise decision. The country would not have been able to cope with the drought conditions prevailing then (1972-73) with a smaller buffer stock. The Food Department concluded by saying that in a tropical country like India where the prospects of agricultural production are not immune from the vagaries of nature, the upward revision of the present size of the buffer stock needed serious consideration.

The Union Cabinet considered the matter in September, 1972 and approved the suggestions of the Food Department, and ordered that a comprehensive note on the question of upward revision of the size of the buffer stock be put up by the Food Department.

WORKING GROUP ON FIFTH PLAN

In April 1972, the Ministry of Agriculture had set up a Working Group on agricultural pricing, marketing, processing, storage, and warehousing with the Food Secretary as its Chairman for formulating proposals for the Fifth Five Year Plan (1974-79). One of the sub-groups was on 'Food Policy and Administration'. In its report submitted in June 1973, this sub-group identified the following as the chief instruments that were being employed in the implementation of the food policy.

(a) the continuance of the public distribution system ;
(b) the acquisition by the public sector of a sizeable percentage of marketable surplus of foodgrains with a view to meeting the commitments under the public distribution system and maintaining the buffer stock at the desired level ;
(c) the imposition of such restrictions on the movement of foodgrains as may be necessary to help the attainment of procurement target, or to prevent in a condition of shortage an excessive rise in prices throughout the country ;
(d) the regulation of private trade to curb speculation and hoarding ;
(e) the regulation of bank advances against foodgrains ; and
(f) the continuance of the ban on forward trading.

The precise role of each of these measures had been changing from time to time but a judicious combination was successful in delivering the goods. Its general recommendation was that these instruments may be continued in the Fifth Plan as well and added that the public distribution system ought to be further strengthened.

WHOLESALE TRADE TAKEOVER

A little before all these deliberations, an important development took place. In its meeting held at Gandhi Nagar (Gujarat) on October, 9-10, 1972, the All India Congress Committee reviewed the economic situation in the country with special reference to the then recent spurt in prices causing great hardship to the poorer sections of the population. The sluggish growth in industrial production had further contributed to limit supplies of many essential commodities. This, coupled with a fall in the foodgrains production by about four million tonnes in 1971-72, the AICC noted, had accentuated the climate of shortages leading to a constant rise in the price level. The Committee recalled that the Party had given to the people a clear and unequivocal commitment that supplies of essential commodities at reasonable prices would be ensured particularly to the vulnerable sections. It, therefore, reiterated the aim of establishing a public distribution system that should cover essential commodities of mass consumption including cereals, sugar, edible oils, kerosene, and standard cloth. It concluded, "a public distribution system can be a success only if government has taken over the wholesale trade in the aforementioned commodities. The AICC would, therefore, reaffirm the promise made to the people on taking over the wholesale trade in foodgrains by the state. Such a takeover achieved through monopoly procurement should be dovetailed into an effective system of retail distribution, holding of buffer stocks and appropriate price policy."

This was a decision of far reaching consequences and one requiring eleborate preparation on the part of the government for its implementation. To begin with, wheat was notified under this scheme and the central government promulgated a control order declaring each state a Wheat Zone and forbidding movement of wheat outside a zone except under an authority of the government. The states were asked to forbid private wholesale dealings in wheat by promulgating a control order within their jurisdiction. Retailers dealing in this commodity in excess of five (and in some states ten) quintals were required to obtain a licence. Stock limits were fixed generally at 100 quintals. Strict stock checking was ordered and traders found violating the aforesaid provisions of law were prosecuted. Wholesale trade in wheat was thus taken over by the government and its agencies. Insurmountable difficulties were faced in implementing this policy and within a very short period, the policy was given up. Extension of this policy to rice from the *kharif* marketing year 1973-74 was stayed and eventually the policy was scrapped.

On the question of the buffer stock, the sub-group referred to the five million tonnes target fixed for the Fourth Plan which was exceeded when the stocks held by the government in June, 1972 reached a figure of 8.8 million tonnes. They recounted the proposal contained in the working paper prepared for the formulation of the Fourth Five Year Plan where it was observed that a buffer stock of about seven million tonnes "would provide reasonable, if not complete insurance against moderate fluctuations in production." It was, however, noted that a buffer of this type and size may not suffice if there is a precipitous fall in production or two successive years of drought.

In addition to the buffer stocks, the size of the operational stocks was reckoned around 3 to 3.5 million tonnes.

In the meantime, a year of scarcity had gone by. On account of the widespread drought (1972-73) and the consequent large scale supplies of foodgrains from the central pool, the stocks with the government had depleted by the end of 1972 to 3.4 million tonnes. The Working Group referred to the views of the APC which were against expanding the size of the buffer indefinitely and finally concluded that since the entire question about the size of the buffer stock was being examined by a high level technical committee (appointed almost at the same time—June, 1973), they did not indicate any quantitative figures for these stocks.

As for the grain-wise composition of the buffer, it endorsed the views of the APC which had said that the components of rice and coarse grain be progressively enlarged.

TECHNICAL GROUP

In June 1973, the Government of India constituted a high level Technical Group to go into the question of the volume of foodgrains to be handled by the public agencies and the reserve stock that would be required to tide over inter-seasonal fluctuations. It was also to examine the question of increasing the size of the buffer stock during the Fifth Plan, particularly when a major structural change had been introduced in the marketing system by nationalization of the wholesale trade in foodgrains.

The time when this group was set up was unfortunately not propitious for its fruitful labours. The drought conditions in 1972-73 which persisted for two years, resulting in an appreciable fall in the agricultural production and heavy drawals on the government stocks had created a situation in which building up of a sizable buffer stock was clearly ruled out. The primary job before the administration during these times was running the public distribution system for which the necessary operational stocks had to be mustered. The Technical Group, therefore, did not pursue the question of reviewing the buffer stock policy. Even the decision to take over the wholesale trade was reversed after a short trial of one year, during which it was confined to wheat only.

TECHNICAL GROUP RECONSTITUTED

With the easing of the food situation in 1975, the question of building up a buffer of adequate size was again taken up and the government reconstituted the Technical Group in December 1975 under the chairmanship of the Food Secretary. The Group studied the figures of gross production for the period 1960-61 to 1975-76 (Table 7.1) and after allowing for seed, feed and wastage and income elasticity of demand arrived at requirements for human consumption. Mean plus one S.D. was calculated to arrive at the quantum required to meet the shortfall in supplies in two out of three years. Mean plus two S.D. represented the quantum needed to cover the deficit in nineteen out of twenty years. Thus, the Group worked out the buffer stock as follows :

(million tonnes)

	Size of stock	Stock as percentage of demand (76.1 million tonnes) : Average for 1960-61 to 1975-76.
(i) Mean + 1 S.D.	9.2	12.1
(ii) Mean + 2 S.D.	13.8	18.1

Assuming normal increases in population and income, the projected demand for 1978-79 was taken at 102.6 million tonnes—the terminal year of the Fifth Plan. The size of the buffer stock for the plan period was accordingly worked out as follows :

(million tonnes)

(i) Mean + 1 S.D.	12.4
(ii) Mean + 2 S.D.	18.6

The Technical Group analysed this question from another angle, namely, the gap between the requirements of the public distribution system and the procurement. It noted that the average public distribution of foodgrains during 1973, 1974 and 1975 worked out around 11 million tonnes. After considering the effect of increase in population and the need for containing prices, normal annual commitment for the public distribution system was estimated betweeu

TABLE 7.1

Year	Mid-year population (million)	Requirements @ 148.6 kgs. Year average rate 1970-71 to 1972-73*	Per capita income at constant prices (Rs.)	% increase/ decrease in per capita income over 1970-71 to 1972-73 Averaged to Rs. 345.9	Additional requirements on account of increase in per capita income (0.5%) elasticity*	Total Requirements Col. 3 & 6*	Net Production*	Gap between production and requirements* d	d^2
1	2	3	4	5	6	7	8	9	10
1960-61	442	65.7	305.7	(—) 11.6	(—) 3.8	61.9	60.6	(—) 1.3	1.69
1961-62	452	67.2	309.3	(—) 10.6	(—) 3.6	63.6	61.9	(—) 1.7	2.89
1962-63	462	68.7	308.2	(—) 10.9	(—) 3.8	64.9	60.2	(—) 4.7	22.09
1963-64	472	70.1	318.2	(—) 8.0	(—) 2.8	67.3	61.8	(—) 5.5	30.25
1964-65	483	71.8	335.1	(—) 3.1	(—) 1.1	70.7	67.3	(—) 3.4	11.56
1965-66	493	73.3	310.9	(—) 10.1	(—) 3.8	69.6	54.6	(—) 15.0	225.00
1966-67	504	74.9	308.2	(—) 10.9	(—) 4.1	70.8	57.7	(—) 13.1	171.61
1967-68	515	76.5	328.4	(—) 5.1	(—) 2.0	74.5	72.6	(—) 1.9	3.61
1968-69	527	78.3	331.7	(—) 4.1	(—) 1.6	76.7	73.2	(—) 3.5	12.25
1969-70	539	80.1	343.1	(—) 0.8	(—) 0.3	79.8	76.8	(—) 3.0	9.00
1970-71	551	81.9	351.8	(+) 1.7	(+) 0.7	82.6	84.5	(+) 1.9	3.61
1971-72	562	83.5	348.4	(+) 0.7	(+) 0.3	83.8	82.3	(—) 1.5	2.25
1972-73	574	85.3	337.4	(—) 2.5	(—) 1.1	84.2	76.2	(—) 8.0	64.00
1973-74	586	87.1	347.2	(+) 0.4	(+) 0.2	87.3	82.9	(—) 4.4	19.36
1974-75	598	88.9	341.4	(—) 1.3	(—) 0.6	88.3	79.4	(—) 8.9	79.21
1975-76	609	90.5	357.2	(+) 3.3	(+) 1.5	92.0	91.9£	(—) 0.1	0.01

1976-77	620	92.1	369.0	(+) 6.7	(+) 3.1	95.2	91.9	(—) 3.3	10.89
1977-78	633	94.1	381.5	(+) 10.3	(+) 4.9	99.0	91.9 (P)	(—) 7.1	50.41
1978-79	644	95.7	394.5	(+) 14.1	(+) 6.9	102.6	91.9 (P)	(—) 10.7	114.49

(*) — relate to cereals only, excluding pulses.

(P) — Provisional.

(£) — Total production of foodgrains 1975-76 118.0

Less production of pulses − 13.0

105.0

Less 12.5% of this Net production −13.1

Net Production 91.9

12 and 13 million tonnes in the next few years. It estimated the distribution requirements in a poor crop year to increase substantially—up to 18 million tonnes—while procurement in such a crop year may be around 6 to 7 million tonnes of rice and wheat. Thus the gap between procurement and public distribution requirement in a bad year might be as much as 10 to 12 million tonnes. To meet the demand in such a year, it concluded, a buffer stock of 12 million tonnes would be called for. For dealing with a situation arising out of two successive bad crops, a buffer stock of still larger size (18 million tonnes) would be needed. But it was felt that the acquisition and maintenance of stocks of this magnitude would be uneconomic, entailing a lot of burden as well as problems of storage and turnover. It was also noted that situations such as the latter occurred once in several years.

The Group finally concluded that a buffer stock of about 12 million tonnes should be built up by the end of the Fifth Plan to meet the situation of normal shortages.

The Group further examined the question whether only a part of the buffer stock should be kept in actual grains and the other could be in terms of foreign exchange reserves to be used to import extra foodgrains in times of shortages. It was noted that while the maintenance cost of the buffer stock was around 15 per cent there had been a very steep rise in prices in the international market ranging on an average to about 33 per cent per year during the period March 1972 to March 1975. Besides, there was also the problem of timely availability of adequate quantities of grain in the international market. The Group, therefore, recommended that the buffer stock of 12 million tonnes should be maintained fully in physical terms within the country. It was further emphasised that the buffer stock should not be drawn down below the level of 5 million tonnes and the replenishment of the stock should be undertaken simultaneously when it is depleted to that level to take advantage of the seasonal low prices in the world market. The Group reinforced this important recommendation by saying that foreign exchange reserves sufficient to cover imports of six million tonnes of cereals may be kept earmarked for meeting abnormal situations arising out of extreme scarcity.

This buffer stock should be over and above the operational stocks which are needed for the maintenance of the public distribution system. The operational stocks were defined as the minimum quantities required for running the public distribution system till the quantities to be procured from the new crop become available for distribution. As on April 1, two months requirements of public distribution for wheat may be adequate to take care of any delays in harvesting, marketing, procurement and transport etc. of the new wheat crop. If the minimum operational stock for a particular grain, at the beginning of the marketing season is taken as equivalent to two months distribution requirement, then, besides a stock equal to two months requirement of wheat, it would be necessary to have on April 1 a stock equal to 9 months distribution requirements for rice as well as coarse *kharif* grains so as to meet the actual distribution requirement for the 7-month period, April-October, and to start the new *kharif* season with a minimum stock of two months. In the case of rice, however, some quantities are procured out of the summer and autumn crop also during the period April-October. The quantities procured during the period April-October may be adequate to meet the distribution requirement for about three months. Thus, the minimum operational stock of rice at the beginning of April would have to be equal to six months distribution requirement.

In regard to coarse grains, it was noted that there was no fixed pattern for their supply through the public distribution system and therefore, in the calculation of their operational stock, the same approach as for rice may be adopted.

OPERATIONAL STOCKS

The Group, with the then existing pattern of grain-wise composition (Rice 4 to 4.5 ; wheat 7.5 to 8 ; and other grains 0.5 million tonnes), worked out the size of operational stocks on 1st April as follows :

1st April :	Rice	2.05 to 2.25
	Wheat	1.20 to 1.30
	Coarse cereals	0.25
	Total	3.50 to 3.80

The size of the operational stocks at the beginning of the *kharif* marketing season (November 1) was computed on the basis of a similar approach. The operational stock for rice and coarse grains as on November 1 was taken at 2 months requirement of public distribution to provide for delay in harvesting, milling and procurement. In the case of wheat, the operational stocks were calculated on the basis of 7 months requirement of public distribution, i.e. to meet 5 months (November-March) actual distribution requirement and to start the new *rabi* season with a minimum stock of two months. The operational stocks as on November 1 were estimated as follows :

	(*million tonnes*)
Rice	0.6 to 0.7
Wheat	4.1 to 4.4
Coarse cereals	0.1
Total	4.8 to 5.2

The size of the operational stocks at the beginning of each calendar quarter following April 1 were also estimated in a similar way.

(*million tonnes*)

	1st July	1st October	1st January
Rice	1.9 — 2.0	0.6 — 0.7	1.7 — 2.1
Wheat	6.1 — 6.6	4.7 — 5.1	2.9 — 3.2
Coarse cereals	0.2	0.2	0.2
Total	8.2 — 8.8	5.5 — 6.0	4.8 — 5.5

Both for an effective monitoring of the stocks as also for proper management of the reserves, this model was indeed a very useful aid.

GRAIN-WISE COMPOSITION

On the grain-wise composition, the Technical Group said that the buffer stock may comprise mainly rice and wheat, as it would be difficult to store coarse grains over long periods because of their poor keeping quality. The exact share of rice and wheat in the buffer stock will necessarily be influenced by the quantum of domestic procurement and availability in world market on the one hand, and by the pattern of public distribution on the other. While the desirable pattern of public distribution would, they observed, suggest a ratio of 40 : 60, considering the relative availability and economics of importing rice and wheat, a ratio of 25 : 75 was considered more feasible at the time they drew up their report. With the expected increase in the production of rice, they said this ratio should progressively improve in favour of rice.

STORAGE CAPACITY REQUIRED

The Group assessed the storage capacity for a stock of 21 million tonnes at around 23 million tonnes, after allowing for the normal occupancy rate and setting apart space for locating weighing machines, keeping fumigation covers and other store articles, which may account for an additional 10 per cent of 21 million tonnes, bringing the total to 23 million tonnes. The Group felt that while the CAP (cover and plinth) storage could probably take care of the peak season accumulations to the extent of about 3 million tonnes, a capacity of 20 million tonnes would still be required for buffer and operational stocks. As against this, the existing storage capacity with the Food Corporation of India, Central and State Warehousing Corporations and the state governments with their current construction programmes added up to 10 million tonnes only. The hired capacity of a reasonably good standard was estimated at not more than 3 million tonnes. The Group, therefore, came to the conclusion that additional capacity of the order of seven million tonnes was required to be set up on a priority basis. Of this, nearly 90 per cent may be of the conventional type and the balance in the form of silos. The capital cost for this additional capacity of seven million tonnes was computed at Rs. 360 crores.

SOME COMMENTS

The Report of the Group was circulated to the various Ministries for their comments. The Planning Commission and the Ministry of Finance raised important points having a bearing on the conceptual frame as also on its empirical aspects. It would be useful to discuss them here.

The Planning Commission raised certain important questions concerning the report of the Technical Group. In the first instance they said that the distinction made between 'Buffer Stock' and 'Operational Stock' does not seem to be maintainable. They suggested that it would be more appropriate to think in terms of minimum and maximum stock holdings of foodgrains.

The Department of Food, however, maintained that conceptually the 'buffer stock' and 'operational stock' have altogether different functions to perform in the management of the food economy. While the buffer stock is needed only to deal with inter-seasonal fluctuation in production and in a normal situation, the recommended size of the buffer stock ought to be available at the beginning of each crop year, the operational stock is intended for the smooth running of the public distribution system and its size is determined with reference to the volume of public distribution and would be different in different months of the crop year. Even from the point of view of practical accounting the Department argued, it is imperative to maintain a distinction between 'buffer stock' and 'operational stock' because it is more appropriate to maintain separate accounts regarding these stocks so as to determine the maintenance cost of the buffer stock and the maintenance and distribution expenses on operational stocks issued through the public distribution system. The total of all this expenditure will finally determine the subsidy that the central government will be required to provide.

As regards the size of stocks, the Food Department were in complete agreement with the recommendation of the Group and said that every effort would be made to keep the buffer stock level at 10 million tonnes for the next 2-3 years.

The operational stocks had been worked out in a range of 3.5 to 8.8 million tonnes, on different dates in the year, based on the assessment of normal level of annual public distribution as 12 to 13 million tonnes. The Food Department believed that for the successful implementation of the new policy of removal of all restrictions on trade in wheat and rice, it was necessary to strengthen the public distribution system so as to contain the prices and to ensure that vulnerable sections of the population get regular supplies of foodgrains at reasonable prices through fair price shops. For this purpose a constant watch would have to be kept on the situation and sufficient stocks of foodgrains would be required to be pumped at a time of speculative rise in prices of foodgrains. In these circumstances, the Department was of the view that while the minimum size of the buffer stock for the next 2-3 years may be placed at 10 million tonnes, the operational stocks should range between 3.5 to 8.8 million tonnes on different dates in the year, as suggested by the Technical Group. They calculated that the peak level stocks on July 1 every year, shall be about 18.8 million tonnes (10 million tonnes buffer plus 8.8 million tonnes operational stocks). This peak level stock more or less corresponded to the maximum level of 18 million tonnes recommended by the Planning Commission.

A point was also raised that the stock levels should not be related to the next 2-3 years as suggested by the group but should be related to a longer time span—say up to the terminal year of the Sixth Plan, viz., 1983-84 (as fixed then).

On this question the Food Department felt that it would be difficult at that stage to project the optimum size of the buffer and operational stocks that would be required by the end of the Sixth Plan period because it would depend upon various factors such as growth of population, increase in income, crop prospects, level of internal production, size of public distribution, ways and means position and other related factors. It would also be influenced by the experience which would be gained in the upkeep and maintenance of buffer stock during the next 2-3 years. It might become necessary to appoint another Technical Group to examine the requirement of buffer and operational stocks from the long range point of view and to obtain the directives of the government in the matter at the appropriate time. Reference was made in the Working Group constituted on storage, warehousing and buffer stocks of foodgrains for the period 1978-83. The Working Group would review, it was hoped, the progress in the Fifth Plan and would consider the main policy issues for the next Plan relating to buffer stocking and creation of additional storage capacity.

The Planning Commission suggested that the total food stocks with the public agencies should not be allowed to fall below 12 million tonnes or to exceed 18 million tonnes. In the former eventuality, steps should be taken to replenish the stocks through imports, while in the latter case, efforts should be made to liquidate the excessive quantities through exports and other appropriate policy measures.

On the proposed ratio of 25 : 75 for rice and wheat the Planning Commission suggested that it should be modified in favour of rice as recommended by the Technical Group, particularly in view of the difficulty in acquiring rice supplies from abroad. It suggested the ratio to be maintained at 40 : 60 from the very beginning. The Food Department accepted this proposal.

Finally, the Planning Commission made two new suggestions outside the framework of the report of the Technical Group. First, a National food budget may be prepared by a high level official group consisting of the representatives of the Ministries of Agriculture and Irrigation, Finance and Commerce and the Planning Commission each year, in the month of January, when firm estimates of production of the *kharif* crop are available and the prospects of *rabi* become reasonably clear. The food budget may include the estimate of total production of foodgrains and the likely order of procurement and distribution by the public agencies in the coming year, keeping in view the level of food stocks as mentioned above. The national food budget may be reviewed in September in the light of latest developments, viz., the prospects of *kharif* crop, the trend of *rabi* procurement and distribution, imports, if any, etc. The food budget should also be considered by the Committee of Economic Secretaries and be brought up for consideration by the Cabinet Committee on Economic Affairs.

This was controverted by the Food Department pointing out that the price and procurement policy is formulated by the government twice a year, i.e., at the time of *kharif* and *rabi* marketing seasons. The APC, which is an independent body, submit, its report on the various aspects of price and procurement policy and other connected matters to the government and after ascertaining the views of the state governments on these recommendations a comprehensive note is submitted to the Cabinet after consulting the concerned Ministries/Departments. The final decision on the various aspects of the food policy is taken by the Cabinet. The crop prospects are subject to rapid change because of the aberrvations in weather and it seems difficult to take a precise view regarding the likely production and the availability during and entire calendar year. Even the APC is able to take a view regarding both the *rabi* and the *kharif* crops, only a few weeks ahead of the commencement of the season, i.e., in the month of March for *rabi* and again in the month of September for the *kharif* season. The entire procurement and pricing policy depends on the production prospects and certain modifications from the previous year very often become necessary. By way of an example the decision that had been taken to remove all restrictions on the movement of rice and paddy was quoted and it was said that such developments have far reaching effects, both on procurement and distribution of foodgrains in the coming months. Because of the rapidly changing position from time to time, it is also difficult to make all the states agree to certain pre-determined targets of procurement and distribution at the beginning of the year. In fact, under any such system, the state governments will tend to pitch their demands very high and their procurement targets on the lower side. It was, therefore, considered that no useful purpose would be served by setting up a high level Official Group for the preparation of the National food budget at the beginning of each year as suggested by the Planning Commission.

The second suggestion was that the stocks of foodgrains with the public agencies should be used more effectively as an instrument for countering the pressure on prices. Accelerated releases of foodgrains from stocks at appropriate times of the year in areas of shortage, and a change in the shares of rice and coarse grains in the composition of the food stocks should enable the authorities to achieve a greater measure of success in controlling the prices of foodgrains, and finally the general price level.

While expressing their general agreement with the broad objectives behind the suggestion, the Food Department observed that in the recent past a number of steps had been taken to strengthen the public distribution system and the state governments have been advised to open more fair price shops so as to make the foodgrains available closer to the door of the consumers. Due to comfortable stock position, the requirements of the state governments for wheat from the central pool are being met in full and the state governments have been authorised to place indent directly on the FCI for any additional requirement of wheat in anticipation of formal allotment from the Department. The allocation of rice was also being made liberally to the deficit states. During the first nine months of 1977, a quantity of 8.7 million tonnes of foodgrains was distributed as compared to 6.6 million tonnes distributed during the corresponding period of the previous year. It was assured that the Food Department would keep a constant watch on the prices and availability of foodgrains and take necessary remedial measures as and when called for.

GOVERNMENT DECISION

Eventually, early in January 1978, the central government approved the following proposals :

(a) the buffer stock of foodgrains should be 12 million tonnes ;

(b) this buffer stock would be over and above the operational stocks needed for the maintenance of the public distribution system which would range between the lowest figure of 3.5 to 3.8 million tonnes on April 1, and the highest figure of 8.2 to 8.8 million tonnes on July 1 ;

(c) the buffer stock of foodgrains would not be allowed to be drawn below the level of 5 million tonnes. Replenishment of the stocks through import should be undertaken simultaneously to take advantage of the seasonal low prices in the world market. Foreign exchange reserve sufficient to cover import of 6 million tonnes of cereals should be kept for meeting abnormal situations arising out of extreme scarcity owing to two successive crop failures ;

(d) the storage capacity should be built up as quickly as possible to 18 million tonnes which would include approved storage in the private sector ; and

(e) while the desirable proportion of the wheat and rice in the buffer stock would be 60 : 40, for the present it may be 75 : 25.

SECOND TECHNICAL GROUP

The framework suggested by the Technical Group and the decisions of the government, thereon constituted for the first time, a scientific food security system for the country. The first test came in 1979 when large parts of the country experienced conditions of severe drought and *kharif* crops suffered a setback. Heavy pressures were generated on the buffer stocks and during a 15-month period—October 1979 to December 1980—which represented the period of real hardship, 18.82 m tonnes—an all time record—were supplied through PDS.

Huge quantities of stocks (in July 1979 the Government Agencies held 21.5 million tonnes) were bottled up in the surplus states where they had been procured. Imported stocks were largely kept under CAP in Maharashtra and Gujarat and their proper maintenance posed a serious problem. Logistics presented by far the most serious constraint because a number of states in the eastern region, viz., Bihar, West Bengal, Assam, and other units in that region and states in the southern peninsular region including Maharashtra, Karnataka, Kerala and Timil Nadu needed stocks at the same time. The movement capacity of the railway system from Punjab, Haryana and certain pockets in western U.P. was limited and even though adequate stocks were available with the government, their movement and stock-building in the aforesaid states posed a difficult problem.

In April, 1981, therefore, the central government appointed another Technical Group with the following terms of reference :—

TERMS OF REFERENCE

(a) To report whether in the light of the experience of the past decade :
  (i) the level of national buffer at 15* million tonnes would be adequate ; and
  (ii) what should be the level of the operational stocks ;

(b) To suggest the grain mix in the buffer and operational stocks ;

(c) To report on the role of state governments in holding a part of these stocks and the manner in which it would be held ;

(d) To examine in the light of the constraints of storage and movement felt in the past two or three years, the requirements of storage capacity and its spatial distribution ; and

(e) To consider and report on any other matter, relevant or incidental to the above points.

The author was a member of this Group and its report is under the consideration of the central government.

*The figure was adopted by the Planning Commission in the Sixth Plan document without having detailed discussions with the Department of Food.

8

The Full Circle

RESPONSIBILITY FOR FAMINE RELIEF

WITH the foregoing narration we have reached the full circle of the famine relief policy which was the starting point in this part of the work dealing with the evolution of the food security system of India. One fact stands out indisputable, namely, famine relief was always considered and accepted as the sole responsibility of the state. The degree to which it was owned and discharged of course depended upon a number of factors, chief of which was the effectiveness of the central government in the country. During the Mauryan Empire, and particularly in the reign of Asoka, because the imperial authority was powerful and strong, the provincial governors undertook relief operations in times of distress. Grain was supplied from government granaries and even bullocks were given on loan for which payments could be made by the farmers in subsequent years in instalments.

During the dark ages which followed the dissolution of Gupta Empire towards the end of the sixth century A.D., no account is available of the state policy on famine relief and the manner in which it was implemented. But it can be fairly assumed that owing to the lack of an imperial authority and absence of means of transportation, the surplus of one region could not have been made available to the famine stricken areas of other and consequently the suffering must have been terrible. All available material points to the fact that, people normally took to flight.

This state of affairs continued right up to the Moghul times when the imperial authority was once again established firmly after a long time. Land revenue administration was improved and perfected during Akbar's time. The historical record shows that the incidence of land revenue assessment was generally excessive, with the result that the peasants preferred to give up cultivation, rather than promote it. This circumstance aggravated the situation during famines. Nevertheless, history further tells up that the rulers maintained government granaries in which the government share of the grain in lieu of land revenue was stored and used in times of famine. We have already given some description of the famine relief undertaken during Shahjahan's reign and particularly during that most devastating famine of 1630-31.

When after the battle of Plassey the British finally got the *Diwani* rights in the Bengal Presidency (comprising the present states of Bihar, Orissa, and West Bengal and Bangladesh) administrators like Verelst, Shore, Grant and Duncan formulated the policy for land revenue administration and drafted detailed instructions for the guidance of the field officers. This was more in the nature of formalizing the system inherited from the Nawabs of Bengal, with minor improvements here and there. The enlightened concepts of assessment and collection of land revenue and their moderation in times of famine were yet to be born. Famine relief, though recognised as a calamity to which the administration could not remain indifferent, was still not a subject of formal policy and action.

By the close of 19th century, and more particularly as a result of the report of the Famine Inquiry Commissions of 1880 and 1897, the land revenue administration policy underwent a material change. By that time the British administrators had gained experience of Indian famines for a little over 100 years and in the Government of India Resolution dated 16.1.1902, the land revenue policy found consummate expression at the hands of Lord Curzon, the then Governor General of India.

LAND REVENUE POLICY AND FAMINE RELIEF

The cardinal principle of this policy, which in its essentials continues to be in force even today is that, "in theory, the government revenue represents the sum that may be fairly demanded on an average of seasons and it is assessed in the belief that cultivators will save from the surplus of good years to meet the deficit in bad." It was emphasised that "assessment should be equitable in character and moderate in incidence ; and that there should be left to the proprietor or to the cultivator of the soil—as the case may be—that margin of profit that will enable him to save in ordinary season and to meet the strain of exceptional misfortune." At the same time, it was recognised that the occasional distress caused by the failure of crops should call forth mitigation of the hardship and moderation in the realization of the revenue. It was stated in the policy Resolution that the government will be prepared, where the necessity is established, to introduce greater elasticity in the revenue collection, facilitating its adjustment to the variations of the season and the circumstances of the people.

Here was a clear enunciation of government policy in regard to famines so far as land revenue administration was concerned. While publishing this policy resolution, the government of the day clearly stated that famine was a calamity to which no civilized government can ever remain indifferent, and that government will take all possible steps to mitigate the rigours of the suffering. The British administrators believed that it was the duty of the state to provide work in times of famine to all able bodied persons who offered themselves for work. Their basic policy was to give famine relief in the shape of employment in the hope that the wages earned by the people would be sufficient to sustain them during the crisis, because by experience they had observed that if purchasing power was available, food supplies were forthcoming. Free feeding was generally discouraged for they rightly believed that it promoted indolence and led to demoralization. At the same, private charity was not ruled out but this, being on a limited scale, was in the nature of a supplement to the government's relief programme.

It was emphasised that there was no greater insurance against famine than thrift and prudence, that a year of bountiful crops was not an occasion for larger expenditure or wasteful consumption, but for saving for the lean years.

Amongst the relief works priority was given to works which in future years would promote agriculture and secure the area from famine. Water conservation schemes, canals, tanks and wells were promoted. In the earlier years, works relating to the spreading of the network of railways were generally encouraged.

GRAIN RESERVE

The concept of a 'grain reserve' for meeting the distress in lean years is noticeable in the British policy from the very beginning. The proposal was seriously examined by the Famine Commission of 1880 but for reasons of finance as well as management they advised against the government holding the reserve by themselves. They believed that once the employment opportunities were organised on a wide scale, the foodgrain supplies would be ensured by private trade. They expressed their trust in the efficacy of private trade and said that given the requisite support and protection, it would maintain a steady flow of supplies. They, therefore, stipulated that the channels of private trade in food should always be kept free and no impediments should be created in their functioning. The district officers, however, had instructions to keep a strict watch on the behaviour of private trade in times of scarcities and government intervention was resorted to when it was necessary. This was done by inducting the government officers in the procurement and distribution of foodgrains, with money from government treasury.

The 1943 famine known as the 'Bengal Famine' was truly a watershed in the evolution of the food policy of the government. It brought about certain fundamental changes in the approach of the government towards famine management. The government was baffled that despite 75 years of railway expansion and general development of means of communications, contrary to their belief, stocks were not forthcoming in deficit areas from the surplus areas. The earlier belief that private trade would play the game and render the service of maintaining the supply line was belied. The government was, therefore, compelled to resort to procedures it had never before adopted. A number of control measures on movement of stocks, limits on holding, prices, sales, etc, were imposed. Likewise a variety of procurement methods in combination with different types of controls on movement were tried. And finally the inevitability of the central government holding a certain buffer by themselves was recognized and laid down as the core of the food policy of the central government. This was a long journey from the 19th century food policy.

This policy continued in free India too. The scarcities of mid-fifties and the two severe scarcities of 1965/1966 and 1972/1973 only served to highlight the magnitude of the food requirements. The vulnerability of a nation 600 million strong, which has to depend on import of food or external assistance was realised all too clearly and in a searing manner. The policy was, therefore, to borrow a metaphor, gone over with a tooth brush ; the methodology was refined and improved ; the model was perfected by the application of modern techniques of quantitative analysis and the commitment of the central government to back up the buffer stocking policy with public funds was declared to be total and irrevocable.

The government has again come a long way from the 1943 Bengal famine. The food policy is now considered not only as a measure for combating famines but as an instrument of fostering agricultural development. The green revolution and the price support operations are now acknowledged as the two wheels on which Indian agriculture is marching forward to newer and higher peaks. They operate as the mutually reinforcing dimensions of the agricultural economy, as it moves on its path of development, giving government means to fight scarcities. The present food policy is the single most crucial economic factor in the universe called 'agriculture' on which it reacts in the most decisive manner. The evolution of the food policy in free India indeed represents that remarkable phenomenon in which a calamity oriented policy got transformed into an instrument of development. And not development alone, it supplies concrete content to the egalitarian concept of food security in the shape of keeping the public distribution system going. In terms of both its coverage as well as content, the buffer stocking policy has acknowledgedly become an instrument of government intervention of widest relevance and of most vital significance. It is now governed by that principle of 'self creation' under which its own working provides this policy its meaning and substance.

PART TWO

EVALUATION

9

Approach to Evaluation

EVALUATION—MEANING AND METHODOLOGY

AN EXERCISE in evaluation bristles with many difficulties. In the first place, concepts have to be clearly stated : what is the meaning of evaluation ; what is the yardstick with which is it to be measured and how is it to be done? Since evaluation basically involves comparison, there has necessarily to be an ideal, a certain value-standard, or in the case of a subject like the present one, quantitative norms, in the light of which the present buffer stocking policy and its working could be evaluated.

But here is our first difficulty. In this universe called the buffer stocking policy, the chief variables are : the population, the production, the demand, the net availability of foodgrains, and, the most important of all, the price—both procurement as well as issue price. These variables keep continually changing and different variables change at different rates, thus rendering comparison with certain fixed norms a difficult exercise. The problem is really one of dynamic equilibrium analysis.

Evaluation also involves both time and space dimensions. The approach would differ in point of time as to whether we are evaluating it in the background of scarcity and shortages, or in times of plenty. Almost of the same genre would be the evaluation with the geographical factor as the principal dimension. What benefits have accrued to heavily surplus states like Andhra Pradesh, Punjab, Haryana, and western U.P. and what benefits have been conveyed to deficit states like Kerala, West Bengal, Gujarat and Maharashtra ?

The two dimensions are intimately connected with and relevant to each other. In the surplus states, heavy procurement has a very direct and visible impact on the producers, on the general price level and the stocks offered for sale. In deficit areas, supplies are short and prices generally remain at a higher level. Drawals are made on the buffer stocks to meet the needs of these areas. In times of plenty, generally speaking, prices tend to dip and if there is no state intervention to maintain the prices at the level of the administered prices, the interests of the producers will suffer irreparably. In lean years consumer prices in deficit states and industrial and mining areas would soar so high that food riots may take place. It is only the public distribution system, fed from the buffer stocks, that keeps the consumer prices in these areas within bounds of sanity.

Evaluation will, again, be different if the approach is to determine, in quantitative terms, the benefits derived by the producers and/or the consumers. This exercise will involve adjustment of transfer payment in the shape of respective benefits gained and/or excess costs incurred by the producers and consumers. In a study done by Kansas State University on Bangladesh, the benefits and adverse effects conferred by variations in prices on the producers and consumers have been computed and after adjusting the two, certain conclusions drawn. One of the conclusions is that beyond a certain range of price variation ($\pm 15\%$) the foodgrains reserve becomes necessary in public interest and is beneficial for the entire economy.

Evaluation will be altogether different if the insurance approach is adopted. Since the costs of insurance are incurred with a view to meeting an anticipated calamity, unforeseen in point of time, there would be no basis for determining the benefits in quantitative terms under this approach. To the extent the system would be able to protect the producers as well as the consumers from the harmful effects of variation in prices and supplies, the insurance would have been redeemed and the efficacy of the system judged accordingly.

Finally, there is the appraisal of this policy as an instrument giving fillip to the general development of the agricultural economy. When this policy has worked itself for nearly two decades a general conclusion seems to emerge in areas where procurement has been done with vigour and surpluses have been mopped up, agricultural production seems to have registered the multiplier effect and has been continually going up, while in states where this has not been done, agricultural production continues to be stagnant. This point has been discussed in detail in Chapter 11—Part B.

PRICING OF AGRICULTURAL PRODUCE

In the strategy for agricultural development in India, the key element is the price factor and since the buffer policy directly impinges on the price factor, it at once becomes an instrument of crucial significance. The real malady of the Indian agricultural development during the past decades has been that foodgrain prices were so low that they were acting as disincentives for the producers. In the agricultural economies of countries like India, the general theory of price does not have the relevance theoretical economists ascribe to it. It does not answer the strange phenomenon of agricultural prices operating in the Indian scene. According to conventional economic theory, price is determined by the relative strength of demand and supply forces. In the case of agriculture, the supply side is inherently weak. The farmers do not have that economic strength or that holding power which may enable them to bargain for a better price. The result is that, as compared to the prices of industrial goods or consumer goods, the agricultural prices do not reflect that level which may reimburse the producers all their costs and also give them their due profit.

It is maintained by the present writer that pricing of the agricultural produce in India does not take place according to the principles of classical theory. It is not explainable even by the refined theory of imperfect competition. There is a great deal of artificiality in the price determination of agricultural commodities in this country. The concept of market that is relevant to them is either 'local' or at best 'regional'. Producers have little hand in marketing as such. All the factors of production, land, labour, capital, organization, and entrepreneur do not get rewarded fully. One circumstance which is peculiar to agriculture—risk from natural calamities which recur with remarkable regularity—is never accounted for in the pricing of agricultural produce. Secondly, the elements like replenishment of soil fertility, prevention of soil erosion and restoration of the soil crust—comparable to depreciation reserve and maintenance of capital in industry—do not get reflected in the costing of these commodities. Relief expenditure in times of famine represents the compounded capital the nation has to provide suddenly at the cost of everything else to make good what was denied to the producers of agricultural commodities in normal times. But it provides only subsistence level relief. Expenditure on projects designed to maintain soil in good condition and to prevent soil erosion are charged to general revenues of the state ; they are not a charge on the industry called agriculture. These circumstances are duly reflected in low yield rates and continued impoverishment of the peasantry.

FUNDAMENTAL CHARACTERISTICS OF AGRICULTURE AND INDUSTRY

There are certain fundamental differences between the industrial or manufacturing activity and agriculture which may be briefly put down here :

(1) Agriculture, including forestry, is the primary industry, while industry is secondary and, in the final analysis, dependent on it ;

(2) The fate of agriculture is directly determined by nature, viz., rainfall, weather conditions, pest attack and agro-climatic factors. Industry does not suffer from these phenomena ;

(3) The factor of uncertainty assails agriculture in a much more diverse and deep manner than is the case with manufacturing and organised industry ;

(4) In predominantly agricultural countries like India, agriculture is the way of life, and the tillers of the soil have no choice or option but to carry on with the activity of cultivation. Factors like 'estimate of demand', 'consumer preference', adjusting production to 'elasticity of demand', etc., do not enter into the calculus of the farmers as they do in the case of industry ;

(5) It is always possible for industry to regulate and adjust its production in relation to market conditions, sometimes even by resorting to artificial embargoes on supplies. Agriculture, on the other hand, largely goes on with the life style of the farmers, and there is no question of regulating the agricultural activity with the demand factor or the market conditions ;

(6) The 'principle of substitution' operates in agriculture within very narrow limits, as compared to industry. The vast multitude of our agriculturists have no means to convert coarse grain producing lands into rice or wheat producing lands or putting them under cash crops. It is

really not possible to do this on any large scale, more particularly in the case of small farmers who constitute a very large majority of the farming community in this country. In the rice producing tracts, limits to convert the areas into wheat growing tracts so as to take a second crop or to diversify the cropping pattern are very narrow and whatever is done at substantial investment, nature (especially agro-climatic factors), lack of experience and the risk factor put severe limitations on it. In the case of industry, however, the principle of substitution is applied to a much greater extent ;

(7) Alternative uses of land are limited in agriculture. Apart from the limitations pointed out earlier, alternative uses cannot be adopted by the farmers ;

(8) Yet one more peculiar feature of the agricultural economy in India and elsewhere too, is the quick off-loading of the produce onto the market, particularly in the post-harvest period. Talking of wheat, the procurement represents roughly one-fifth to one-fourth of the total produce and this is accomplished within a short period of three months, namely April, May and June. Even within this limited period when bulk of the marketable surplus is off-loaded onto the market, nearly 80 per cent is procured in one month, i.e., May. The procurement figures for the wheat marketing season (April to March) for 1978-79 and 1979-80 bear out this phenomenon :

(*in million tonnes*)

Month quarter	1978-79	% to total	1979-80	% to total
April	0.220	4.02	0.428	6.29
May	4.329	79.03	5.525	81.15
June	0.846	15.44	0.855	12.56
July-Sept.	0.072	1.31	—	—
Oct.-Dec.	0.003	0.15	—	—
Jan.-March	0.008	0.05	—	—
Total	5.478		6.808	

The story of rice is the same as would be seen from the procurement figures for the 1977-78 and 1978-79 marketing season :

(*in million tonnes*)

Month/ Quarter	1977-78		1978-79	
	Quantity procured	% to total	Quantity procured	% to total
October	0.232	4.78	0.670	11.24
November	1.188	24.47	1.200	20.14
December	0.934	19.24	1.174	19.70
January	0.803	16.54	1.061	17.80
February	0.538	11.08	0.704	11.81
March	0.427	8.80	0.571	9.58
April-June	0.619	12.75	0.580	9.73
July-Sept.	0.114	2.34	—	—
Total	4.855		5.960	

Of the total procurement of rice in these two years, 65.03 per cent and 68.88 per cent was procured respectively in the first-four months of the season. This trend persists even now. A proper marketing system hardly exists in this country, much less an effective participation by producers in it. Does such a phenomenon happen in any other industry—whether manufacturing heavy or light consumer goods ? The consequences of this phenomenon may detain us for a while. The most disastrous consequence is a fall in the prices of these commodities in the immediate post-harvest months. And this happens for no other reason but for the glut in the market. In other words, the prices have no relationship with the cost of production. And once the rush is over, the very same cultivators have to purchase, as consumers, the grain at a much higher price ; the seed is purchased at 2½ to 3 times of the consumer price. This is the status of the agricultural prices about which the economists have said with a lot of solemnity that they are the kingpin of the general price mechanism and that on them the latter is largely determined. It is just not true. Had it not been for the massive state intervention in the shape of price support operations in respect of wheat and rice, and to a limited extent in the case of gram also, their prices would have just crashed. But that is no economic mechanism ; it is an administrative policy based on wider considerations ;

(9) An agriculturist is both a producer as well as a consumer of his commodity. Talking of 70 per cent of the farmers who fall in the category of small and marginal farmers,

they buy foodgrains in the market for the better part of the year for their own consumption. The fluctuations in the prices of agricultural produce, therefore, affect them in the same manner and with the same severity as they do an ordinary consumer. Food being a vital need, there is no means to mitigate this rigour ;

(10) In India, the agricultural economy is structurally different from the industrial economy. The principles which govern the size and organization of an industry do not operate in the agricultural sector. Consequently, the operational part of the agricultural economy is fundamentally different from that of the industrial economy and hence, the theory of pricing too. In India 88.6 per cent of the total holdings are of 5 hectares and below (which was once considered a size just sufficient to keep the body and soul together) accounting for nearly 47 per cent of the total area under occupation. Hence the phenomenon of 'economies of the scale' does not operate in it. The managerial and entrepreneurial dimensions of this economy are qualitatively different from those of the industrial sectors, with the result that the theory of pricing of our economic science which allocates the share of earnings to the factors of production, fails to answer the phenomenon that characterize Indian agriculture ;

(11) The inherent flaws in the price determination of agricultural produce, coupled with the risks and hazards, affect the agricultural entrepreneur in a much more serious and damaging manner than an industrial entrepreneur. When a bad year hits the former, all his working capital is lost. He becomes a pauper and he folds up his 'industry'. Not only this, his capacity to carry on in future years is seriously impaired. This vulnerability of the agricultural entrepreneur to the vagaries of nature is peculiar to him alone ;

(12) Exhaustion of fertility, erosion by wind and rain, and deterioration of land by deposit of sand in the event of inundations and submergence by floods and cyclones are extremely damaging factors which change the very character of agriculture. The capacity of the farmers to tackle these dangers which threaten their very capital is severely limited, with the consequence that depletion in

the fixed capital (land) is, by and large, unabated. The result is that there is a continual impoverishment of the agriculturists. Industry does not suffer from these threats, nor does any depletion in its capital takes place on account of these causes. Normal wear and tear is the general rule of depletion in the industrial capital which is covered by depreciation reserves. The other form in which this depletion takes place is through technological obsolescence. But that is a different matter altogether ; and

(13) Of late the farm economists have started talking in terms of parity in the terms of trade between agricultural on the one hand and manufactured and industrial goods on the other. The argument is that the prices received by the farming community for their produce are much less than the prices paid by them for the goods purchased. As compared to 1970-71, the index of procurement price of wheat has risen from 100 to 154 in 1980-81. As against this, the cost index of some of the important agricultural inputs have risen more as shown below :

Index Numbers of prices of agricultural inputs as on September 27, 1980

(1970-71 - 100)

Item	*Index*
Fertilizers	259.0
Insecticides	321.6
High speed diesel oil	285.7
Tractors	274.6
Agril. power	296.7
Agril. sprayer	189.4
Diesel engine	165.7
Electric motor	211.5
Power driven pumps	230.5
Electricity	231.0

Another aspect to which the leaders of public opinion and farmers' organization draw attention is the growing disparity in the prices of foodgrains and those of non-agricultural commodities which implies a deterioration in the terms of trade of the agricultural sector vis-a-vis the other sectors and fall in the real income of the producers of foodgrains.

The data on index number of wholesale prices of foodgrains, manufactured products and non-agricultural commodities as a whole, reveal that the terms of trade have increasingly turned unfavourable to the producers of foodgrains, more particularly since 1979 as is evident from the table below :

Average Annual Wholesale Price Index

(*Base 1970-71 = 100*)

Year	Foodgrains	Manufactured products	Non-agricultural commodities*
1975	187	173	184
1976	150	172	186
1977	167	179	193
1978	173	178	193
1979	180	203	221
Aug. 1980	200	242	269

*Fuel, power, lighting, minerals, etc.

It is obvious that the price structure (which determines the income pattern) has moved significantly against the interests of the farmers and the agricultural economy in general.

The question the present writer wishes to pose is—are the costs listed in the foregoing paragraphs reflected in the process of price determination of agricultural produce? In industrial pricing, depreciation, research and development, innovations, and all overheads are fully accounted for. If there is slump, production is reduced and labour retrenched. A part of the capital no doubt becomes idle, but these losses are passed on to the society and are ultimately reckoned as social costs, but not so in agriculture. In this sense it is maintained that the agricultural pricing in India is artificial.

The course of events which marked the production and pricing in the sugar and jute industries during the past few years amply bear out the fact that the industry prospered at the cost of the farmers growing these two important crops.

U.N. STUDIES

These basic conclusions get support from the studies conducted by certain expert bodies of the United Nations. The Sub-Commission on Economic Development of the Economic and Employment Commission set up in 1949 under the United Nations Economic and Social Council* undertook a study of the post war appreciation of the price of goods imported by under-developed countries—especially capital goods, machinery and equipment—relative to the post-war price appreciation of the exports of under-developed countries, predominantly primary products. This Sub-Commission studied the material available for the latter part of the nineteenth century right up to the beginning of the Second world war, covering a period well over fifty years in relation to the Latin American countries and came to the conclusion that "there was a secular downward trend in the prices of primary goods relative to the prices of manufactured goods." Prices of primary commodities had been declining relative to manufactured goods over a long period of time prior to the Second World War. In addition to the secular decline, the price of primary goods had been subject to especially severe price pressure during the depression of thirties. In other words, it found that a "given quantity of primary goods exported would pay, at the end of this period, for only 60 per cent of the quantity of manufactured goods which it could buy at the beginning of the period."

Exports of the underdeveloped countries, they observed, were almost entirely composed of primary commodities and very little processing is done in the exporting countries. These very countries import back substantial quantities of food items in processed form, besides the capital goods and manufactured articles. The Sub-Commission stated that special conditions often intervene to affect the prices at which the underdeveloped countries dispose of their primary products through which they pay for the imported manufactured goods in their trade relations with the industrialised countries. While in the case of under-developed countries changes in the terms of trade are largely determined by the general trend of prices in international trade of the primary products, the same was not true of the imported manufactured goods to an equal degree. The absolute rise in the post-war price level, has however, had an additional adverse effect upon the financial resources available to under-developed countries for imports that aid their economic development. The post-war price inflation depreciated the purchasing power of their foreign exchange accumulated largely during war time. Their purchasing power was much

*Post War Price Relations in Trade between Under-Developed and Industrialized Countries No. E/CNI/Sub.3/WS/United Nations.

reduced in the post-war period as compared to the period during which they were accumulated. Copious statistics have been furnished to substantiate these conclusions.

The Sub-Commission dilated upon the importance to the under-developed countries of the changing price relation of goods and observed that the effect of this phenomena upon the financial resources of these countries for their economic development is crucial. The adverse long term trend in the prices of primary goods relative to manufactures will mean a continuing increase in the amount of primary goods a country must supply in order to obtain a given quantity of capital goods for economic development. This unfavourable trend in the price of primary materials relative to capital goods further cripples the under-developed countries to discharge their debt services on foreign loans and withdrawal of earnings of foreign financed investments thereby leading to curtailment of foreign investment in these countries. The result is that these countries are faced with harsh alternatives ; serious reduction in already low living standards, or default on debt service which will impair the possibility of foreign financing for economic development ; with practically very little choice between the two.

The Sub-Commission concluded that this unfavourable trend in the terms of trade brings about a situation in which the foreign trade of under-developed countries tends to be larger in proportion to the total national income than in the case of developed countries. This signifies a phenomenon in which larger volume of resources move out of the under-developed countries which could otherwise be available to them for their economic development. The Sub-Commission, referring to the under-developed countries mentioned in Appendix 'A' to their report, stated that pre-war exports of these primary producing countries were valued at $ 7000 to $ 7500 million annually. Corresponding exports in 1947 were approximately equal to the pre-war volume but the export prices of these goods were more than twice the 1938 level (in United States dollars). The value of these exports was, therefore, conservatively estimated at roughly $ 15000 million. Even a 10 per cent change in their terms of trade would modify the ability of under-developed countries to import by as much as $ 1500 million. This is a measure of the dimensions of the terms of trade between the primary (agricultural) goods and industrial (manufactured) goods, and how the agricultural commodities suffer decline in their value.

OBJECTIVES OF THE BUFFER STOCKING POLICY

The approach to evaluation would also depend on how we define the objectives of the buffer stocking policy. What purposes the buffer stocks are to subserve ? what objectives has the government kept before itself while setting up these stocks ? In his book *Buffer Stocks and Storage of Foodgrains in India*, Dr. A.M. Khusro speaks of price stabilization as an obvious objective. But he finds this to be in competition, and sometimes in conflict, with other objectives. The first in this category is stabilization of farmers' income. The conflict between these two objectives comes to surface alternately in good and bad years when, as a result of changes in the farm output, the prices fluctuate accordingly. Dr. Khusro observes, "Thus buffer stocks can be instruments of price stabilization, farm income stabilization and consumer income stabilization ; but a razor's edge balancing of these various objectives is required if serious conflict is not to develop amongst these."

Dr. Khusro poses the question : "What range of price fluctuations within a year and what range between a good and bad year is it desired to tolerate?" He believes that a tolerance of a certain order of magnitude of price fluctuations is an absolute necessity both for reasons of financial limitations on the government as well as for fundamental economic reasons. Complete price stabilization through buffer stock operations is, in his opinion, not only an enemy of buffer stock policy itself but is also an enemy of economic efficiency in production and consumption. The objective can be to eliminate the unduly low price trough of the post-harvest period, especially in a good year, and to eliminate the unduly high price peaks of the off-season, especially in a bad year, he concludes.

It should be clear that the origins of the buffer stocking policy essentially lay in the experiences of famines and compulsions of famine relief policy. This is the basic fact that ought not to be forgotten while examining the objectives of the buffer stocks. In other words, insurance against famine is the first and foremost objective. To mop up the surplus grain from a bountiful year and to store it for meeting the misfortune of a lean year is the obvious policy that any enlightened government could adopt in a sensitive area like food. The break-up of these stocks into the national buffer and the operational stocks is a question of secondary importance. This conceptual distinction has been introduced purely for considerations of administrative and operational convenience. There is nevertheless a fundamental rule governing the national buffer since it represents insurance against famine in future years; it must be maintained at all times and when drawn down, must be replenished at the earliest opportunity. The operational stocks represent the month-to-month requirements of the public distribution system and their level varies from time to time.

Price stabilization is not the primary objective of the buffer stocking policy. In fact, it is beyond its capability. Price is a highly complex phenomenon which is spread over innumerable sectors of the economy. A large number of factors—totally diverse yet inter-related —enter into this phenomena called the price structure. Money supply, demand and supply of the various commodities and their elasticities, cost structure, market conditions, speculative operations, international developments, and a host of other visible and invisible forces impinge on and determine the price structure. In the second place, though the price system of every single commodity is an individual and separate phenomenon, there is a high degree of unity in the price structure of all the commodities which we call the general price level. In this matrix there is a definite relationship between the prices of all the commodities and as a rule the entire price matrix moves together and in the same direction. Occasionally there are aberrations when, as pointed out earlier in this chapter, prices of different goods behave differently. These aberrations are sometimes seasonal ; sometimes there are valid explanations for them ; while at others there are none. In the causation of price, the cause and effect cycle operates relentlessly and to suggest that the buffer stocking operations could pierce this cycle is really expecting too much. These operations relate only to a few items of foodgrains and to control a complex phenomenon like the general price level is beyond their power.

When Dr. Khusro says that price stabilization is the aim of the buffer stocks, it is not clear as to which price he is referring to. There are wholesale prices and there are retail prices : there are prices for industrial and agricultural inputs and there are prices for consumer items ; there are prices at the level of the national market while the prices that rule in regional or local markets are quite different. Fertilizers are an important input in agricultural production. Is it the argument that buffer stocking operations would stabilize the price of fertilizers ? Would these operations regulate and stabilize the water rates or the electricity tariff which also enter into the calculus of agricultural prices and finally in that of general price level? Obviously no. Or, is the argument that the end-price of foodgrains—whatever it is—would be stabilized by these operations? But if the prices of inputs are beyond the pale of buffer stocking operations, the agricultural prices would keep fluctuating and the buffer stocking operations will have to adjust themselves to their level, rather than the other way about. The history of buffer stocking operations during the past two decades bears this out.

As regards farmers income stabilization, the correct way to state it is that through these operations the producers are assured a certain basic minimum which they can turn to, on their choice; for the rest the normal market mechanism still operates. Procurement has been the central policy of the government all along. When the concept of procurement price got transformed into support price and the government announced its commitment to purchase all stocks conforming to the prescribed specifications at that price, the objective to build up stocks still remained unchanged; only the means to achieve it were given a new direction and a new orientation. This became necessary as the green revolution got underway and production registered higher and higher levels. The support price is fixed and price support operations are organized not with a view to achieving farm income stability but to assuring minimum price to the farmers. They are free to put their produce in the market and get a higher price if it is obtaining there. Barely 20 to 25 per cent of total wheat production and 10 to 12 per cent of rice have been picked up under this policy; the rest of the quantities have passed through the normal market mechanism. Actually, the market behaviour in deficit and marginally placed states has been such that the open market prices of wheat and rice have generally ruled higher than the support prices and the intervention by public agencies was but rarely required. It is only in heavily surplus states like Punjab, Haryana, and western U.P.—and there too in the immediate post-harvest period, when large surpluses are released onto the market in a very short period—that intervention of the government agencies has been found to be necessary for supporting the prices from falling below the support level

The stocks thus acquired are primarily designed to provide insurance against famine and secondly to moderate, to the extent practicable, the fluctuations in supplies and prices of foodgrains owing to seasonal causes. But here the prime mover of the moderating influence is the central subsidy. If the market mechanism were truly efficient as the economists assume while discussing the theory of equilibrium, there would indeed be no problem. Taking the demand for wheat on a countrywide basis, including that of the roller flour mills, the surplus in the three states—Punjab, Haryana and western U.P.—is not in excess of the demand, so that when production increases, prices ought to fall, as Dr. Khusro argues. Secondly, if the purchasing power of that section of the community which is below the poverty line is brought at a reasonable level of consumption (or the effective demand is generated), the demand for foodgrains will be still more. In other words, what is being said is that the supply phenomenon viewed purely in the localized markets of Punjab, Haryana and western Uttar Pradesh would give one set of conclusions ; if the same phenomenon is transposed on the national market taking into account the total effective demand factor, it will give an entirely different set of conclusions. While carrying on the buffer stock operations the government is trying to correct the aberrations of the behaviour of the market. By purchasing and storing the grain and moving it into the needy areas, the government is in fact trying to extend the supply line so as to make it coincide with the demand factor, thereby extending the market both in spatial as well as time dimensions. For what is market but a state in which the buyers and sellers are in relationship with each other.

It is neither feasible nor desirable for the government to work on, what Dr. Khusro says, a mean price determined out of the troughs and peaks. As a matter of fact, to talk of troughs and peaks in relation to the Indian agriculture is unrealistic and has little relevance. A critical study of the marketing and price policy experience of Indian agriculture for the past fifty years, if not more, would clearly show that the chief malaise which accounted for the stagnation in agriculture was that prices of the agricultural produce had all along been too low and were operating as disincentives to the producers. This is an incontrovertible genesis of Indian agriculture which explains its low capital formation. Suggestion of deriving a mean price out of the troughs and peaks is born of a thinking wholly contrary to this lesson of history.

This approach further assumes that the food prices could be thought of in isolation from other prices. Prices of all commodities behave in an integrated manner and in a situation as at present, when the economy is caught up in a continuously rising price spiral, it would not be possible to think of a mean price level at which buffer stocking operations could be done. The support prices announced by the government are determined upon a large number of assumptions and approximations and are enforced in the hope that they will provide support to the prices of foodgrains in general. They are calculated to firm up the commodity market and to give an assurance to the producers that if the market prices fall below the support prices, the government is committed to step in and purchase stocks at the support prices. The representatives of the farmers' organizations and the state governments have frequently voiced their criticism of the support prices saying that they do not take care of the total costs of production and thus do not reimburse the farmers their real costs—much less a remunerative price. There is no *a priori* reason for applying the technique of mean price level of agricultural produce for buffer stocking operations. Likewise, any judgement on the tolerable range of price fluctuation in a year or between good and bad seasons is bound to be arbitrary and completely lacking in economic justification. In practical administration it would be well nigh impossible to successfully conduct buffer operations on a moving average of good and bad seasons as suggested by Dr. Khusro.

BASIC OBJECTIVES

To conclude this discussion, the basic objectives of the buffer stocking policy could be stated as follows :

(a) to acquire stocks for providing insurance against scarcities ;

(b) to assure a minimum support price to the farmers and thereby foster agricultural development ; and

(c) by extending the spatial and time dimensions of the market, to correct, to the extent possible, the aberrations in the commodity market.

Does this narration indicate any lines of inquiry ? It points to one important fact, namely it is difficult to evaluate the buffer stocking policy of the government based on the technique of support prices or administered prices from the standpoint of theoretical economics. The general concepts of economic analysis such as cost-benefit analysis, maximization of benefits (which, in other words, means reducing costs to the minimum), comparison of alternatives, and the kindred standards will no doubt be applied. But the evaluation has to be on the basis of the law of comparative advantages or balance of public gain. As explained in Part I, the origins of this policy lie essentially in the horrors of famine and the wide fluctuations in prices which inflict great hardship on the consumers, including a very large number of small and marginal farmers. In times of abundance, prices tend to fall to unremunerative levels which phenomenon does not conduce to the good of the farmers.

It will be chiefly these factors which will guide us in evaluating the efficacy of the government action in entering the market and influencing it through its buffer stocking operations.

10

Cost of Buffer and Operational Stocks

STOCKS

IT has been explained in sufficient detail in Chapters 5 and 7 that the central government was in effect conducting buffer stock operations much before the Technical Group formalized the framework in 1976. This policy was put into effect almost immediately after the government of India took the decision in January 1978, thanks to the comfortable stocks position with government and other public agencies. As a result of a series of good harvests in the country as well as because of heavy imports (see table below) made from 1973 onwards, the stock position with the government was very nearly in terms of the limits prescribed under the buffer stocking policy resolution (see also table 10.1*).

(*in million tonnes*)

Year	Wheat	Rice	Milo	Total
1973	2.41	—	1.20	3.61
1974	4.20	—	0.67	4.87
1975	7.01	0.13	0.26	7.40
1976	5.83	0.15	0.53	6.61

COSTS

In order to have an idea of the total costs involved in the acquisition, maintenance, and holding of these stocks, it would be necessary to

*In this table figures from 1975-76 onwards have been adopted. The reason is that the system of payment to the FCI subsidy on operational stocks and carrying costs of buffer stock was introduced from this year. Since the question of costs is being studied in this chapter, the figures which are relevant for this purpose have been adopted.

TABLE 10.1 : **Statements showing stocks of foodgrains (in the Central Pool as well as with States' Agencies) during the financial years 1975-76 to 1981-82**

(in million tonnes)

Year	Opening stocks (as reported)	Procurement	Total stocks	Total offtake	Closing stocks (derived)
		WHEAT			
1975-76	0.97	4.05 +6.57	11.59	6.92	4.67
1976-77	4.86	6.60 +4.82	16.28	5.53	10.75
1977-78	11.15	5.16 +0.18	16.49	7.06 +0.48	8.95
1978-79	8.59	5.48	14.07	6.75 +0.73	6.59
1979-80	6.31	8.00	14.31	8.04	6.27
1980-81	5.32	5.86	11.18	7.51	3.67
1981-82	3.07	6.60	9.67	6.69	2.98
		RICE			
1975-76	1.86	5.96 +0.14	7.96	3.00	4.96
1976-77	4.72	5.23 +0.15	10.10	4.06	6.04
1977-78	6.34	4.57	10.91	4.32 +0.04	6.55
1978-79	6.65	6.22	12.87	3.22 +0.01	9.64
1979-80	9.65	3.84	13.49	4.37	9.12
1980-81	8.40	4.09	12.49	5.44	7.05
1981-82	6.65	6.09	12.74	6.30	6.44
		COARSE GRAINS			
1975-76	0.22	0.34 +0.72	1.28	0.34	0.94
1976-77	0.90	0.28	1.18	0.59	0.59
1977-78	0.74	0.04	0.78	0.64	0.14
1978-79	0.11	0.12	0.23	0.07	0.16
1979-80	0.15	0.11	0.26	0.12	0.14
1980-81	0.15	0.10	0.25	0.15	0.10
1981-82	0.11	0.22	0.33	0.16	0.17

GRAND TOTAL

YEAR	TOTAL STOCKS	TOTAL ISSUES	CLOSING STOCK
1975-76	20.83	10.26	10.57
1976-77	27.56	10.18	17.38
1977-78	28.18	12.54	15.64
1978-79	27.17	10.78	16.39
1979-80	28.06	12.53	15.53
1980-81	23.92	13.10	10.82
1981-82	22.74	13.15	9.59

(+) Indicates import under procurement and export under issues.

briefly explain the various components that normally enter into the calculus. First and foremost is the capital cost of the stocks at which they are procured from the producers, millers, etc. This is calculated at the procurement price or the support price fixed by the government from year to year. This price is fixed for the naked grain, and the procurement costs or 'incidentals' as they are called, are separately determined. These are determined both for the FCI which is the central agency as well as for the state agencies which procure these stocks in the first instance and subsequently hand over to the FCI. The stocks retained by the states for their requirements do not form part of the central pool and, therefore, their costs are not being considered here. These costs for the past seven years have been compiled in Table 10.2.

TABLE 10.2 : **Quantity and capital cost of foodgrains procured/imported by government (central pool only)**

(Quantity in million tonnes)
(Value in crores of rupees)

PART A

Year	Indigenous		Imported		Weighted Average cost (per tonne)	
	Qnty.	Value	Qnty.	Value	Indegs.	Imptd.
			WHEAT			
1975-76	3.827	475.19	6.521	1006.55	1241.68	1543.55
1976-77	5.420	658.52	4.819	721.24	1214.98	1496.66
1977-78	5.286	632.96	0.179	26.93	1197.43	1504.47
1978-79	5.771	718.50	—	—	1245.02	—
1979-80	7.536	992.65	—	—	1317.21	—
1980-81	5.748	787.34	0.490	6.31	1369.76	1287.76
1981-82	6.810	1016.79	2.25	452.13	1493.08	2010.36
			RICE			
1975-76	4.230	580.78	.141	31.85	1373.00	2258.79
1976-77	4.730	656.67	.146	37.52	1338.31	2569.66
1977-78	4.060	546.72	—	—	1346.60	—
1978-79	5.703	839.96	—	—	1472.84	—
1979-80	3.844	611.74	—	—	1591.42	—
1980-81	4.085	723.18	—	—	1770.33	—
1981-82	6.022	1200.60	0.730	12.38	1993.69	1695.89
			COARSE GRAINS			
1975-76	0.035	2.91	0.261	24.36	831.43	933.33
1976-77	0.010	0.88	0.533	67.75	880.00	1270.00
1977-78	0.006	0.67	—	—	1116.67	—
1978-79	0.011	1.15	—	—	1045.45	—
1979-80	0.022	2.10	—	—	954.55	—
1980-81	0.008	0.76	—	—	950.00	—
1981-82	—	—	—	—	—	—

TABLE 10.2 : *Contd.*

Weighted average cost of all foodgrains

(*Rs. per ton*)

Year	Indigenous	Imported	Weighted average of total stocks
1975-76	1308.55	1535.10	1413.01
1976-77	1295.34	1503.30	1368.36
1977-78	1262.14	1504.46	1266.69
1978-79	1559.61	—	1357.95
1979-80	1606.49	—	1408.95
1980-81	1511.28	6.31	1534.47
1981-82	2217.39	464.51	1769.76

Explanation :

(i) The quantities relate to the stocks procured/imported during that particular year and do not include the carry-over stocks.

(ii) Values include the purchase price plus the procurement incidentals (as shown in Table 10.3)

Source : Annual Reports of the FCI.

PART B

Weighted average cost of respective grains

(*Rs. per tonne*)

	Wheat	Rice	Coarse Grains
1975-76	1431.63	1401.89	921.28
1976-77	1347.42	1422.52	1263.90
1977-78	1208.59	1346.60	1116.67
1978-79	1245.02	1472.84	1045.45
1979-80	1317.21	1591.42	954.55
1980-81	1369.07	1770.33	950.00
1981-82	1621.50	1990.12	—

TABLE 10.2A : **Total Foodgrain stocks handled by FCI—carry over stocks and purchases (including imports)**

Opening Stocks

(*Qty. in million tonnes*)
(*Value in crores of rupees*)

Year	Wheat	Rice	Coarse grain	Total
1975-76	2.09 (311.41)	1.43 (181.66)	0.07 (7.10)	3.59 (500.17)

Year	Wheat	Rice	Coarse grain	Total
1976-77	5.70 (818.28)	3.61 (495.70)	0.62 (76.70)	9.93 (1390.68)
1977-78	9.77 (1355.00)	5.58 (781.00)	0.39 (48.69)	15.74 (2184.60)
1978-79	7.49 (991.61)	6.05 (844.93)	0.02 (1.85)	13.56 (1838.39)
1979-80	5.35 (697.77)	9.17 (1342.41)	0.02 (1.63)	14.54 (2041.81)
1980-81	3.95 (828.22)	8.19 (1255.02)	0.03 (2.58)	12.17 (1785.82)
1981-82	1.83 (252.99)	6.34 (1049.40)	0.02 (1.67)	8.19 (1304.06)

Total Stocks handled

Year	Carry over stocks	Purchases and imports	Total stocks handled
1975-76	3.59	15.49	19.08
1976-77	9.93	14.24	24.17
1977-78	15.74	9.53	25.27
1978-79	13.56	11.49	25.05
1979-80	14.54	11.40	25.94
1980-81	12.17	9.90	22.07
1981-82	8.19	15.15	23.34

Source : Annual Reports of the F.C.I.

PROCUREMENT INCIDENTALS

Procurement incidentals comprise the following :

(a) *Obligatory charges* : Such as mandi charges, local taxes, and cost of the gunny. Every mandi levies a fee for the utilization of the facilities provided by it and is, therefore, in the nature of service fee. Then there are commission agents—*kacha arthia* and *pucca arthia*—who are supposed to be licensed and who operate within the mandi performing specific tasks, The *kacha arthias*, by their definition, are supposed to serve the seller of the goods while the *pucca arthias* serve the purchasers. The commission agents realize their commission on a prescribed percentage basis which is included in the overall mandi charges. Thirdly, local taxes which are imposed by the state government on the purchase and sale of the various commodities are also required to be paid at this stage. Finally, the cost of the gunny is also included in the obligatory charges because the foodgrains are bagged in the mandi and thereafter removed to the storage points ;

(b) *Storage and interest charges* : A certain minimum time—varying from 15 days to 75 days—elapses between the purchase of stocks in the market and their transference to the FCI for buffer stocking. It often happens that either the stocks are kept in the mandi itself or are moved to a temporary storage from where they finally move to the warehouses. Therefore, proportionate costs of such temporary storage and interest on the capital invested by the purchasing agencies in these stocks are computed as procurement expenses. It also happens that because of constraints of storage or difficulties in rail movement the stocks are carried by the state procurement agencies for longer periods and in such cases the reimbursement made by the FCI covers the carrying costs incurred by such agencies by way of storage and interest on capital. These charges also go into the costing of procurement expenses ;

(c) *Handling charges* : Costs incurred on payment made to the mandi labour for handling the stocks in the market, stitching the bags and stenciling them, internal movement, and forwarding charges representing despatch of these stocks to the temporary godowns or warehouses are grouped under this head ;

(d) *Establishment charges* : Proportionate costs of the staff employed by the procuring agencies and other administrative expenses, viz., stationery, telephone, postage, miscellaneous office expenses, etc., are determined and included in the procurement costs ; and

(e) *Others miscellaneous items* : These include items like bank commission, depreciation on stock articles, and other unforeseen items.

All these items taken together constitute the procurement incidentals. Actuals for the past seven years are shown in Table 10.3.

DISTRIBUTION INCIDENTALS

After the stocks have been acquired and put into the godowns/ warehouses, they have to be maintained in good condition, moved to

TABLE 10.3 : **Details of procurement incidentals of wheat and rice**

(*Rs. per tonne*)

Item	1975-76		1976-77		1977-78		1978-79		1979-80		1980-81		1981-82	
	Wheat	Rice	Wheat	Rice	Wheat	Rice	Wheat	Rice	Wheat	Rice	Wheat	Rice	Wheat	Rice
1. Obligatory charges (Mandi charges, cost of gunny and sales tax).	118.10	67.80	114.00	67.80	117.6	59.10	119.70	68.60	122.20	81.10	145.40	76.70	144.00	73.20
2. Storage and interest charges	34.70	0.20	19.60	4.30	20.70	15.40	23.80	0.60	24.20	0.10	25.80	2.20	30.10	0.20
3. Handling charges (Mandi labour, forwarding charges, internal movement etc.)	30.30	7.70	29.20	9.10	27.60		33.30	15.80	30.90	9.90	32.40	8.00	38.40	11.60
4. Establishment charges	11.00	4.30	10.60	5.60	9.60	4.00	10.50	4.00	10.70	10.20	9.50	9.60	10.70	10.40
5. Other miscellaneous items (Bank commission etc.)	0.90	0.60	1.50	1.00	0.70	—	0.90	—	—	—	—	4.00	—	—
Total	195.00	80.60	174.90	87.60	176.20	78.50	188.20	89.00	188.00	101.30	213.10	100.50	223.20	95.40

Explanation :

Difference in the rates of wheat and rice in respect of certain items such as serial Nos. 2 and 3 would appear to be significant. The reason is that whereas in the case of wheat the stocks are held by the state agencies for considerable length of time necessitating payment of incidentals, in the case of rice the deliveries are taken from the millers almost on day-to-day or week-to-week basis. Consequently these charges are much less.

As regards item No. 1, the obligatory charges are incurred by and large at the paddy stage which are included in the rate of paddy per quintal while working out the conversion ratio. Hence they are not reflected at the rice stage. In the case of wheat they are all reflected at one stage.

Similarly establishment charges in the case of rice are also quite low. Rice deliveries are taken from the millers and they have to hold the stocks so long as they are not lifted by the state agencies.

all parts of the country, and issued through the public distribution system. Costs incurred on all these operations are computed under the head distribution incidentals. The principal heads of expenditure under these operations are as follows :

(a) *Freight* : The stocks have to move in bulk from the procurement areas to the deficit areas and within the procurement areas to the various places in the state for feeding the public distribution system. The freight costs are therefore, worked out on a pooled basis and a per tonne rate determined ;

(b) *Interest* : Since the stocks are purchased with borrowed money the interest charges are computed on an average basis and added to the costs ;

(c) *Transit and storage loss* : A certain quantity of grain is necessarily lost in transit as well as in storage. Loss during storage is also due to pests and rodents as well as by natural deterioration. Costs on these accounts are included under this head ;

(d) *Storage charges* : Rent paid for godowns, maintenance costs in the shape of fumigation, standardization, re-bagging, and the like are included under the head 'storage' ;

(e) *Handling expenses at the godowns* : Handling of stocks both at the time of issue to the public distribution system as well as for mintaining the buffer is inevitable and these expenses are computed under this head ; and

(f) *Administrative overheads* : These charges shown under procurement incidentals pertain to the reimbursement given to the procurement agencies. In the distribution operations the proportionate cost of staff deployed by FCI alongwith other administrative expenses is computed and added to the distribution incidentals. Details are shown in Table 10.4.

ECONOMIC COST

Taking the capital cost of the stocks, the procurement incidentals, and the distribution expenses together, the economic cost

TABLE 10.4 : **Details of storage, movement and distribution incidentals (wheat and rice) incurred during years 1975-76 to 1981-82**

(Rs. per tonne)

Storage, distribution and movement etc.	1975-76	1976-77	1977-78	1978-79	1979-80	1980-81	1981-82
Freight	61.10	45.10	41.70	83.70	85.30	96.40	139.20
Interest	30.80	46.10	46.50	87.00	60.90	71.60	79.60
Transit and storage loss	20.60	13.60	12.70	30.50	33.30	52.40	68.90
Storage charges	9.10	7.20	8.90	18.00	16.70	27.70	32.80
Handling expenses at the godowns	12.10	13.50	13.10	14.90	14.60	21.10	33.30
Administrative overheads	26.70	27.60	25.40	16.70	15.80	21.30	24.90
Total	165.40	153.10	148.30	250.80	226.60	290.50	378.70

TABLE 10.5A : Economic cost of wheat

(Rate Rs. per tonne)

Cost Component	1795-76			1976-77			1977-78		1978-79	1979-80	1980-81	1981-82
	Indigenous	PL480	Imported	Indigenous	PL480	Imported	Indigenous	Imported	Indigenous	Indigenous	Indigenous	Indigenous
Procurement/ acquisition cost.	1046.68	1392.20	1456.10	1040.08	1567.00	1442.10	1021.23	1415.20	1114.80	1143.60	1165.30	1277.50
Procurement incidentals (Port clearance charges) (Table 10.3).	195.00	88.80	88.80	174.90	89.20	89.20	176.20	143.70	188.20	188.00	213.10	223.20
Total purchase. cost.	1241.68	1481.00	1544.90	1214.98	1656.20	1531.30	1193.43	1558.90	1303.00	1331.60	1378.40	1500.70
Add distribution incidentals (Table 10.4)	165.40	165.40	165.40	153.10	153.10	153.10	148.30	148.30	250.80	226.60	290.50	378.70
Economic cost	1407.08	1646.40	1710.30	1368.08	1809.30	1684.40	1345.73	1707.20	1553.80	1558.20	1668.90	1879.40
Issue price	1250.00	1250.00	1250.00	1250.00	1250.00	1250.00	1250.00	1250.00	1250.00 (upto 30.11.78) 1300.00 (from 1.12.78)	1300.00	1300.00	1450.00

Note: The economic cost shown above does not include the effect of opening and closing stocks.

Explanation : The economic cost has been worked out separately for indigenous, PL480 and imported (commercial) stocks which quantities include the carry over stocks also. Hence there is no exact link between Table 10.2 and these two tables.

The difference between the economic cost and the issue price shown in these two tables (10.5A and 10.5B) would not tally with the rate adopted in Table 10.6 for calculating the quantum of subsidy. In that table the quantities and values have been worked out on the basis of the available stocks, including the stocks carried over from the previous years ; whereas in these two tables the quantities and values have been worked out on the purchases made in that particular year.

of the stocks is calculated (tables 10.5A and 10.5B). If the stocks could be sold at this rate the operations would break even. But these costs will obviously push up the issue price so high that it will defeat the very purpose of the system, especially in relation to the vulnerable sections of the society. It is, therefore, the policy of the government to supply these grains in the public distribution system at a subsidized rate, which is fixed keeping a host of considerations in mind : the open market prices of the grain, the general availability in the market, the likely impact of the issue prices on the general price level, requirements of the vulnerable sections of the people, availability of stocks with the government, etc. The issue prices are uniform throughout the country.

TABLE 10.5B : **Economic cost of rice**

(*Rs. per tonne*)

Year	Indigenous rice	Imported rice	Pooled issue price
1975-76	1548.90	2426.10	1555.6
1976-77	1591.80	2720.60	1512.4
1977-78	1578.70	—	1527.0
1978-79	1808.60	—	1511.9
1979-80	1928.30	—	1556.7
1980-81	2161.30	—	1592.9
1981-82	2454.00	—	1805.6

Note : (i) The economic cost shown above do not include the effect of opening and closing stocks.

(ii) Since procurement price varies from variety to variety (earlier four and now three varieties are procured for public distribution) and state to state, the format adopted in the case of wheat has not been adopted here for the sake of convenience. Weighted average figures were adopted and total all-India costs have been worked out.

SUBSIDY

Inevitably, therefore, the issue prices are lower than the economic cost of the respective grains necessitating subventions from the public exchequer. This represents the 'food subsidy' from the general revenues of the government. This subsidy is in two parts—one relating to the operational stocks which are issued from the central pool through the public distribution system or are otherwise sold on central account such as to the roller flour mills, Army Purchase

TABLE 10.6 : **Total subsidy on operational stocks sold from central pool**

(Quantities in million tonnes)
(Rate Rs. per tonne)
(Amount in Rs. crore)

	Quantities Sold*			Rate of Subsidy Per qtl.			Total amount of subsidy			Grand Total Amount
	Wheat	Rice	Coarse grain	Wheat	Rice	Coarse grain	Wheat	Rice	Coarse grain	
1975-76	6.62	1.56	0.19	31.85	(—) 0.90	19.87	210.95	(—) 1.40	11.52	221.07
1976-77	5.16	2.44	0.23	28.14	1.26	61.52	145.33	3.08	14.15	162.56
1977-78	7.72	2.95	0.36	24.32	1.91	71.88	187.65	5.64	26.02	219.31
1978-79	7.74	2.16	0.010	32.12	19.05	48.00	253.50	41.09	0.48	295.07
1979-80	8.76	4.37	0.011	28.14	17.71	34.55	246.47	77.30	0.38	324.15
1980-81	7.61	5.27	0.017	40.19	34.02	27.65	306.05	179.35	0.47	485.87
1981-82	6.81	5.97	0.012	53.73	42.94	31.88	365.96	256.45	0.38	622.79

* The quantities are different from those shown in Table 10.1. because the quantities shown in this table relate to the central pool, while those in Table 10.1 include issues from stocks held by all the public agencies—central as well as state.

(—) Denotes profit.

TABLE 10.7 : **Statement showing details of costs of carrying buffer for the years 1975-76 to 1981-82**

(*Rs. per tonne*)

Storage, distribution and movement etc.	1975-76	1976-77	1977-78	1978-79	1979-80	1980-81	1981-82
Freight	61.10	35.00	33.00	—*	—*	—*	—*
Interest	150.70	160.20	177.70	150.10	156.20	182.40	222.40
Transit and storage loss	27.50	14.70	17.50	13.90	16.40	42.80	53.40
Storage charges	38.10	25.00	33.80	57.70	54.20	83.00	98.30
Handling expenses at the godowns	12.10	10.50	10.40	11.40	11.20	15.80	25.00
Administrative overheads	49.70	21.50	20.10	12.70	12.10	16.00	18.70
Total	339.20	266.90	292.50	245.80	250.10	340.00	417.80

Note : Variation in the carrying costs from year to year would deposed upon :

(i) The quantities carried ;

(ii) Acquisition cost of the stocks ;

(iii) Servicing charges, including credit ; and

(iv) general cost structure of the various items ralated to the maintenance of stocks.

* From 1978-79 the entire freight is charged to the operational stocks, on the ground that there has been no net accretion to the buffer.

Organization, and other organizations (Table 10.6), and the other relating to the buffer stocks (Table 10.8). In the case of the former which is called the consumer subsidy, the extent of subsidy is determined by the difference between the economic cost and the issue price. In the case of the latter, only the carrying costs in the shape of freight, interest, storage charges, transit and storage loss, handling and administrative charges are computed (Table 10.7) and paid to the central agency for holding the stocks.

TABLE 10.8 : **Carrying costs of buffer stock**

(Quantity in million tonnes)
(Value : Rs. crores)

	Quantities Carried (Average buffer)				Carrying Costs* (Rs.) (Pooled cost)
	Wheat	Rice	Coarse Grains	Total**	
1975-76	1.75	0.51	—	2.26	76.54
1976-77	7.87	2.68	0.41	10.96	292.56
1977-78	8.69	3.06	—	11.75	343.64
1978-79	5.22	5.46	0.01	10.69	262.77
1979-80	3.50	7.10	0.01	10.61	265.30
1980-81	0.65	4.51	0.02	5.18	176.08
1981-82	1.01	2.69	—	3.70	154.81

* Quantities multiplied by the rates shown in Table 10.7.

** The quantities represent average stocks carried in the year, determined in the manner described on pages 155-6. Hence they will not tally with the figures of actual stocks adopted in other tables derived from actual purchases and actual sales.

In the overall computation of the total subsidy bill, there are five parameters : the anticipated quantity to be procured, the procurement price, including the costs, the distribution costs, the anticipated supplies through the distribution system, and the issue price. As explained in Chapter 7, after the APC submits its report and by the time consultations with the states conclude, a fair assessment of the crop prospects is available to the Food Department. Based on past trends, an estimate is made of the likely quantity that will be procured. This quantity multiplied by the second parameter—the procurement price and procurement costs—gives the total funds required. But for determining the extra outgo of funds over the level of the previous year's, what is relevant is the differential between the previous year's procurement costs, and the price proposed for the current year's multiplied with the quantity anticipated to be procured. In the case of wheat, the calculations are simple because wheat is classified only in one variety (qualitatively it is graded into two—Grade I and Grade II, depending upon the refractions.) But in the case of rice* the calculations are rather complicated, because the levy price (which is different for different varieties) at which rice is procured from the mills varies from state to state. The levy price of rice is derived from the hulling/milling ratio (which again varies from variety to variety and state to state) of rice and thereafter adding to it costs like statutory and obligatory charges, handling expenses, and a margin for milling.

The impact of the procurement/support prices on the central exchequer in a particular year in the shape of subsidy is determined in the following manner—Weighted average costs (purchase costs plus distribution costs) of the anticipated procurement are calculated statewise (because different tax and cost structures prevail in the states) at old and suggested prices. The difference between these two costs divided by the anticipated procurement gives the per tonne rate of additional financial burden, if any, over that of the previous year's. The total bill is later split into the consumer subsidy (related to issues) and the carrying costs of the buffer (the stocks that go in the reserve) as explained a little later.

The next set of calculations relates to the sale realization through the issue prices, on the anticipated offtake through the public distribution system. This is done for determining the level of consumer subsidy. The opening stocks of foodgrains (October 1 in the case of rice and April 1 in the case of wheat) are next computed to which the anticipated quantities to be procured are added with a view to determining the weighted average procurement costs by distributing them over this total quantity, thus arriving at the per tonne cost. Against this rate is adjusted the rate of realization through sales giving the net per tonne rate of consumer subsidy that will be necessary in that particular year with reference to the five parameters listed above. This quantity can be both in plus as well as in minus depending upon the parameters. The two sets of hypothetical calculations are shown in Table 10.10. They relate to rice which, on account of a number of varieties, are somewhat complicated.

*Until 1978-79 rice was classified into five varieties with different issue prices. From 1979-80 *kharif* season these were reduced to three—Common, Fine and Superfine, the classification depending on the length-breadth ratio.

It would be relevant here to dwell upon the principles according to which this total subsidy bill is allocated between operational and buffer stocks. The quantity of operational stock is first determined. The formula adopted at present is that average issues of two months of wheat, average issues of six months of rice, and average issues of seven months of coarse grains based on the annual offtake are calculated and treated as operational stocks. The next step is to compute the opening stocks of foodgrains on the first of a month. From these, the operational stocks aforesaid are deducted. The balance is treated as the buffer stock for the month. In the next month, the opening stock is again determined on the first of that month from which the operational stocks worked out on the basis mentioned above are deducted, giving the buffer stock for that month. The buffer stock carried in the previous month is added to the buffer quantity of this later month and the carrying costs as shown in Table 10.7 are multiplied with this quantity and divided by 12 so as to yield the carrying costs of the total buffer for one month. The amount so determined is reduced by the amount determined and paid in the previous month by way of carrying charges thereby giving the net carrying costs for that month. Below is given the example relative to the year 1978-79 :

Provisional bill for subsidy payment by Govt. of India for April 1978**

Commodity	Quantity (lakh allotted tonnes)	Quantity (lakh sold tonnes)		Rate of subsidy Rs. qtl.*	Amount (Rs. in crores)
Wheat imported / Wheat indigenous	11.82	7.78		25.61	19 92
Rice imported / Rice indigenous	3.83	—		18.02	—
		1.70		(—) 2.21	(—).38
Milo Imported	0.05	—		72.62	—
Coarse grains	—	—		13.25	—
Subsidy on normal operations :			19.55		
Cost of holding buffer stock :			24.04		
Total claim :			43.59		

NB : For wheat, pooled rate has been adopted.

(—) Indicates profit.

* These figures represent the difference between the economic cost of the foodgrain and the sale realizations of the FCI.

Provisional bill for subsidy payment by Govt. of India**
for the period 1-4-1978 to 30-5-1978

Commodity	Quantity allotted (lakh tonnes)	Quantity sold (lakh tonnes)	Rate of subsidy Rs./qtl.	Amount (Rs. in crores)
Wheat imported / Wheat indigenous	22.37	10.52	24.93*	26.23
Rice imported / Rice indigenous	7.45	—	18.02	—
		(—) 3.60	(—)2.21	.79
Milo imported	0.05	—	72.62	—
Coarse grains	—	—	13.25	—

Subsidy on normal operations :	25.43
Cost of holding buffer stock for May 78 :	45.72
Total claim:	71.15
Less amount paid for April :	(—) 43.59
Net for May :	27.56

(—) Indicates profit.

* This figure is different from the corresponding figure of the previous month, as it varies slightly from month to month depending on the sale realizations, fresh purchases and certain items of expenditure that come up.

** This is the format in which FCI prefers its monthly bills in respect of the subsidy on operational stocks as well as carrying cost of the buffer. Allotment figures are as per the allocations made by the Central Government. The figures are reported by FCI and shown in the bills. Some explanation is needed in regard to per quintal rate of subsidy shown in column 4 of the above Tables. The rate is relevant to the sales, i.e., supplies made through the P.D.S. and to the roller flour mills. This rate is worked out by the FCI every month and is incorporated in the bills. (In the two tables reproduced above, the minus figure against indigenous rice shows that there was profit on it). The subsidy rate is worked out by computing the value of the opening stock at the beginning of the month plus the value of the purchases made during the month, which after being added together give the average acquisition cost. To this are added storage, movement and distribution costs which finally determine the economic cost. This minus the issue price is the per quintal rate of subsidy that is claimed by F.C.I.

Calculation of the subsidy which is on actual sales is relatively simple. The subsidy rate is multiplied by actual sales and the amount determined. Normally what happens is that the actual sales for the month for which the claim is being made by FCI are not known, so the actuals of the previous months are adopted, subject to the condition that the actual sales should not be more than the allotments made by the department, and necessary adjustment to be made in the next month. The subsidy calculations are also done on progressive basis minus the amounts paid by the end of the previous month.

These two items, namely, the subsidy on actual sales or issues and the carrying costs of buffer, enter into the final food subsidy bill. (Table 10.9).

The principles explained in the foregoing paragraphs were codified in 1978 by an Expert Committee. The Committee was asked to examine in depth the various components that constituted the recurring cost of maintaining the buffer stocks and to identify areas where the incidence of these charges could be reduced. The Committee's recommendations were processed by the Comptroller and Auditor General of India and finally prescribed in January 1979 for the FCI to be adopted for apportionment of the various costs.

(***Contd.*)

The details of the calculation of the subsidy rate shown in the Table pertaining to April, 1978 in respect of wheat are given below :

	Quantity (*lakh tonnes*)	*Value* (*Rs. in crores*)	*Rate* (*Rs. per Quintal*)
Opening stock 1.4.78 (imported & indigenous wheat)	76.84	1042.33	135.65
Purchase from 1.4.78 to 30.4.78			
Indigenous wheat	2.38	30.91	129.86
Total	2.38	30.91	129.86
Average Acquisition cost	79.22	1073.24	135.48
Storage, movement and distribution cost	—	—	15.13
Economic cost	—	—	150.61
Issue price	—	—	125.00
Subsidy	—	—	25.61

As regards the carrying cost of the buffer, the rate remains unchanged throughout the year. The details are shown in Table 10.7.

The principles governing some of the important costs are reproduced below :

TABLE 10.9 : **Subsidy paid for handling foodgrains on central account (consumer subsidy and carrying costs)**

(*Rs. in crores*)

Year	On operational stocks (consumer subsidy)	Carrying costs of buffer	Total
1975-76	221.07	76.54	297.61
1976-77	162.56	292.56	455.12
1977-78	219.31	343.64	562.95
1978-79	295.45	262.77	558.22
1979-80	324.15	265.30	589.45
1980-81	485.87	176.08	661.95
1981-82	622.79	154.81	777.60

Note : Progressive reduction in the carrying costs of buffer is indicative of declining level of buffer in physical terms :

TABLE 10.10 : **Model calculation for determining subsidy (Rice)**

Model I

Parameters for 1978-79		Parameters for 1979-80 Assumed Procurement—550 million tonnes* Assumed offtake—3.80 million tonnes	
Procurement Prices			(in Rs./tonne)
Common	1420	Common	1490
Fine	1500	Fine	1550
Superfine	1590	Superfine	1656.9
Issue Prices			
Common	1500	Common	1500
Fine	1620	Fine	1620
Superfine	1720	Superfine	1720

	(crores)
(A) Additional outgo of funds on procurement (from last year's level of procurement prices)	36.01
(B) Increase in per tonne rate of procurement	65.40
(C) Weighted average price increase of old and new stocks	25.72

TABLE 10.10—*Contd.*

Opening stocks on 1.10.79	8.5 million tonnes	
Anticipated procurement	5.5 million tonnes	
Total	14.0 million tonnes	
(D) Net per tonne subsidy		25.72
(E) Addition to subsidy bill	25.72×3.8 m. tonnes	= 9.77

* For variety wise details, see the calculation sheet at the next page.

Model II

Parameters for 1978-79		Parameters for 1979-80 Assumed Procurement—5.5 million tonnes Assumed offtake—3.8 million tonnes	
	Procurement Prices		(in Rs./tonne)
Common	142	Common	149
Fine	150	Fine	155
Superfine	159.43	Superfine	165.69
	Issue Prices		
Common	150	Common	155
Fine	162	Fine	168
Superfine	172	Superfine	180

		(Crores)
(A) Additional outgo of funds on procurement (from last year's level of procurement prices)		36.01
(B) Increase in per tonne rate of procurement		65.40
(C) Weighted average price increase of old and new stocks		25.72
Opening stocks on 1.10.79	8.5 million tonnes	
Anticipated procurement	5.5 million tonnes	
Total	14.0	
36.01/14=25.72		
(D) Per tonne extra realization on account of revision of issue prices		62.00
(E) Total extra realization on assumed offtake 3.8 × 62.0 = 23.56		
(F) Decrease in per tonne subsidy (Rs. 62—25.72)		= 36.28
Decrease in total subsidy bill 36.28 × 3.8 m. tonnes = 13.79 crores		

TABLE 10.10—*Contd.*

Calculation Sheet

Variety	Quantity (in million tonnes)	Procurement Cost				Model I		Model II	
		Pre-revised		Revised					
		Rate (per tonne)	Amount (in crores)	Rate (per tonne)	Amount (in crores)	Rate (per tonne)	Amount (Rs. in crores)	Rate (per tonne)	Amount (Rs. in crores)
Common	3.5	1420	497.00	1490	521.50	1500	525.00	1550	542.50
Fine	0.8	1500	120.00	1550	1240	1620	129.60	1680	134.40
Superfine	1.2	1594.3	191.32	1656.9	1988.3	1720	206.40	1800	216.00
Total	5.5		808.32		844.33		861.00		892.90
Rate per tonne (Weighted)		1469.7		1535.1		1565.5		1623.5	

TRANSPORTATION COSTS

Transportation costs should be allocated in the first year in the ratio of sales plus operational stocks to average buffer. In the subsequent years, the allocation should be in the ratio of sales plus accretion to operational stocks to accretion to buffer (accretion in the case of both buffer and operational stocks would be with reference to the highest level reached during the year).

TRANSIT LOSSES

The same principle as for transportation costs should be applied in the case of transit losses.

HANDLING CHARGES

The distribution of handling charges may be made in the ratio of sales plus average operational stocks to average buffer stock.

STORAGE CHARGES

These charges may be apportioned in the ratio of operational stock to average buffer stock (in terms of quantities).

STORAGE LOSSES

Storage losses may be apportioned in the ratio of average operational stocks to average buffer stocks, on value basis.

INTEREST CHARGES

The interest on the value of average buffer stock should be first worked out at the appropriate rate of borrowing and the amount so determined should be charged to the average buffer stock. The balance amount should be taken as representing the interest charges to be allocated to operational stock.

ADMINISTRATIVE CHARGES

Administrative charges may be allocated on the basis of ratio of sales to average buffer stock for the first year and the ratio of sales plus average operational stocks to average buffer stock for the subsequent years.

STATE OPERATIONS

There is one more operational dimension to the exercise of allocation of these costs. In many states the FCI is also operating under a separate agreement as an agent of the state government in the matter of retail distribution of foodgrains. In Madhya Pradesh, West Bengal, Rajasthan, Andhra Pradesh, Kerala, and Delhi, the FCI does retail distribution while in states like Gujarat, Uttar Pradesh, Maharashtra, Karnataka, Punjab, and Haryana, the state agencies take the stocks from the FCI in bulk and themselves do retail distribution. In the former, the movement of stocks, storage, losses, and handling costs are all charged to the state account and recoveries made through issue prices. In this arrangement certain points are designated as Central Storage Depots (CSDs) to which places the movement and handling takes place on Central account. The remaining points are treated as distribution points operated on state account. The transit and storage losses, handling costs, and other incidental expenses are likewise allocated between the two heads of accounts in accordance with the principles laid down by the Central Government. Analysis of the costs charged to states on account of retail distribution is beyond the scope of this treatise and the economics of these costs has therefore not been examined.

COSTS ANALYSIS

In absolute terms, for financing central pool purchases, the central government had to stand guarantee to the Banks for making available to the FCI working capital of the following order :

	(Rs. in crores)
1975-76	1525.48
1976-77	2303.28
1977-78	2238.33
1978-79	2541.01
1979-80	2384.94
1980-81*	1823.63*
1981-82	2324.14

*Poor procurement owing to the severe drought in 1979.
Source : Annual Reports of FCI.

The total subsidy quantum shown in Table 10.9 can be considered to be the cost of working the buffer stocking policy on central account which the public exchequer has borne in those years.

Of the two components of this subvention, it is not possible to work out the per capita incidence of consumer subsidy for the reason that the exact number of beneficiaries is not known. But the per capita incidence of the carrying cost of the buffer which provides food security to the nation can certainly be worked out.

Another way to look at these costs is the per ton annual cost to the public exchequer in terms of total purchases made for the central pool in a year and the stocks carried over from the previous year :

Year	Total subsidy (Rs. in crores)	Population* (in million)	Per capita cost (Rs.)	Incidence of carrying cost (per capita) (Rs.)
1975-76	297.61	606	4.91	1.26
1976-77	455.11	620	7.34	4.72
1977-78	562.95	634	8.88	5.42
1978-79	558.22	648	8.61	4.06
1979-80	589.45	663	8.89	4.00
1980-81	661.95	678	9.76	2.60
1981-82	777.60	693	11.22	2.23

*Projected @ 2.26% p.a. as on 1st Oct.

(*in million tonnes*)

Year	Total purchases in the year	Carry over stocks	Total stocks handled	Total subsidy (Rs. in crores)	Cost per ton (Rs.)
1975-76	15.49	3.59	19.08	297.61	155.98
1976-77	14.24	9.93	24.17	455.11	188.30
1977-78	9.53	15.74	25.27	562.95	221.77
1978-79	11.49	13.56	25.05	558.22	222.84
1979-80	11.40	14.54	25.94	589.45	227.24
1980-81	9.90	12.17	22.07	661.95	299.93
1981-82	15.15	8.19	23.34	777.60	333.16

Yet one more approach could be to evaluate the subsidy in relation to the value of the total stocks handled by the FCI and to determine as to what fraction the expenditure in the shape of subsidy is to the total turnover. This has been done in the table given below :

(*Rs. in crores*)

Year	Total purchases	Carry over stocks	Total turnover	Total subsidy	Col. 5 as % to Col. 4
1	2	3	4	5	6
1975-76	2121.64	500.17	2621.81	297.61	11.35
1976-77	2142.58	1390.68	3533.26	455.11	12.88
1977-78	1207.28	2184.69	3391.97	562.95	16.60
1978-79	1559.61	1838.39	3398.00	558.22	16.43
1979-80	1606.49	2041.81	3648.30	589.45	16.16
1980-81	1517.59	1785.82	3303.41	661.95	20.04
1981-82	2681.30	1304.06	3985.36	777.60	19.51

It would be seen that the total subsidy works out to no more than mere service charges of the capital in the shape of total value of the stocks. In other words, the percentage figures roughly represent the rates at which commercial credit is advanced by the scheduled banks. It would thus be seen that in the shape of subsidy from the public exchequer, the Government of India is providing the service charges on the total investment on the stocks handled by the FCI in a year.

Finally, let us relate the subsidy bill to the total turnover-purchases plus sales :

(*Rs. in crores*)

Year	Purchases	Sales	Total turnover	Subsidy	Col. 5 as % to Col. 4
1	2	3	4	5	6
1975-76	2121.64	1219.90	3341.54	297.61	8.9
1976-77	2142.58	1120.79	3263.37	455.11	13.95
1977-78	1207.28	1731.50	2938.78	562.95	19.16
1978-79	1559.61	1354.84	2914.45	558.22	19.15
1979-80	1606.49	1968.73	3575.22	589.45	16.49
1980-81	1517.59	1910.23	3487.82	661.95	18.98
1981-82	2681.30	2288.68	4970.58	777.60	15.64

It is clear from Table 10.2 that the weighted average cost of the imported foodgrains is much higher than that of the stocks procured internally. Experience has shown that, to the extent internal procurement is done effectively and stocks built up, the need for imports in lean years is considerably diminished. The desirability of building up the buffer stocks, which, as is shown in the next chapter, besides providing food security, is beneficial to the national economy as a whole is, therefore, clearly established.

This is a rough and ready measure of the costs the public exchequer has to subsidize for enabling the central and state agencies to continue operating in the market for giving effect to the price support and buffer stocking policy of the government. For a country of the size of India and for the role these stocks play in the overall management of the country's food economy as well as the insurance they provide against scarcities, the costs are certainly not substantial.

11

Impact of Buffer Stocking Operations on Prices Production and Regional Disparities

PART A

PRICES (BENEFITS TO CONSUMERS)

SUPPORT AND PROCUREMENT PRICES

THERE has been a gradual shift in the buffer stocking policy of the government during the past few years as far as the concept of support and procurement price is concerned. As explained earlier, the policy was conceived principally in the context of scarcities and shortages and to protect the vulnerable sections of the population from the disastrous consequences of fluctuations in prices and supplies. But over the years, as the green revolution made its headway, the price concept underwent a gradual change.

In the sixties, the government had been fixing the minimum support prices of foodgrains and announcing them before the commencement of the respective sowing seasons. These minimum support prices were not intended to serve as the basis for procurement of foodgrains but were actually purported to remove price uncertainties for the producers and to serve as a long-term guarantee to them so that, in the event of a shortfall in the open market prices consequent on increase in production or due to any other factor, their incomes did not fall unduly.

A little later, before the marketing season commenced, the government was also announcing procurement prices for these commodities. Targets were fixed and the government purchases were made at the procurement prices. These prices were generally higher than the minimum support price announced before the sowing

TABLE 11.1 : **Minimum support prices/procurement prices of foodgrains according to marketing year**

(*Rate Rs. per tonne*)

Commodity	1967-68	1968-69	1969-70	1970-71	1971-72	1972-73	1973-74	1974-75
Paddy	420 to 440	NA	450.00	460.00	460.00	NA	630.00	NA
	450 to 562.50	450 to 562.50	450 to 562.50	460-580	470-580	490-580	700.00	740.00
Wheat-								
Red	495.00	520.00						
Common	527.50	550.00						
White	535.00	560.00	NA	NA	NA	NA	NA	800-850
Superior	575 to 607	600-630						
	650-950*	760-810*	760*	760*	760*	760*	760*	1050
Coarse	420.00	NA	440.00	450.00	450.00	NA	630.00	NA
Grains (Jowar)	430-560	470-560	550	550	550	580	700	740

* All varieties except indigenous Red.

NA — Stands for 'not announced.'

season. A statement showing the procurement prices fixed by the government during the period when the system of support prices was in vogue is reproduced in Table 11.1.

In 1968 the government decided to purchase all foodgrains of fair average quality offered for sale by the farmers at the procurement price fixed by it which included an element of incentive to the farmers. This policy of two official prices being announced continued, with some variations, up to 1973-74 in the case of paddy. In the case of wheat, it was discontinued from 1969, but revived in 1974-75 for one year only. Experience in pursuing a dual pricing policy showed that in course of time demands were made for stepping up the minimum support prices to the level of the procurement prices, and thus the procurement prices themselves tended to become the minimum support prices. In view of this, the government decided that there was no point in announcing minimum support prices in respect of foodgrains which were being procured for the government stocks. Thus evolved (in 1975-76) the present system in which only one price is announced for each of the cereals like paddy and other *kharif* grains, and wheat which are being procured for buffer stocks. In the case of gram and barley as also pulses, no procurement for public distribution is being done and in their case the practice of announcing minimum support price is being continued. But since the open market prices of these commodities have generally been ruling higher, the question of price support operations in their cases does not normally arise, except in remote areas and during the peak season of market arrivals.

BENEFITS TO CONSUMERS

While examining the efficacy of the buffer stock policy in relation to the prices, a distinction has been made between surplus states and deficit states. In surplus states the problem of prices is chiefly in relation to the producers, while in the deficit states open market prices are of vital concern for the consumers. The former has been dealt with in Part B of this chapter ; in this Part we would be looking at the impact of the buffer stocking policy from the point of view of the consumers. The benefits to this sector would be apparent if it can be shown that the supplies through the public distribution system were made available at prices considerably lower than the open market prices. Conversely, if it is established that, but for the supplies channelised through the public distribution system, the prices in the open market would have ruled at a higher level, the efficacy of the policy would stand vindicated. Another yardstick could be that by making supplies available at a fixed price in all seasons and throughout the country, the system has conferred enormous benefits on the population served by it.

The spread of the supply network and its coverage is shown below :

(As on January 1981)

Number of Fair Price Shops			Population Covered (in millions)		
Urban	Rural	Total	Urban	Rural	Total
55,186	2,17,273	2,72,459	147.7	456.9	604.6

The total offtake during the past six years has been of the following order :

TABLE 11.2 : **Total offtake during past six years**

(in million tonnes)

Year	Supplies from Central Pool				Total Supplies through Public Distribution System			
	Rice	Wheat	Coarse grains	Total	Rice	Wheat	Coarse grains	Total
1975-76	1.58	6.56	0.18	8.32	3.00	6.92	0.34	10.26
1976-77	2.36	4.99	0.24	7.59	4.06	5.53	0.59	10.18
1977-78	2.85	6.67	0.35	9.87	4.32	7.06	0.64	12.02
1978-79	2.07	6.50	0.01	8.58	3.20	6.75	0.07	10.02
1979-80	3.66	7.81	0.01	11.48	4.81	8.09	0.12	13.02
1980-81	3.87	5.78	0.01	9.66	4.34	5.90	0.11	10.35

Note : Difference between the two figures represent supplies from stocks held by the states. The above figures do not include exports on Government account, which were as follows :

Year	Wheat	Rice
1977-78	0.49	0.04
1978-79	0.78	0.01
1979-80	0.64	0.40
1980-81	0.06	0.16

If the figures of total supplies are judged in the light of the total requirements of foodgrains shown in Table 7.1 it would appear that the system has been able to supply in a range of 11 to 15 per cent of the total requirements. It should be remembered that this volume of supplies has been made available to the consumers alongside the free market which is also functioning. A supplementation of the supply factor to this extent is really worthwhile.

While making a study relating to the population below the poverty line while drafting the Sixth Five Year Plan, the Planning Commission noted that in terms of the expenditure, the cutoff points turn out to be Rs. 61.8 and 71.3 for rural and urban areas at 1976-77 prices. By this standard, the percentage of population below the poverty line for the year 1977-78 was estimated at 47.85 for the rural and 40.71 for the urban areas ; the all-India figure being 46.33. In the case of this population reckoned at 289.37 million, it is estimated that as much as one-third of the demand was met by the public distribution system.

MARKET PRICE AND ISSUE PRICE

The difference between the market price and the issue price of the government stocks is a concrete measure of the benefit conferred on population served by the system. Tables 11.1 and 11.2 show the relative position of these two prices for the past decade and the difference between the two represents the quantum of benefit.

TABLE 11.3 : **Index Numbers of Wholesale Prices and Issue Prices**

Base : 1970-71 100
Base Price : Rice Rs. 106.00 per qtl.
Wheat Rs. 82.80 per qtl.

Year	Index Numbers* of Wholesale Prices		Index Numbers of Issue Prices		
	Rice	Wheat	Rice Coarse	Rice Medium	Wheat
1970-71	100.0	100.0	93.8	104.1	94.2
1971-72	103.0	99.5	93.8	104.1	94.2
1972-73	116.0	106.5	93.8	104.1	94.2
1973-74	140.2	108.2	103.6	115.4	100.2
1974-75	183.2	183.1	119.6	133.7	151.0
1975-76	178.8	159.6	126.6	140.7	151.0
1976-77	156.9	152.0	126.6	140.7	151.0
1977-78	162.0	156.5	126.6	140.7	151.0
1978-79	160.8	153.8	126.6	140.7	153.0
1979-80	183.8	160.7	126.6	140.7	153.0

*Office of the Economic & Statistical Adviser, Ministry of Industry, Govt. of India.

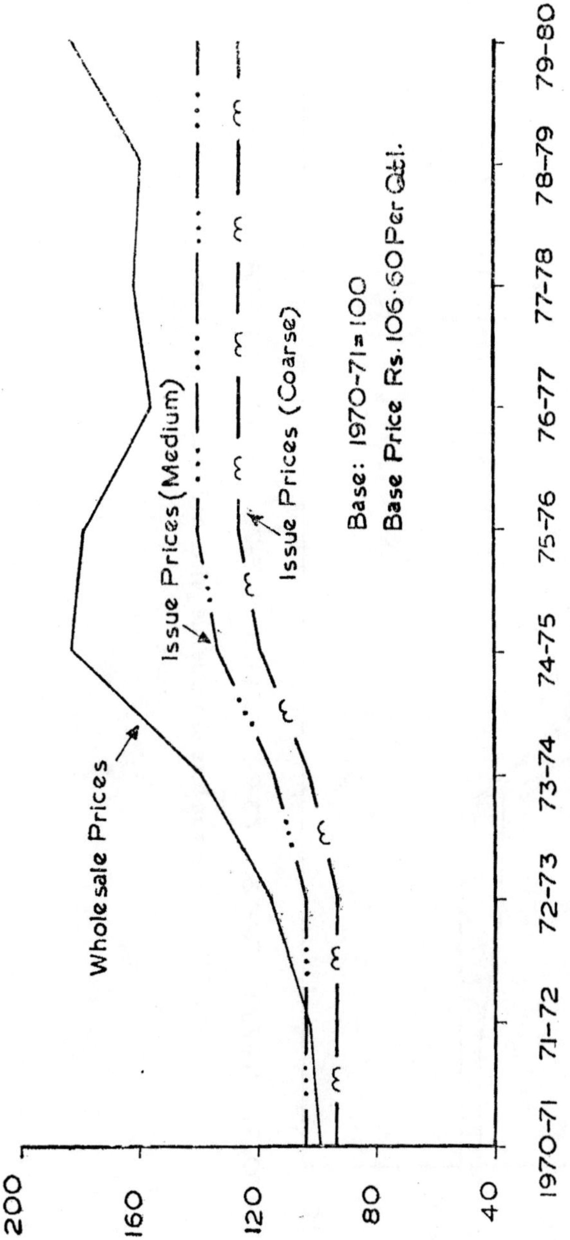

FIG. 11.1 : Index numbers of wholesale prices and issue prides of Rice

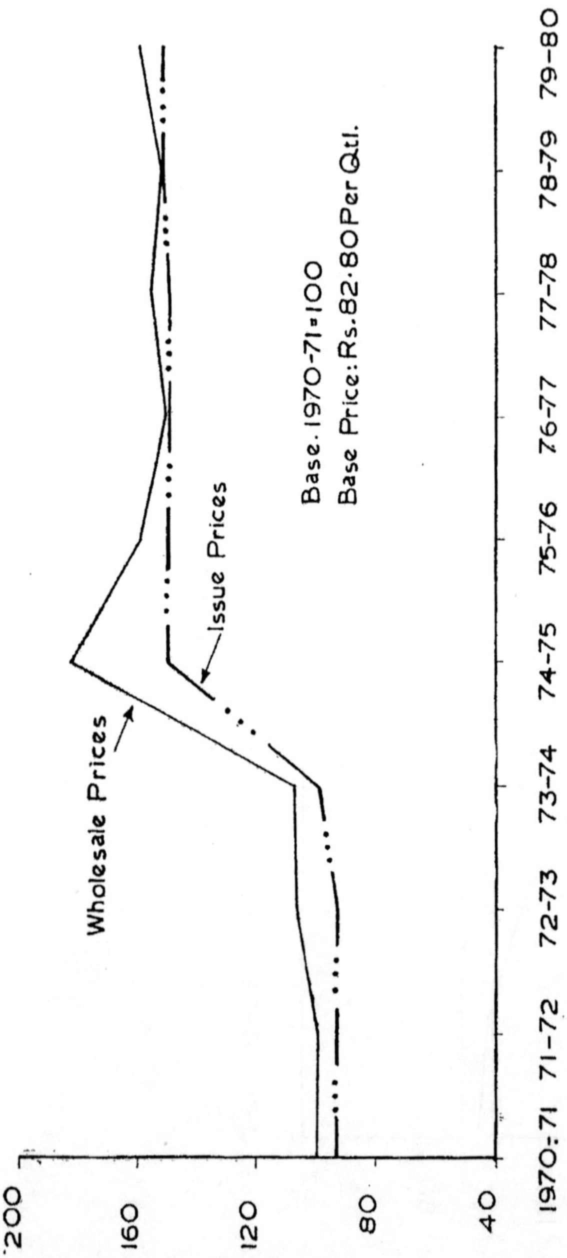

FIG. 11.2 : Index nnmbers of wholesale prices and issues prices of wheat

Certain interesting conclusions are apparent from Tables 11.1 and 11.2 and the graphs as follows :

(a) In the case of both wheat and rice the graphs start almost from the same point. This is a mere coincidence brought about by the selection of the base year, namely, 1970-71, which was a year of bountiful crops and abundant supplies in the market. The result was that the market prices were ruling at comparatively lower levels ;

(b) The divergence between the two curves is more pronounced in the case of rice than in that of wheat. Rice is a highor priced commodity compared to wheat and its yield is more susceptible to weather conditions than is the case with wheat. Slight deficiency in rainfall or little longer gaps between the falls and, most important of all, deficiency of rainfall at the milking stage affect the rice crop much more seriously than wheat. The net result is that rice is extremely susceptible to the availability and price factor and hence the divergence between the two curves ;

(c) The year 1975-76 is a kind of landmark in this study because in that year the curve of the open market prices started falling markedly. Thereafter the two curves run almost parallel with a tendency to gravitate towards each other. In the case of wheat they almost overlap each other while in the case of rice the divergence is considerably narrowed down and the two curves run almost completely parallel to each other. It is understandable because from that year till June/July 1979 the country had been exceptionally fortunate in having a run of bumper crops, with abundant supplies available in the market and the open market prices maintained an even keel. Yet the divergence between the two curves in the case of rice even in these exceptionally good years represents the inherent susceptibility of this commodity to the market phenomena ; and

(d) When in September 1979 the signs of drought appeared unmistakably, duly reflected in the table showing wholesale index numbers, the government issue price having remained unchanged, the divergence between the two curves appears again.

A simple measure in monetary terms of the benefit to the consumers could be made by multiplying the quantities supplied

TABLE 11.4 : Computation of benefit to consumers

Rate : Rs. per quintal
Quantity : in '000 tonnes
Benefit : in crores of Rupees

Items	1970	1971	1972	1973	1974	1975	1976	1977	1978
RICE									
*Average market price	111.21	108.68	122.52	150.14	203.52	201.80	155.35	169.55	158.36
Issue Price of government stocks	100.00	100.00	100.00	110.40	127.50	135.00	135.00	135.00	135.00
Net difference	11.21	8.68	22.52	39.74	76.02	66.80	20.35	34.55	24.61
Quantity sold during the year	1645	2050	2403	1715	1828	1510	2096	2968	2087
Benefit to consumers	18.44	17.79	54.12	68.15	138.96	100.87	42.65	102.54	51.36
WHEAT									
Average market price	88.65	80.91	86.93	89.61	140.90	146.99	126.21	125.22	128.50
Issue Price of government stocks	78.00	78.00	78.00	83.00	125.00	125.00	125.00	125.00	126.65
Net difference	10.65	2.91	8.93	6.61	15.90	21.99	1.21	0.22	1.85
Quantities sold during the year	5191	4283	7026	7048	5725	7411	4525	7720	6635
Benefit to consumers	55.28	12.46	62.74	46.59	91.03	162.97	5.48	1.30	12.27
Grand Total	73.72	30.25	116.86	114.74	229.99	263.84	48.13	103.84	63.63

*Derived from yearly averages given for each market in different States—Bulletins on Food Statistics, Directorate of Economics & Statistics, Ministry of Agriculture and Irrigation.

through the public distribution system with the difference between the average market price and the issue price of government stocks. This exercise has been done in Table 11.4.

We have briefly referred to the benefits that have acccrued to the consumers from the public distribution system. From the consumers' point of view the efficacy of this system would lie in times of scarcity when prices tend to rise unduly. This aspect has been studied with the help of empirical data relating to the open market prices for two scarcity periods, namely, 1965-66-67 and that of 1972-73-74. Data have been compiled in Tables 11.5 and 11.6 in respect of the states which are not self-sufficient in foodgrains.

TABLE 11.5 : **Average wholesale open market prices of wheat in selected deficit states (quarterly averages)**

(*Rate Rs. per quintal*)

State/Year	March	June	Quarter Ending Sept.	Dec.
1	2	3	4	5
Bihar				
1965	96	94	110	107
1966	106	102	112	126
1967	142	131	156	120
1973	100	103	120	143
1974	220	187	201	200
1975	203	NA	144	142
1979	151	121	145	164
1980	159	146	161	174
Gujarat				
1965	79	76	79	76
1966	70	72	75	91
1967	94	107	112	111
1973	148	146	149	185
1974	184	177	189	188
1975	182	195	184	188
1979	145	152	155	175
1980	164	166	163	180
Karnataka				
1965	120	104	122	125
1966	136	159	151	134
1967	140	148	166	170
1973	159	155	NA	326
1974	290	247	230	260
1975	246	208	198	203
1979	182	180	183	208
1980	223	198	200	217

TABLE 11.5—*Contd.*

(*Rate Rs. per quintal*)

State/Year	March	June	Quarter Ending Sept.	Dec.
1	2	3	4	5
Maharashtra				
1965	103	96	116	122
1966	113	112	112	112
1967	107	114	126	151
1973	128	167	202	245
1974	241	194	194	200
1975	209	197	204	203
1979	146	145	153	168
1980	169	170	171	200
West Bengal				
1965	75	85	128	98
1966	107	101	101	118
1967	107	124	—	—
1973	85	87	87	95
1974	99	135	135	135
1975	135	136	136	136
1979	132	129	143	147
1980	145	142	157	178

Issue prices of wheat

1965	59	59	59	60
1966	60	62	63	63
1967	63	63	63	63
1973	78	78	78	86
1974	90	125	125	125
1975	125	125	125	125
1979	130	130	130	130
1980	130	130	130	130

TABLE 11.6 : **Average wholesale open market prices of rice (coarse) in selected deficit states (quarterly averages)**

(*Rate Rs. per quintal*)

State/Year	March	June	Quarter Ending Sept.	Dec.
Bihar				
1965	82	100	123	108
1966	118	122	132	146
1967	163	180	204	146
1973	164	171	188	185

TABLE 11.6—*Contd.*

State/Year	March	June	Quarter Ending Sept.	Dec.
1974	241	254	290	149
1975	215	217	216	183
1979	163	176	201	219
1980	216	230	235	211
Gujarat				
1965	69	68	68	86
1966	103	106	108	130
1967	175	185	185	176
1973	177	188	213	228
1974	232	230	318	297
1975	298	288	245	167
1979	153	156	169	178
1980	179	182	192	188
Karnataka				
1965	71	85	111	117
1966	114	129	143	99
1967	100	115	118	115
1973	138	159	189	182
1974	232	228	202	183
1975	253	252	240	214
1979	179	178	188	194
1980	181	191	204	207
Orissa				
1965	—	—	—	—
1966	75	78	80	78
1967	82	88	95	84
1973	108	125	130	131
1974	137	172	212	172
1975	184	246	215	145
1979	142	159	182	179
1980	183	202	211	187
West Bengal				
1965	74	88	118	116
1966	115	132	155	143
1967	119	146	219	169
1973	145	166	222	209
1974	209	261	298	254
1975	224	241	238	192
1979	182	199	228	225
1980	213	224	236	218

TABLE 11.6—*Contd.*

(*Rate Rs. per quintal*)

State/Year	Quarter Ending March	June	Sept.	Dec.
Madhya Pradesh				
1965	63	62	64	77
1966	139	166	180	173
1967	168	189	180	105
1973	126	131	139	171
1974	165	192	238	234
1975	236	273	279	218
1979	167	184	202	196
1980	194	208	208	213

This data has also been plotted on the graphs.

Issue prices of rice (coarse)

1965	58	58	58	60
1966	61	62	62	68
1967	75	75	78	80
1973	100	100	100	117
1974	125	125	125	125
1975	135	135	135	135
1979	135	135	135	150
1980	150	150	150	150

Figures 11.3 and 11.4 show how violently the prices of both the cereals have been fluctuating during the three scarcity periods. Rice prices have been fluctuating more than those of wheat. The issue prices of the government stocks, on the other hand, were kept, as a measure of public policy, at stable levels represented by the shape of their curves which, over stretches of time, are horizontal. The divergence between the two graphs is quite striking. In the same measure, it reflects the benefit afforded to the consumers by government supplies at fixed prices.

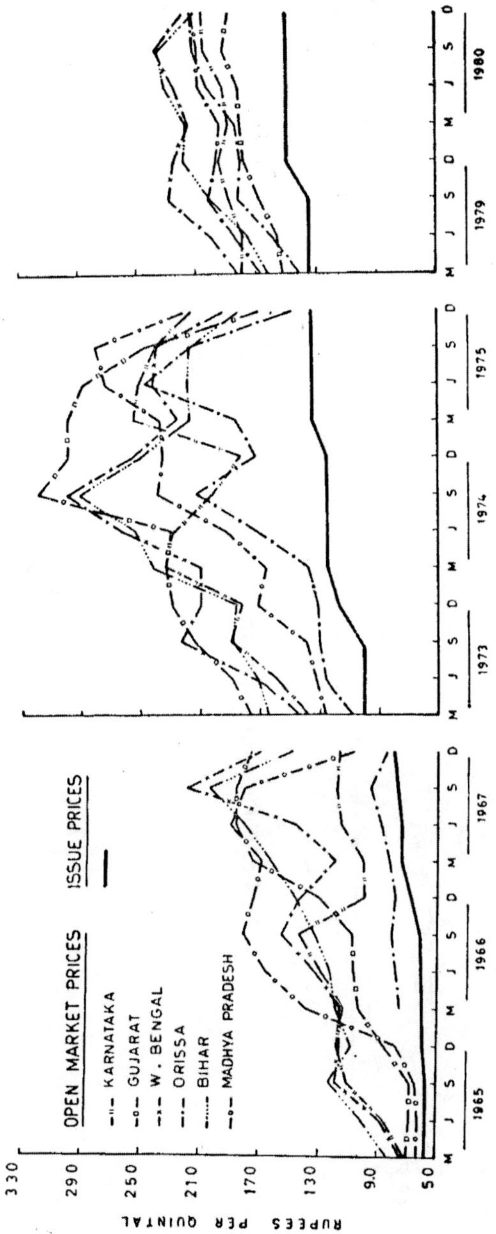

FIG. 11.3 : Wholesale open market and issue prices of rice

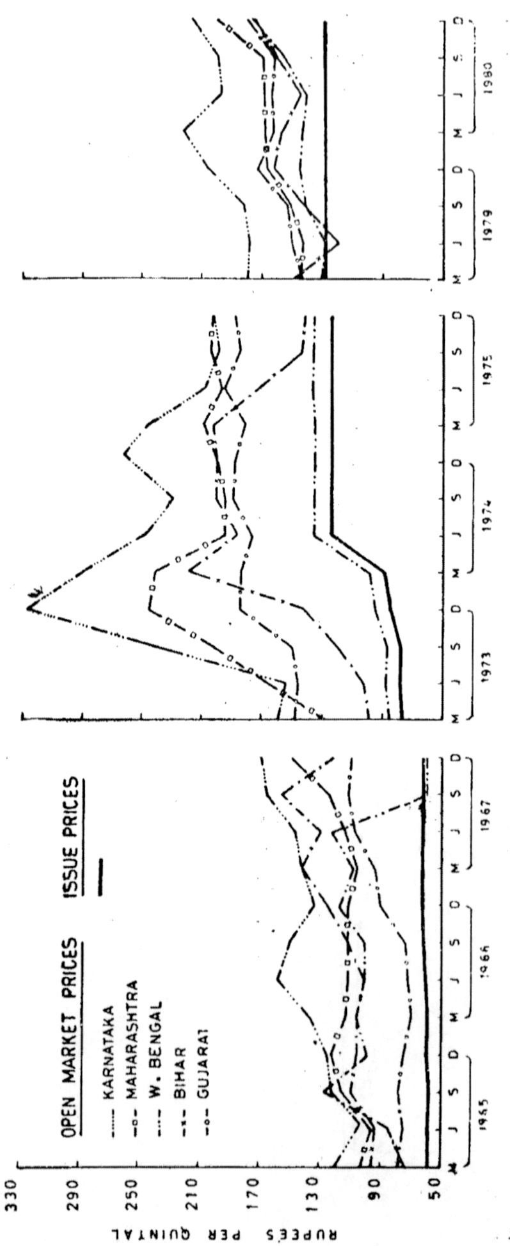

FIG. 11.4 : Wholesale open market and issue prices of wheat

PART B

IMPACT ON PRODUCTION

BENEFITS TO PRODUCERS

As far as the producers are concerned, the benefit would be manifest when it will be shown that, but for the price support operations by the state agencies, the price of their produce would have crashed to such levels as would have rendered the practice of agriculture totally uneconomic for them. This would be particularly true of surplus states like Punjab and Haryana and surplus pockets in others where multipurpose irrigation projects have brought about such a situation. A review of the procurement policy followed by the government particularly during the past two decades clearly brings out the conclusion that the announcement of the procurement prices and the state intervention to enforce them have operated entirely to the benefit of the producers. The effect of announcing a support/ procurement price has been that the market has remained stable and a psychology was created that the prices would not be allowed to fall below a certain level. This assurance has enabled the farmers to bargain for their produce from a better position than was the case in earlier decades when no such policy was being pursued. Concerted efforts by public agencies like the Food Corporation of India, the State Civil Supplies Corporations and the Cooperative Societies in states like Punjab, Haryana, Uttar Pradesh, Rajasthan, Tamil Nadu, Maharashtra and Madhya Pradesh have amply demonstrated that this policy can be implemented effectively to the benefit of the farmers. No other factor has contributed so much to the firming up of the market in the past few years as the awareness of the existence of this support operation by the public agencies, always present and visible in the background to both the producers as well as the private trade. Let us have a look at Table 11.7.

The years for which the average wholesale prices have been summarized in this Table have been one of exceptionally good harvests. For rice, the relevant period from the point of view of the behaviour of prices in a surplus state is December onwards. Likewise, for wheat, it is from April onwards. A comparison of these figures with the procurement/support prices would show how close the two are. Their closeness in the case of wheat is particularly

TABLE 11.7 : **Average wholesale open market prices of wheat and rice (coarse) in selected surplus states**

(Rate Rs. per quintal)

		For the quarter ending							
		March		June		September		December	
State	Year	R	W	R	W	R	W	R	W
Punjab	1975	150	121	152	107	164	108	152	124
	1976	133	131	133	106	147	106	154	118
	1977	152	128	154	110	154	110	141	120
	1978	142	127	150	113	152	116	148	125
	1979	146	127	152	115	—	—	—	—
Haryana	1975	184	147	186	107	182	106	186	109
	1976	166	114	165	105	—	107	—	111
	1977	—	127	150	110	166	114	169	125
	1978	163	127	166	113	169	114	163	123
	1979	159	129	160	115	—	—	—	—
U.P.	1975	213	196	222	134	216	122	159	106
	1976	135	107	147	105	158	105	142	111
	1977	150	130	161	112	174	118	161	126
	1978	159	131	170	112	177	117	160	121
	1979	154	126	164	112	—	—	—	—

R—rice W—wheat

Source : Directorate of Economics & Statistics, Ministry of Agriculture.

Procurement/Support Prices

		1975	1976	1977	1978	1979
Wheat		105	105	110	112.50	115
Rice						
Punjab	SB	124	127	126	130	139
	LB	126	130	129	134	142
	MS	138	141	139	144	152
	S/L Slender	147-172	152-178	150-172	155-172	163
Haryana	SB	124	127	126	131	144
	LB	126	130	129	134	147
	MS	138	141	139	145	158
	S/L Slender	147-172	152-178	150-172	156-172	169
U.P.	SB	117	117	117	123	134
	LB	122	122	122	127	139
	MS	133	133	133	136	148
	S/L Slender	143-154	143-154	143-154	148-159	160-171

Explanations :

(*i*) Procurement prices of the various varieties of rice are fixed statewise because of varietal differences from state to state and allowing for traditional price differential.

(*ii*) SB—short bold ; LB—long bold ; MS—medium slender S/L—short slender/ long slender. These varietal classifications are based on the standards laid down in the Ramiah Committee Report,

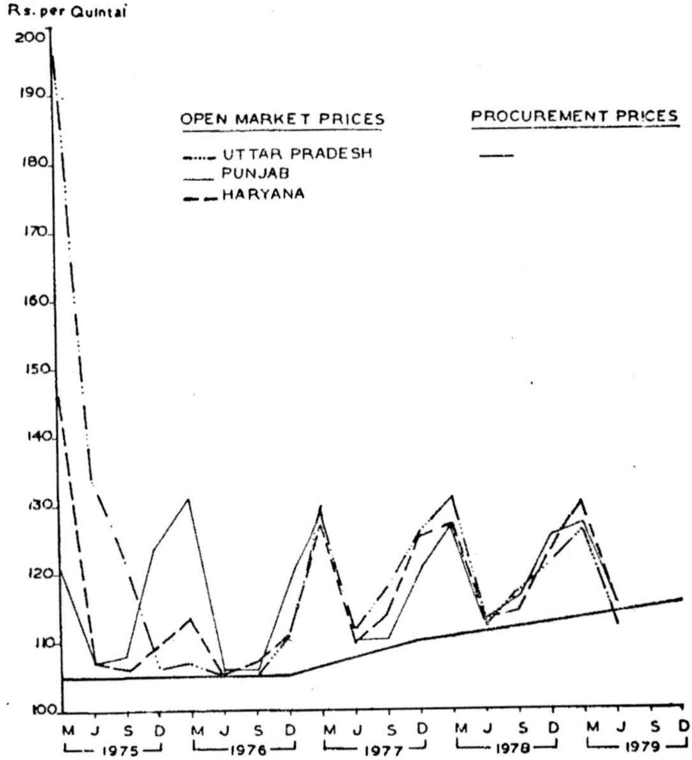

FIG. 11.5 : **Wholesale open market and procurement price of wheat**

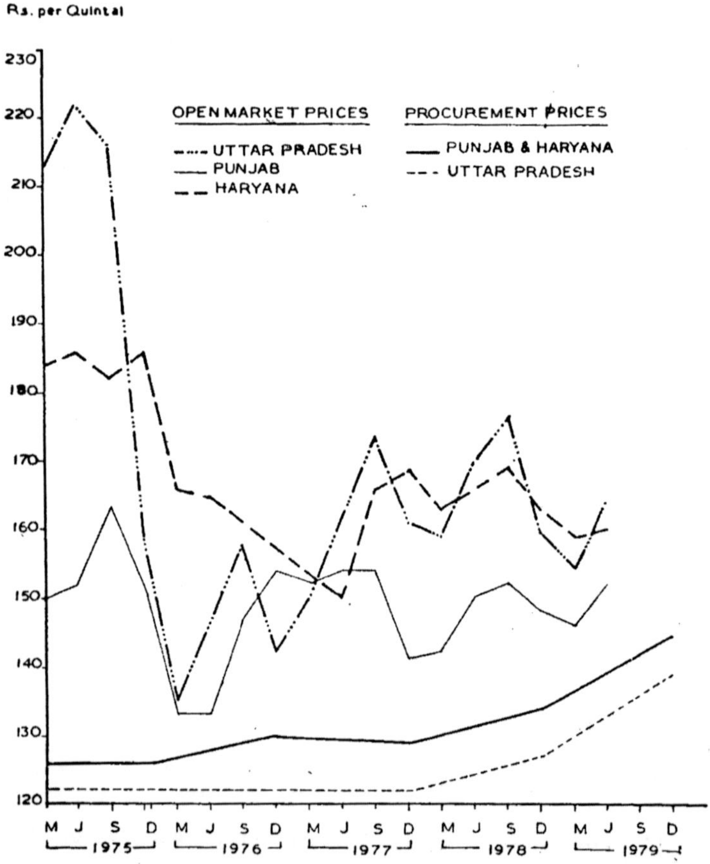

FIG. 11.6 **Wholesale open market and procurement price of rice**

striking. In fact, in a number of instances, they are almost identical. In the case of rice, owing to its inherent sensitivity to the agro-climatic and market factors, the fluctuations are somewhat pronounced.

Figures 11.5 and 11.6 bring out in one glance the fact that the open market prices never came down to a level lower than the one represented by the official procurement prices. In the case of wheat, the peak of the curves in the three states has unfailingly been in the months of March and thereafter right up to September the prices have remained at considerably lower levels. In fact, practically in all these years the price level during this period (April-September) almost touches the horizontal curve of the support price. In the case of rice, the curves faithfully show that the prices during the season (September to March and slightly thereafter too) remained low, though unlike wheat, they do not touch the procurement price. From the shape of the two graphs, namely, the fluctuating curves, with their peaks and troughs—of the open market prices and those of the support prices—it is clear without doubt that the latter have served as a kind of a base supporting the former ; as an underpin to the entire open market price structure, supporting it, as it were, on its shoulders. The significance of this phenomenon should be realized in the light of the fact that the states in question are heavily surplus and the period studied was one of exceptionally bountiful harvests and, had it not been for the massive intervention by the state agencies, the prices would have slumped causing grievous loss to the farmers in these states which contribute nearly 88 per cent of wheat and 70 per cent of rice to the total procurement. The fact that the open market prices have remained above the procurement prices vindicates the thesis propounded in the foregoing paragraphs. The efficacy of the support price policy backed by the buffer stocking operations thus stands proved.

PROCUREMENT AND PRODUCTIVITY

Elsewhere it has been said that this policy has acted as the most effective instrument as well as an incentive for boosting agricultural production particularly in respect of wheat and rice which are directly covered by it. The administration of support prices (details are shown in Table 11.8) and the building up of buffer stocks have jointly operated as a very effective plank, providing buoyancy to the

TABLE 11.8 : **Support price of wheat (all varieties)**

(Rate Rs. per quintal)

Year	Rate
1975-76	105.00
1976-77	105.00
1977-78	110.00
1978-79	112.50
1979-80	115.00
1980-81	117.00
1981-82	130.00

Support Price of Paddy

1975-76 Owing to varietal differences, as also different cost structure prevailing in different states, different support prices were fixed for different varieties in the states. Procurement prices of rice were derived from
1976-77
1977-78 the paddy price on the basis of hulling ratios which again were different in different states. Only from 1979-80, government standardized the paddy in three categories—common, fine and superfine and
1978-79 announced support prices accordingly.

(Rs. per quintal)

	C	F	SF
1979-80	95	99	103
1980-81	105	109	113
1981-82	115	119	123
1982-83	122	126	130

TABLE 11.9 : **Production and procurement of wheat and rice in selected states**

(in million tonnes)

State	1968-69 Prod.	Proc.	Col. 3 as % to Col. 2	1978-79 Prod.	Proc.	Col. 6 as % to Col. 5	% increase in prod.	Increased proc. as % to increase in prod.
1	2	3	4	5	6	7	8	9
				WHEAT				
Punjab	4.52	1.87	41.37	7.42	4.20	56.60	64	88
Haryana	1.52	0.27	17.76	3.42	1.38	40.35	125	58.42
U.P.	6.08	0.20	3.29	11.23	1.88	16.74	85	32.62
Rajasthan	1.18	neg.	0.42	2.87	0.30	10.45	143	17.75
				RICE				
Punjab	0.57	0.37	64.91	3.13	2.72	86.90	449	91.80
Haryana	0.37	0.24	64.86	1.24	0.88	70.96	235	73.56
A.P.	4.70	0.17	3.61	7.30	0.97	13.28	55.32	30.76
U.P.	3.53	0.21	5.94	5.89	0.83	14.09	66.85	26.27

agricultural prices and thus safeguarding the interests of the producers. The efficacy of this policy as a spur to higher agricultural production has clearly been established. Figures of production and procurement (Table 11.9) for the past one decade relative to Punjab, Haryana, western Uttar Pradesh and Andhra Pradesh—the four states known for their efficiency in procurement—would bear out this thesis.

These figures are indeed revealing. Taking wheat first, one is struck with an impressive increase in the overall production ; in the case of Haryana and Rajasthan, it is more than double. As the production increased, so did procurement. Excepting Punjab where even in 1968-69 as much as 41.37 per cent of the total production was collected in procurement, in the remaining three states, the percentage of procurement to total produce has registered a very substantial increase. Still more revealing is the fact that, a very high proportion of the increase in production is reflected in the increased procurement. This phenomenon is strikingly prominent in the case of rice where nearly 92 per cent in the case of Punjab and 73.56 per cent in the case of Haryana of the increased production has found its way in the procurement.

A brief explanation about the lower figures for Uttar Pradesh in respect of both wheat and rice and for Andhra Pradesh in respect of rice seems necessary. In the case of Uttar Pradesh, even though wheat production has increased by 85 per cent only 32.62 per cent of the increased production was secured in procurement. In the case of rice, it was still less ; against 66.85 per cent increase in production, only 26.3 per cent additional came into procurement. The reason is that the surplus pocket of Uttar Pradesh is limited to only the western region of the state, while most of the central and practically the entire eastern region ranges from marginal to large deficits. The result is that the prices generally rule high and substantial quantities are moved through trade channels, thus accounting for lower collection in official procurement.

As regards rice, the phenomenon that is reflected in the above table is generally true of all rice producing states. In the first instance, rice crop is more susceptible to the vagaries of nature than wheat. Unusual variations in the agro-climatic factors are much more damaging to the rice crop than to other crops. Secondly, rice being the staple food of the people in these states, larger quantities are usually retained for personal consumption. Varietal differences and consumer preference for them are predominant in rice trade. Even a slight variation in the agro-climatic factors accentuates these preferences, leading to smaller quantities being available for public procurement.

Nevertheless, the positive trend in production and higher levels of procurement are clear indications of the phenomenon that in fostering the green revolution in the Indian agriculture, the price support operations have played their critical role.

The treatment of this particular aspect of the productivity phenomena would be incomplete if mention of one more crucial fact is not made. The past two decades have witnessed, together with the rising productivity, a continuous rising trend in the general prices of agricultural produce. The malady with the Indian agriculture in the forties and the fifties was basically the low level of prices which acted as disincentives to higher production. The combined operation of the procurement policy of the government and the rising trend of agricultural prices has indeed resulted in the happy position today when the agricultural production, particularly of wheat and rice, has made spectacular strides. The following Table 11.10 speaks for itself.

TABLE 11.10 : **Production figures of wheat and rice (all India)**

(*in million tonnes*)

Year	Wheat	% increase	Rice	% increase
1970-71	23.83		42.25	
1971-72	26.41		43.07	
1972-73	24.74		39.25	
1973-74	24.10		44.05	
1974-75	24.10		39.58	
1975-76	28.85		48.74	
1976-77	29.01		41.92	
1977-78	31.75		52.68	
1978-79	35.51		53.80	
1979-80	31.83		42.33	
1980-81	36.31		53.63	
1981-82	37.83	60	53.59	27

Increase in productivity is, no doubt, also a function of two important variables, namely area under cultivation and the per hectare productivity. These figures for the period covered in the above Table are summarized below :

(*in million ha*)

	Area under cultivation		Productivity per hectare (in kgs)	
	Wheat	Rice	Wheat	Rice
1970-71	18.24	37.59	1307	1123
1981-82	22.31	40.71	1696	1317

In the case of wheat, whereas the increase in area was 24 per cent, the productivity registered an increase of over 29 per cent. In terms of total production, the increase was 46 per cent. In the case of rice the area increased by little less than 8 per cent but productivity rose by 18 per cent. In absolute terms the production rose by 27 per cent. These are some of the interesting facts about wheat and rice and they bring out the inherent characteristics of these two economies. However, this is not the occasion for commenting on the peculiar features of these two economies ; the conclusion that emerges is that the sustained level of higher production in these two cereals has been due, in no small measure, to the two forces—favourable prices and procurement activity—happily operating in a conjunctive manner, and inducing the Indian farmer to set new records in agricultural production. The price factor has indeed operated as the catalytic agent in triggering off the productivity phenomena in Indian agriculture, and the state intervention in the form of procurement activity acted as a bolstering operation supporting, as it were, the rising wave of this basic industry.

In contrast, let us have a look at the situation in some other states where administration of support prices and the procurement drive have been known to be not so vigorous. Bihar, Orissa, Madhya Pradesh, Karnataka, West Bengal, and Assam have been considered in this example. The relevant figures are shown in Table 11.11.

TABLE 11.11 : **Production and procurement of wheat/rice in selected states**

(*in million tonnes*)

	Wheat				Rice			
	1968-69		1978-79		1968-69		1978-79	
	Prod	Proc	Prod	Proc	Prod	Proc	Prod	Proc
Assam	Neg	Neg	—	—	2.25	0.19	2.18	0.08
Bihar	1.26	0.01	2.51	0.09	5.20	0.07	5.54	0.01
Karnataka	0.16	Neg	.22	—	2.00	0.07	2.30	0.11
M.P.	2.01	0.02	3.27	0.10	3.00	0.32	3.48	0.30
Orissa	0.02	—	0.11	—	4.70	0.29	4.44	0.05
West Bengal	0.30	Neg	1.00	—	6.25	0.44	6.31	0.14

In their own way, these figures are also revealing. In almost all states the production over the decade has remained more or less stagnant. Procurement too has not only remained stagnant but has significantly come down in Bihar, Orissa and West Bengal. If the figures given in the preceding paragraphs substantiate the conclusion that vigorous procurement and implementation of the price support operations have acted as a catalytic agent in boosting the production, the same conclusion is substantiated here also though in the contrary fashion. Where procurement is not done vigorously and the price support operations are kept in the low gear, agricultural production has remained stagnant.

The conclusion is obvious : the buffer stocking policy has engendered such economic stimuli which have conferred immense benefits on the two principal cereal crops namely wheat and rice. The multiplier effect of this increase in production and the benefits that have accrued to the ancillary and tertiary sectors have had their full play. The change that has swept over the rural areas in these states, especially the modernization of agriculture and multiple cropping, flow of capital in agriculture and its allied sectors, and *mandi* development are only patently visible. In Punjab and Haryana realizations on account of *mandi* fee alone have gone up from Rs. 67.5 million in 1975-76 to Rs. 346.2 million in 1979-80. This income is being spent by the state governments on the development of the rural economy. This indeed is the classic example of the multiplier effect in which the income generated at the primary source is being ploughed back for the general development of the agricultural economy. In the same proportion the earnings of the commission agentshave gone up—both private as well as public agencies like the co-operatives and government corporations employed in the procurement work.

Another index of the multiplier effect of benefits flowing from this policy is increase in warehousing activity. In March 1975 the Food Corporation of India had 1.98 million tonnes equivalent of godown accommodation on hire from private parties as well as from the central and state werehousing corporations, paying them rent in a range of Rs. 3.2 to Rs. 4.0 per tonne per month. In August 1979, this capacity increased to 8.88 million tonnes, representing more than a four-fold increase conferring all round benefits in that proportion.

PART C

IMPACT ON REGIONAL DISPARITIES

FOOD MAP OF INDIA

In the food map of India, there are green areas (heavily surplus) and white areas (deficit), interspersed with grey areas (marginally surplus or marginally deficit). Punjab, Haryana, western U.P., M.P., Orissa, coastal areas of Andhra Pradesh and Tamil Nadu are the surplus areas, while Rajasthan, Gujarat, Maharashtra and Kerala in the western belt; and West Bengal in the eastern sector continue to be net deficit states. Bihar, plateau districts in M.P., Andhra Pradesh and Karnataka and the hill states like Jammu and Kashmir constitute the grey areas.

Regional disparities insofar as procurement is concerned, have been dealt with in Part 'B'. Nearly 75 to 80 per cent of wheat and 60 to 65 per cent of rice in the national pool comes from the small area comprising the states of Punjab, Haryana and western U.P. The breakthrough in rice production has come not in rice producing states like West Bengal, Tamil Nadu, Andhra Pradesh, and Orissa, but in wheat producing states of Punjab, Haryana and western U.P. The rice producing states have somehow not achieved the same kind of breakthrough, whether in terms of yield or in terms of diversification of agriculture. The warning is clear : if the nation has to depend for its food security on a limited area and has to draw more and more from it, the marginal cost of production of each additional unit of production will be higher, as is already happening. In the context of the overall national food economy, such a policy will not be prudent. National food security cannot be secured without some semblance of regional self-sufficiency. In fact the spurt in both production as well as procurement should now, in the coming years, occur in states like eastern U.P., Bihar, West Bengal, Maharashtra, Gujarat, Rajasthan, Karnataka and Assam. There is considerable potential in these states which can easily be tapped, given the resolve and will to do it at the political and administrative level. It will result in all-round benefits and reduction in costs as well. Marginal cost of production in these states would be much lower and this economic surplus must be reaped for the benefit of the nation. Beginnings have been made in this direction (of late, Gujarat and Maharashtra are making serious efforts in stepping up the production and procurement of foodgrains) ; what remains is a quickening of the pace. As and when these regional disparities in production and procurement are reduced to as narrow limits as human effort would render it practicable, the disparities in the per capita availability will also narrow down in the same proportion.

PER-CAPITA AVAILABILITY

However, regional disparities that are proposed to be treated in this Part are mainly from the angle of per capita availability of foodgrains in some of the heavily deficit states and the role played by the buffer stocking operations in supplementing that availability. Since the buffer stocking operations and releases from the government stocks for feeding the public distribution system are conducted on state basis, the per capita availability for the state as a whole has been considered here. Actual per capita availability for individuals has not been examined because that is materially affected, among others, by income and employment parameters.

Total availability in a state would be equal to total production in that state plus/minus exports/imports, minus procurement within the state, plus releases from the government stocks, and plus/minus changes in stocks with the public and private agencies. Authentic data on all these transactions, particularly relating to exports and imports in respect of various states are not available. Prof. A.C. Minocha of Bhopal University has, in one of his papers* compiled a table from different sources showing state-wise per capita availability of cereals and found that there were sharp differences. In 1971, the highest per capita availability of foodgrains was obtained in Punjab, followed by M.P., and the lowest in Maharashtra, preceded by Kerala and Gujarat. He found the co-efficient of variation as 45.3 per cent in 1971, which showed a significant increase over the previous years. According to him "state-wise variability was higher during 1961 and 1963 and then in 1971. In the years 1961 and 1963, there were no movement restrictions and free trade was allowed but this widened the gap between the surplus and deficit states in per capita availability. The state-wise variability started declining from 1964 and at the peak of government operations in 1966—the year

*"Public Distribution of Foodgrains in India," *Indian Economic Journal,* Vol. 23, No. 5, Conference Number, 1975.

TABLE 11.12 : **Per capita net availability of cereals in Kerala and West Bengal**

Year	Mid-year population ('000 persons)	Production Gross ('000 tonnes)	Production Net ('000 tonnes)	Per capita net production (kgs. per Yr.)	Issues From Central Pool ('000 tonnes)	Issues From Central Pool % to All India issues	Contribution to C. Pool ('000 tonnes)	Change in State Govt. stocks	Total availability ('000 tonnes)	Per capita availability (kgs. per year)
1	2	3	4	5	6	7	8	9	10	11
KERALA										
1970	20919	1227	1074	51.3	842	12.1	—	—	1916	91.6
1975	23418	1342	1174	51.1	1024	11.2	—	(+) 10	2208	94.3
1976	23885	1372	1201	50.3	1152	16.9	—	(—) 9	2344	98.1
1977	24341	1260	1103	45.3	1447	15.6	—	(+) 4	2554	104.9
1978	24787	1298	1136	45.8	936	10.7	—	(+) 7	2065	83.3
1979	25227	1268	1110	44.0	659	6.6	—	—	1769	70.1
1980	25666	1287	1126	43.9	924	6.7	—	(+) 7	2057	80.1
WEST BENGAL										
1970	43702	6861	6003	137.4	1144	16.5	—	(—) 72	7075	161.9
1975	49405	7491	6555	132.7	1514	16.5	—	(+) 36	8105	164.1
1976	50578	8182	7159	141.5	1388	20.3	—	(+) 74	8621	170.5
1977	51739	7102	6214	120.1	1831	19.7	—	(—) 7	8038	155.4
1978	52885	8636	7557	142.9	1349	15.4	—	(—) 73	8833	167.0
1979	54023	7777	6805	126.0	1776	17.7	—	(+) 1	8582	158.9
1980	55163	6574	5752	104.3	2090	15.1	—	(—) 13	7829	141.9

NOTES : 1. Production figures relate to Agriculture year (July-June) 1970 figures correspond to the production of 1969-70 and so on for the subsequent years.

2. Net production has been arrived at 87.5 per cent of gross production, the balance being provided for feed, seed requirements and wastage.

of severe scarcity—it was the lowest at 14 per cent, per capita availability ranging from 103.8 kg. in Kerala to 174.3 kg. per year in Punjab." He concluded : "the effect of government distribution on state-wise co-efficient of variations in cereal availability was highly significant. Had there been no public distribution, state-wise variability would have been as high as 29 per cent between 1961-68. On an average, a 10 per cent increase in distribution reduced variability by 5 per cent."

IMPACT OF GOVERNMENT SUPPLIES ON KERALA AND WEST BENGAL

Let us have a look at the impact made by the supplies from the buffer stocks in Kerala and West Bengal, the two most notable deficit states in the country. These have been worked out in Table 11.12.

Certain interesting conclusions emerge :

(a) the per capita availability, without taking into reckoning the supplies from buffer stocks, is much lower than the minimum adopted by the Technical Group on Buffer Stocking Policy. Even as bare necessity, it is far too inadequate ;

(b) the supplies from the buffer stocks made a difference in the per capita availability on an average of nearly 90 per cent in the case of Kerala and little less than 24 per cent in the case of West Bengal which only serve to establish that, but for these supplies, the position would have been worse. A system which supplements the per capita availability by such a margin is manifestly indispensable ;

(c) the coefficient of variation in the case of Kerala comes to 12.3 while in the case of West Bengal it is 5.43. These values show that the variation in the per capita availability in Kerala has been more while in the case of West Bengal it has been somewhat steady. The reason perhaps is a stronger and wider agricultural base in West Bengal than in Kerala ;

(d) even though total supplies in these states from the government stocks varied between nearly a fourth and above a third of the all-India supplies, the per capita availability has been coming down in the second-half of the seventies ; and

(e) the gap in the food security is obvious, notwithstanding the green revolution and higher levels of production. The above data give an unmistakable warning against complacency and bring out in sharp relief that the goal of food security is still far and a large part of the population, particularly in remote and isolated tribal and rural areas, remains hungry and underfed.

RURAL-URBAN DISPARITIES

Another aspect of regional disparities is reflected in the pattern and quantum of foodgrain consumption in the rural and urban areas respectively. Unfortunately, lack of authentic data prevents us from, dealing with this question in any greater detail. However, Prof. Minocha, in his paper referred to earlier, has examined it with the help of available price indicators. He proceeded on the assumption that the magnitude of supply deficiency in rural and urban areas would be reflected in the comparative state-wise consumer price index series for agricultural and industrial workers. On the basis of these series compiled from the *Reserve Bank of India Bulletin* covering the period 1966—1973, he came to the conclusion that the variations in the agricultural labour price index between the years and states were statistically significant with the exception of 1972. The highest difference in the coefficient of variation was in 1966 when public distribution was also the highest, domestic production of foodgrains declined significantly, and peak level imports were resorted to. He found that, except in 1972, in all the years, the coefficient of variation was higher in respect of consumer price index for agricultural labourers as compared to industrial workers. He observes : "At the time of shortages, significant deficiencies occurred in rural areas than in urban areas. Public distribution was withdrawn from rural areas in 1967 and as a result price variability again increased. About 20 per cent of population live in urban areas and a large number of them are in the organised sector where workers get dearness allowance and other benefits to offset increase in cost of living index. The rural areas are plagued with large under-employment and unemployment and include disproportionate share of low income people in the

TABLE 11.13 : **Consumer Price Index for industrial workers and agricultural workers**

(*Base : 1960-100*)

State	1974		1975		1976		1977		1978	
	(a)	(b)	(a)	(b)	(a)	(b)	(a)	(b)	(a)	(b)
(1)	(2)	(3)	(4)	(5)	(6)	(7)	(8)	(9)	(10)	(11)
Punjab	310	312	328	329	316	296	336	325	346	332
Assam	294	310	320	338	307	282	331	335	338	319
Bihar	306	392	299	349	282	282	314	331	319	333
Jammu & Kashmir	238	301	270	355	298	324	318	337	330	339
Rajasthan	N.A	333	N.A	348	N.A	261	N.A	309	N.A	327
Madhya Pradesh	338	374	347	484	316	306	347	339	354	339
Uttar Pradesh	310	354	311	343	286	262	325	315	336	336
Gujarat	294	278	301	329	276	261	305	277	320	288
West Bengal	279	320	288	330	290	304	318	337	326	315
Andhra Pradesh	312	280	355	327	323	268	356	297	372	293
Karnataka	305	310	338	352	314	296	344	318	314	296
Maharashtra	275	311	303	385	294	314	315	316	323	314
Orissa	285	337	311	430	292	338	309	354	312	346
Kerala	317	323	356	404	309	338	299	317	311	321
Tamil Nadu	N.A	326	N.A	404	N.A	289	N.A	306	N.A	299
Coefficient of Variation	7.96	9.28	7.44	11.99	4.77	8.58	5.14	5.80	5.24	5.62

(a) — Consumer price index for industrial workers.

(b) — Consumer price index for agricultural labourers.

N.A.— Not available

Source : Bulletin on Food Statistics published by Directorate of Economics & Statistics, Ministry of Agriculture, Government of India.

country. At present public distribution system has been mainly biased in favour of urban consumers and has widened disparities in the availability of foodgrains at reasonable prices among rural and urban areas."

In order to verify the above conclusions we have compiled the consumer price indices for industrial and agricultural workers and the coefficient of variation for the period 1974-78 which are given in Table 11.13.

The figures show that in Andhra Pradesh, in all years the price index for agricultural workers was lower than that of industrial workers. The same is the case of Gujarat with the exception of 1975, which was most probably due to the fact that it was a lean year for that state. In the case of Punjab, M.P. and also to a certain extent in Karnataka and Assam, the consumer price index for agricultural workers was low during the period 1976-78, a situation contrary to Minocha's findings. In other states, however, the index in respect of industrial workers has been lower, almost as a general rule, than that of agricultural workers. The years in which the price index for agricultural workers was lower than the one for industrial workers were years of exceptional bumper harvest and food availability in the rural areas was generally good. This was also the period of three continuous good harvest seasons. Nevertheless, the conclusion drawn by Minocha is, by and large, correct, and is reflected in the values of coefficient of variation. These values are higher in respect of agricultural workers in all these years—the peak difference being in 1975 when the scarcity conditions forced this value to go as high as 12 approximately. Food is generally scarce in the rural areas and the disparity that is created by this phenomenon is adequately reflected in the indices.

These are some of the tentative studies of this important aspect of food security system which only indicate the vital gaps both in the system as well as in our awareness of them. Food security system cannot be built up unless there is complete awareness of the areas and the income groups of people who are in need of its protection. Obviously, detailed studies and compilation of data will have to be undertaken for ascertaining the true picture of regional disparities in the availability of food, its variation over time, and the structure of population affected by it. Even in the commonly called surplus or self-sufficient states, there are pockets—particularly the remote and isolated areas inhabited by the tribals and areas poorly served by means of communication—where food shortage is almost a permanent feature. Plateaus and uplands which comprise major parts of Madhya Pradesh, Andhra Pradesh, Maharashtra, Karnataka, and Tamil Nadu are generally deficient in food supplies. The local produce of these tracts lasts but for a few months and for the rest the food supplies have to be drawn from outside. Detailed information about the situation of these areas is not available in a systematic manner and this is one more area which could be the subject matter of a separate and indepth study worthy of urgent attention ; for, a sound and authentic data base alone could be the foundation of a sound Food Security System.

FLOUR MILLING INDUSTRY

Roller flour milling industry has always been treated as a part of the public distribution system in a wider sense. Of the many industries that directly depend on agriculture, the roller flour milling industry is dependent entirely on wheat production. In India this industry has been, for more than two decades, a sheltered industry, in the sense that supply of its raw material has been ensured by the government. Even in times of acute scarcities when the country was living from 'shop-to-mouth', a certain minimum quantity of imported wheat was made available to these mills so as to enable them to do the minimum of grinding. In times of plenty also, while the mills are sometimes permitted to purchase their requirements in the open market (this happened during 1971 to 1973 and for a small period in 1979), the option is available to them, particularly in states where wheat production is not substantial, to draw their supplies from government stocks. Of course, when this option is exercised, purchases in the open market are prohibited.

DEVELOPMENT OF THE INDUSTRY

In the traditional rice growing states, these mills have played a pioneering role in not only popularizing consumption of wheat and wheat products, but also in evening out regional disparities in the availability of wheat products. The comparative development of this industry as between wheat producing (Punjab, Haryana, U.P., M.P., and Rajasthan) and non-producing areas (the rest of the country) as it has taken place during the past two decades is shown in Table 11.14.

TABLE 11.14 : **Annual installed capacity**

(*in million tonnes*)

	1958	1960	1965	1970	1973
Wheat producing areas	1.43	1.46	1.52	1.79	1.92
Non-producing areas	1.30	1.54	2.49	3.61	4.03

In 1973, a ban was imposed on the expansion of this industry which continued up to June 1979 when a relaxation was made in favour of small units up to 30 tonnes grinding capacity per day. However, a total ban was imposed again from May 1980.

Total quantities of wheat supplied to Roller Flour Mills from Central stocks during 1969—1980

(*All India*)
(*in million tonnes*)

Year	Quantity supplied to mills in wheat producing states	Quantity supplied to mills in non-wheat producing states	Total
1969	0.45	1.58	2.03
1970	0.56	1.93	2.49
1971	0.34	2.07	2.41
1972	0.71	2.29	3.00
1973	0.46	1.65	2.11
1974	0.17	1.07	1.24
1975	0.12	1.13	1.25
1976	0.20	1.22	1.42
1977	0.56	2.19	2.75
1978	0.80	2.51	3.31
1979	0.60	2.47	3.07
1980	0.74	2.90	3.64

The position is strikingly clear. Supplies to the mills in the non-wheat producing states exceed those made to the ones located in the wheat producing belt by three to four times. In the lean years of 1974 and 1975 the excess was very substantial, indicative of the government policy of reducing the disparities in the availability of wheat products in the non-wheat producing areas. Indeed, few other sectors would reflect in such unambiguous terms the working of the policy of the government in evening out disparities in food supplies as th's one. This would not have been possible had there been no buffer stocks.

This industry has received direct protection and benefit from the buffer stocking policy of the government as would be evident

TABLE 11.15 : **Capacity utilization by Roller Flour Mills in selected States**

(*in percentage*)

States	1972	1973	1974	1975	1976	1977	1978	1979	1980
Andhra Pradesh	47.6	37.3	15.0	27.4	40.4	45.5	67.8	64.7	61.1
Assam	55.4	28.1	13.3	11.6	0.6	44.6	48.3	4.3	38.1
Delhi	64.0	61.7	43.8	54.8	25.4	62.86	81.3	80.3	111.5
Goa	32.6	50.7	40.0	14.1	61.6	61.6	61.6	59.2	33.3
Gujarat	41.4	26.9	11.0	12.1	2.2	45.5	45.0	39.4	78.1
Haryana	35.5	34.1	15.9	—	3.2	13.5	24.6	21.1	19.1
Karnataka	63.4	24.9	13.5	16.4	28.9	62.33	77.4	83.3	96.0
Madhya Pradesh	41.3	21.8	5.0	18.8	14.3	46.5	52.6	48.0	49.5
Maharashtra	71.4	56.9	47.8	57.3	63.7	67.5	77.8	87.4	80.5
Tamil Nadu	56.8	26.4	12.6	20.1	26.8	58.6	67.8	68.6	51.3
West Bengal	52.9	46.2	22.4	35.1	32.8	57.2	57.2	51.6	57.3
All-India	52.7	35.5	20.9	21.1	23.9	46.3	55.6	51.6	61.2

N.B. : The years from 1973 to 1976 were characterized by acute shortage of wheat. Hence supplies to the mills were low resulting in lower capacity utilization.

from the supplies made from the buffer stocks and capacity utilized. (Table 11.15). It will be noticed that against the all-India percentage of 61.2 in 1980, the capacity utilization in Delhi was as high as 111.5, in Karnataka 96, in Andhra Pradesh 61.1, in Maharashtra 80.5 and in Tamil Nadu 51.3 (it was around 68 in the previous two years). These figures represent the highest levels achieved by this industry. Higher capacity utilization in the non-wheat producing areas confirms the beneficial role of buffer stocks in improving the food availability in those states and evening out regional disparities.

FOOD FOR WORK PROGRAMME

The role of the 'food for work' programme started in 1976-77 and converted into the national rural employment programme in 1980-81, in mitigating regional disparities in food availability is very considerable. Shortage of food has two aspects—physical shortage of food and shortage owing to lack of purchasing power. Both these features assail rural areas nearly in all the states in the country—surplus and deficit alike—though in a varying degree. The NREP has been designed to reach foodgrains in interior areas characterized by food shortage and to supply to labour engaged on development projects as part of their wage. Under this scheme foodgrains are allotted by the central government to the states which the latter utilize for financing these works in the rural areas. Population of marginal and landless workers and the size of the population below the poverty line are the two criteria for determining allocation of resources to the different states. Thus it aims at bridging the gap in per capita availability of food by financing works which create employment opportunities for small and marginal farmers and landless labourers. It would be no exaggeration to say that this programme is a direct and frontal attack on the regional disparities so far as food availability is concerned.

The allotment of foodgrains and man days generated during the four years since the inception of the programme has been as shown in the table below.

BENEFITS

The foodgrains were supplied from buffer stocks at the subsidized price. Their value is one measure of the benefit conferred on the

Allotment—All India

(in lakh tonnes)

	1977-78	1978-79	1979-80	1980-81
Wheat	2.0	12.1	13.7	2.81*
Rice	—	1.9	13.5	10.07
Total	2.0	14.0	27.2	12.88
Value (in million Rs.)	257.0	1842.5	3991.2	1889. 8
Man days generated (in millions)	44.43	353.85	591.12	420.81

*Includes a small quantity of coarse grains.

states. Local irrigation works, rural roads, schools, dispensary buildings, soil conservation works, flood protection works, maintenance of community assets, forest plantations, social forestry, etc. have been taken up under this programme on an extensive scale. Since a part of the wage is paid in kind, these stocks mean an additional resource for the states and create assets in a range of 33 to 50 per cent over and above the cash value provided in their budgets, depending upon the proportion of grain to cash.

In the rural areas the labour remains self employed for some time and also gets private employment during the crop seasons. N.R.E.P. comes to his aid in the lean season when he is unemployed. It would be safe to assume that this programme provides employment for 150 days in a year, thus giving an average for the four years of nearly 23.5 million persons per day who received foodgrains as part of their wage.

WFP are also supporting a number of development and welfare projects with commodity assistance in the shape of cereals, pulses, edible oil and DSM. In respect of the cereals, the arrangement is that wheat is issued to the project authorities from the FCI stocks which are replenished later by WFP. Thus continuity in food supplies is ensured. A 'plan of operations' is signed between the Government of India and WFP in respect of each project according to which it is administered.

A major fall-out of these projects is the accumulation of funds generated through sale of commodities to the labour. These funds are ploughed back for the general development of the area in accordance with guidelines issued by the Government of India.

Through this programme foodgrains have reached the remotest corners of the country, thereby enabling the poorest of the poor to earn two square meals a day. Secondly, the foodgrains having been supplied in a mix of wheat, rice, pulses and oil, the nutritional intake of the people has improved. Thirdly, with the spread of government works, backed by these food stocks, the agricultural and landless labour has been placed in a better bargaining position. Lastly, the surplus labour population has been provided with employment for a longer period of time in a year than was the case before, thereby leading to reduction in under-employment. The efficacy of this programme has indeed been amply demonstrated and the exploitation of the rural poor has been reduced. These are some of the fall-out effects of this programme which would have been unthinkable in the absence of buffer stocks with the government.

The 'food for work' programme has thrown up many valuable lessons in developmental strategy in countries like India. It has been proved that gainful employment of a higher order can be provided to the vast labour force with the help of food stocks, which may not be feasible if the conventional monetary approach were to be continued. Community assets which were in a state of utter neglect for decades for want of funds have been restored and put to good use. By far the most important lesson is that public spending in this form is anti-inflationary. The general price level of foodgrains remains on an even keel and the disastrous consequences of spiralling monetary expenditure are avoided. The common and well-known evils that attend upon ever-increasing monetary expenditure by the government are totally absent in this system. The programme has indeed given a new orientation to the development strategy in the country.

These are some of the visible and invisible benefits of this programme—the multiplier effect of the foodgrain stocks operating in the employment programme in the various regions of the country.

12

Relevance of the Distribution System

COMPONENTS OF DISTRIBUTION SYSTEM

THE efficacy of any food security system can be judged only with reference to the distribution system through which it is translated into action. In a free economy the distribution network consists of millions of traders and other persons at various levels engaged in this activity. At the apex are the big wholesalers who operate countrywide and purchase and sell foodgrains on a large scale almost throughout the year. It is these people who move, in the shape of commercial transactions, the surplus of one region to meet the deficit in others.

Then there are smaller wholesalers who, by reason of their resources operate on a limited scale and undertake similar transactions on a smaller scale. Their field of operation is either confined to a state or to a well defined agro-economic region in a state. They marshal their stocks received through the first category of wholesalers as well as on their own and handle them so as to make them available to the retailers spread out in the villages and interior areas. The number of these middle level wholesalers is indeed very large.

At the lowest rung are the retailers who draw their supplies from the middle level wholesalers in smaller quantities and carry them for retail vending. They operate on a short term basis—say a week or a fortnight—in the sense that with their meagre resources they obtain at a time, supplies which would last for a short period of time—after exhausting which they purchase fresh supplies from the wholesalers.

This is half of the marketing network ; the other half is the large body of producers who bring their marketable surplus on to the market. Since the producers are spread all over the country—in developed and well connected areas, in villages and also in remote hills where tribals reside—the grain market, both conceptually as well as in physical dimensions, is spread all over the country in the same fashion. At the bottom are the tradition and custom regulated village-level weekly *hats*, while at the top are highly organised and commercially regulated markets and in between are markets with varying structure and size. In these markets the producers (sellers) and the traders (purchasers) of all description operate and through this twin network, integrated in these markets, the supplies reach the consumers.

Excepting certain licensing procedures prescribed for the traders and the organizational and functional regulations pertaining to the market as such, the marketing system in the country functions freely and without any interference. The licensing system for the traders has been prescribed more with a view to keeping a check on the stocks coming in the market and available for the consumers as well as for curbing hoarding which creates artificial scarcity. Control or regulation of price is not the intention of this system. Excepting in the case of state trading, there has never been any price control in respect of the stocks moving on trade account.

The stresses and strains in the distribution system are felt more acutely in times of scarcities when supplies tend to dwindle and prices show an upward trend. In times of plenty, the stresses and strains are of a different kind, namely, the surplus stocks coming in huge quantities depressing the prices,' thereby adversely affecting the interests of the producers. Problems of storage and movement also arise and accentuate the stresses and strains. But here, we are chiefly concerned with analysing this distribution system through which the purposes of the buffer stocking policy are translated into action.

CONTROL METHODS

As stated earlier, the marketing system comprising the traders (purchasers) and producers (sellers) has existed in this country from times immemorial and has functioned with varying degrees of efficiency, directly related to the stage of development of the economy as a whole. This distribution system, according as the need arose from time to time, was controlled and regulated by the government of the day to meet the urgent requirements thrown up by the situation. During World War II, rationing, an extreme form of control over distribution of foodgrains, was enforced in a number of cities and urban areas in the country. Rationing in the orthodox sense, is always backed by the force of a statute. The area in question is completely cordoned off and movement of foodgrains into that area takes place only on government account ; movement of stocks on private account is completely prohibited. In other words, availability of stocks is strictly controlled and the government takes upon itself the responsibility of feeding the populace in the area. Here there is complete control on stocks as well as on prices and normally supplies are made in specified quantities to individuals identified on the basis of ration cards. For the obvious difficulties inherent in the system, the government has thought of rationing only as the last resort and when it is unavoidable.

Experience has shown that rationing creates a number of problems which often prove intractable. As an alternative, therefore, a system called modified or informal rationing has been introduced in some urban areas. The distinction between statutory rationing and modified rationing is that unlike the total prohibition on the open market functioning under the former system, the traders are allowed to legitimately function under the latter. The government, for its part, makes available a part of the requirements of the consumers supplied through fair price shops. As stated in the Foodgrains Policy Committee Report of 1966, the objectives of these two systems are different. Statutory rationing aims at isolating the areas of high purchasing power so as to reduce the pressure on supplies and prices elsewhere. Under modified or informal rationing on the other hand, the objective of organizing supplies through fair price shops is to supply a part of the needs of the consumers at reasonable prices, allowing, at the same time, the open market to function normally.

The licensing procedures for the traders and the market regulations are relevant—rather essential—for such a dual marketing system. Under a system of strict reporting and supervision, stocks on private account are also allowed to come into the market along with government stocks. This system was devised mainly because government policy has always been to do away with statutory rationing as far as practicable. The distribution system that obtains in this country at present, excepting in Calcutta and Durgapur and the Asansol industrial complex, is of informal rationing. Fair price shops are fed from the stocks held by the government, the object being to make a part of the requirements of the people available at controlled prices which are generally lower than the open market prices. Under this system the foodgrains market is allowed to function freely, except, insofar as the licensing procedures and regulations relating to the *mandis* have to be observed by the traders. Fair price shops, run by the agents of the government also function and supply foodgrains at fixed prices. These agents are bound by the condition that so long as they sell government stocks, they will not deal in those grains on private account. This condition is imposed obviously to ensure that government stocks are not put to any misuse. A choice or a facility is, therefore, available to a consumer that if he finds the price in the open market going beyond a certain level, he could turn to the fair price shop for drawing a certain minimum of his requirements at controlled prices. This is a situation where a dual market is operating—one in which private trade and the price mechanism are operating according to the normal laws of demand and supply, and the other embodying the measure of government intervention in the market as a deliberate corrective to the aberrations created by situations of scarcity.

The objective is to provide some protection to the vulnerable sections of the population.

PRIVATE TRADE

The question of associating private retailers with the public distribution system was raised in 1978 by the Federation of All-India Foodgrain Merchants Association. They said that the network of the fair price shops was not wide enough and was not operational in the interior areas, whereas a petty trader existed almost everywhere. To make the distribution system effective, government stocks should be issued to all such private traders and this network of private trade would be able to reach the supplies to the farthest and the remotest corners of the country. They tried to justify this change in the distribution system on the ground that the overheads in this system would be less and the final issue price for the consumer would be lower than what it is at present.

Government did not find this proposal acceptable. They found that there would be no effective control on the distribution of these stocks by the private retailers unless they gave up dealing in those foodgrains on private account. In the second place the assurance about the price discipline was also found to be un-enforceable, unless the retailers bound themselves by the Control Order. Lastly, it was pointed out to the Federation that the government stocks would not suffice for keeping the entire retail trade going ; they barely meet 12 to 14 per cent of the total demand, the balance being met by the stocks moving on private account which the trade handles on its own. No useful purpose would, therefore, be served by channelising the government stocks through private trade. It would, on the other hand, disrupt the channels of trade and upset the market.

ESTIMATE OF QUANTITIES

An estimate of the marketed surplus and its distribution between the public agencies and private trade can be had from the Table 12.1.

These data reveal that the average marketed surplus in rice is approximately 28 per cent of the production while in wheat it is 31 per cent. The position, however, varies materially from state to state. In Punjab much higher proportions of the total production of wheat and rice arrived in the market—66 per cent of wheat and 93 per cent of rice ; in Haryana the figures work out to 41 per cent and 92 per cent respectively. In the case of Andhra Pradesh—a surplus state in rice—the marketed surplus comes to about 35 per cent. Low marketed surplus in the rice growing states can be attributed to the fact that these areas are, by and large, monocrop areas and rice being the staple food of the people, a large proportion of the produce is retained for personal consumption. In the case of wheat, however, it does not happen that way. In Punjab more than half of wheat produced is marketed. Ultimately, the explanation may be found in the factors responsible for productivity and the state of the agricultural economy in a state or region.

The marketable surplus in coarse grains is very limited because they are generally grown on inferior soils and are retained mostly for personal consumption. The surplus is estimated between 10 and 15 per cent.

From the above data, it can be concluded that the organised sector handles about 26 million tonnes of rice and wheat alone to which can be added about 5 to 6 million tonnes of coarse grains and about 5 million tonnes of pulses, taking the total to 36-37 million tonnes. Besides, local transactions also take place between the producer on the one hand and the consumer and the retailers on the other. It will, therefore, be safe to assume that the Indian foodgrains market handles about 43-44 million tonnes of foodgrains every year in the organised and unorganised sectors. Handling of imported grain is additional to this. During 1982-83, 4 million tonnes of wheat was imported, thus pushing up the total quantity to around 48 million tonnes. The distribution system has, therefore, to handle quantities

TABLE 12.1 : **Production, marketable surplus and procurement of rice and wheat : 1978-79***

('000 tonnes)

State	Rice				Wheat			
	Production	Marketed surplus.	Public procurement	Market operations	Production	Marketed surplus	Public procurement	Market operation
Andhra Pradesh	7432	2561	1042	1519	13	—	—	—
Assam	2172	32	32	—	68	—	—	—
Bihar	5490	770	12	758	2502	250	88	162
Gujarat	535	221	—	221	1192	402	neg.	402
Haryana	1128	1040	887	151	3398	1389	1389	—
J&K	546	58	58	—	204	22	22	—
Karnataka	2175	396	106	290	264	19	—	19
Madhya Pradesh	3562	817	306	511	3523	360	100	260
Maharashtra	2201	187	31	156	951	184	—	184
Orissa	4402	132	58	74	122	—	—	—
Punjab	3091	2874	2726	148	7423	4923	4200	723
Rajasthan	234	71	17	54	2874	652	301	351
Tamil Nadu	5559	1888	71	1817	1	—	—	—
Uttar Pradesh	5964	1651	837	814	11458	2392	1883	509
West Bengal	6677	1200	145	1055	998	3	3	—
INDIA	53773	15003	6334	8669	35508	11150	8000	3150

*Bulletin on Food Statistics, 1981-82, Directorate of Economics and Statistics, Ministry of Agriculture, Government of India.

of this order and to satisfy the beneficiaries by the service offered, and the consumers by the quality of the commodity and the prices charged.

COSTS

The foregoing analysis highlights the importance of the distribution system as also its costs to the buyers and sellers. In private trade operations, the margins of the various handling agencies come to about 18 per cent of the retail price. This is over and above obligatory costs such as market fee, purchase/sales tax, and other levies. In respect of wheat procured by the FCI, the economic cost for the whole year means an addition of nearly 30 per cent to the support price at which it is purchased from the producers. Incidentals for retail distribution differ from state to state. Local taxes and commission of the intermediaries form a major portion of these expenses. Taking the central issue price of the government stocks as the base, and after adding the distribution costs, it has been found that the retail price for the consumer is lowest in Punjab (Rs. 136.50 per quintal) and highest in Himachal Pradesh (Rs. 214 per quintal). In the Andaman and Nicobar Islands, the issue price works out to Rs. 169.25, but after adjusting the central subsidy of Rs. 6.75, the retail consumer price is Rs. 163 per quintal. The variations are indeed many and of different character. But it is clear that items like transport, commission to wholesalers and retailers, and administrative and establishment charges levied by the state governments, are items which can bear scrutiny as well as some slashing. Sales tax seems to be excessive in Orissa, Andhra Pradesh, Karnataka, Chandigarh, Bihar, and Punjab. In Tamil Nadu the state government has been adding a lump sum of Rs. 15 per quintal to the central issue rate towards retail distribution.* In the overall reckoning, these distribution incidentals have varied between 2 and 8 per cent of the cost of the grain handled, excluding the abnormally high transport costs in hill states ; in the case of private trade these margins have varied between 3 and 15 per cent.

The distribution system as well as its operational costs differ from state to state. What is the relative share of the regulated and unregulated markets in the marketing of the produce in a state, what costs are added at every stage of the operations, what is the efficiency of these operations and whether there is scope for reducing costs and

*These conclusions are based on the data collected in 1978.

improving the system—these should form appropriate subjects for further study.

OBJECTIVES

The basic question that is to be answered before devising a distribution system is what are the purposes that this system is expected to serve. What sections of the community should it serve ? It is obvious that it cannot meet the requirements, even partially, of the entire population. The foodgrains stocks available with the government being limited, make it imperative that they are put into a distribution system which is directed towards well-defined sections of society in need of protection against the fluctuations of market conditions. Historically speaking, commitment of the state to the policy of procurement and distribution has had its origin in the egalitarian concept of state subsidization of food supplies to vulnerable sections in times of scarcities, except in the case of rationing. But, as seems highly probable, we have said goodbye to statutory rationing and are now faced again with the question as to which sections of society the public distribution system should be directed to. In the past two decades some states had applied income criteria, favouring the low income groups. It entailed extensive field enquiries about the economic status of the beneficiaries and at times was commented upon as cumbersome as well as irksome and also unfair to certain salaried income groups. Nevertheless, the system worked satisfactorily, especially in times of acute scarcities. Towards the end of 1976 when the stock position was comfortable, the central government advised the state governments to withdraw the *income restriction on the drawal of foodgrains and per unit scale of* ration was also liberalized.

Of late, another dimension has been added to the objectives of the buffer stocking policy. Distribution of food through works taken up under the employment generation programmes is increasingly posing problems which the system has to cope with. Injection of foodgrains in the NREP has reinforced this dimension. Foodgrains have to be made available to the labour through employment programmes as part of their wage on a continuing basis. The size of the NREP has grown substantially from 0.20 million tonnes in 1977-78 to 1.40 million tonnes in 1978-79 and to 2.50 million tonnes in 1979-80. It should be obvious that to move such enormous quantities and reach them to the beneficiaries would require strengthening of the distribution system with an eye on the costs.

There is a broader aspect of the food policy in relation to the dimension of distribution. Article 47 in Part IV of the Constitution setting forth the Directive Principles of State Policy enjoins upon the state as its primary duty, to raise, among others, the level of nutrition. In this constitutional direction is contained the sanction for evolving a distribution system which should satisfy the enlarged needs of the society. The system will have to reckon with the total 'food basket', viz., items like processed foods and fortified and enriched items such as vitamins, salts, and other nutrients. Pre-school going children and lactating and pregnant mothers have to be covered under the supplementary nutrition programme. These wider considerations call for a serious study for determining a suitable distribution system and appropriate policy options.

Problems of logistics will always constitute the most crucial aspect of the distribution system. Movement of supplies—whether procured internally or imported—would impinge on the logistics network. Apart from the transportation network, various ancillary activities like loading, unloading and storage will pose additional problems. In many food importing developing countries these problems stem mainly from inadequacy of transportation, storage and handling capacities, near absence of all-weather roads in the interior and inadequacy of port clearance and off-take facilities. In such situations the extra strain put upon the existing facilities may create serious congestion in the food distribution chain and thereby exacerbate the effects of food shortage. A close coordination of procurement, handling, storage, transport and distribution functions is needed to ensure smooth flow of supplies.

13

Management of the Food Economy

FOODGRAINS reserve as a backstop for national food security is now the cardinal element in India's Food Policy. The national food security and the overall regulation of the food economy of the country is the paramount duty of the central government. As early as 1943, the central government declared that the various provinces of India "are so interrelated in food matters that 'give and take' physically and administratively is imperative . . . that public opinion will not tolerate 'hands-off' attitude by the centre, and in consequence, the centre cannot accept any situation which involves its having responsibility without power." The decisions on the procurement and management of buffer stocks have to be taken with a country-wide focus. The operational apparatus has also to be basically with the central government which may exercise strategic control over stocks and their deployment in the areas where they are needed. These objectives are achieved through the Food Corporation of India, and to the extent expedient, through the state governments or their designated agencies. The location of the stocks would naturally have to be planned in relation to the availability of storage capacity, movement feasibility and the requirements of the various states, depending on their food habits and their basic character of being surplus, marginally surplus or deficit and deficit under normal conditions.

Entries 33 and 34 in the Seventh Schedule to the Constitution (Concurrent List) give the central government power to control trade and commerce in and distribution of foodstuffs and enforcing price control. An elaborate set of control orders have been promulgated both by the central and state governments—in the case of the latter with prior approval of the central government—under the enabling provisions of the Essential Commodities Act, 1955, for the regulation of trade and commerce in and distribution of foodgrains and for price control. Food represents that sensitive department of administration where the delicate framework of the centre and state relations enshrined in the Constitution has to be maintained with utmost care, thought, and ingenuity.

This delicate yet vital function is performed through an elaborate system of laws and procedures, involving mutual consultation, delegation of powers, and continuous monitoring. In a country of the size and diversity of India, the methods of procurement will naturally vary from state to state, and even in a state, from region to region. In food administration the local conditions are always the guiding considerations in determining the instruments as well as the modes of procurement. Generally speaking, therefore, the modes of procurement are left to the judgement and discretion of the state governments with the central government doing counselling and coordination. The broad parameters of the national food policy are determined by the central government, such as what should be the support price, whether there should be free trade or zonal restrictions have to be imposed, the magnitude of procurement and matters of that nature. Within these broad parameters the states are free to devise such means as would best answer the local conditions.

MODES OF PROCUREMENT

The following methods were adopted at different times, singly or in combination, for procurement of foodgrains in the different states of the country :

(a) levy on millers and wholesale dealers in the case of rice ;
(b) levy on wholesale traders in the case of wheat ;
(c) levy on producers ;
(d) monopoly purchase/procurement ;
(e) open market purchases ;
(f) purchases through pre-emption in the regulated markets ;
(g) procurement from producers through requisitioning ; and
(h) price support operations.

Briefly, rice, which is a processed commodity, is procured from the millers and the modality is that a fixed percentage of the quantity milled daily, is prescribed by law to be delivered by the millers to the appointed agent of the government. In Punjab and Haryana where paddy is grown totally as a cash crop and local consumption is negligible, the millers do not mind handing over as much as 80 to 90 per cent of the rice milled by them to the state agencies. In states like Tamil Nadu and Andhra Pradesh where rice is the staple food of the people, the state governments have by experience found that the lower the levy, the more would be the availability in the open market at a fairly reasonable price. In these states, therefore, the levy has ranged in the past between 10 and 20 per cent. As larger and larger surpluses have emerged in states like Andhra Pradesh, this percentage went up as high as 50 per cent in 1980. Orissa has adopted a novel system in which the rice millers are given the licence on a condition that during the entire season they will deliver the stipulated quantity of rice as the levy. In Bihar more or less the same method is followed, under which levy is compounded for the whole season with every rice miller and wholesale dealer. These two states have perhaps found that, owing to the day-to-day fluctuations in the arrivals as well as prices of paddy in the market, the millers must have the flexibility to adjust their business as they consider best while the state's demand in terms of levy should be assured during the season as a whole.

In the rice trade the pattern throughout the country is that the paddy is usually purchased by the rice millers who process it into rice. It would be very difficult for the government agencies to store paddy and thereafter convert it into rice ; the hazards in the storage of paddy are indeed numerous. For these reasons, the system of monopoly purchase has never been employed so far as paddy trade is concerned. Monopoly purchase system has, however, been adopted in relation to procurement of wheat. But, as the very title suggests, this method of procurement is so drastic that it shuts out all purchases by private trade and hence it should be resorted to only in times of exceptional difficulty. It will never be a wise policy to dry up the channels of private trade by adopting such draconian methods of procurement and the history of food administration affords hardly one or two instances when this measure was adopted. It was adopted for the first time during the 1943 Bengal famine but no sooner was it adopted than it was found that it created more problems than it sought to solve and was consequently given up.

A variation of this method, namely purchases through pre-emption, has been adopted with relatively greater success. Under this system the government agencies are vested with an option to purchase a specified proportion of the arrivals in the market at the prices determined in open competition. While, therefore, the price is left to be determined by forces of demand and supply, the choice is available to the public agencies to acquire a prescribed percentage of the market arrivals for public distribution. This mode was adopted in many states in the past two decades, especially during the severe scarcities of 1965-66 and 1973-74. The experience of this method has been that it is no unmixed good ; it is after all a variation of the monopoly purchase system and therefore where some zealous governments tried to prescribe a higher percentage which could be purchased at their discretion, conditions very similar to the monopoly purchase system were created.

Likewise, procurement by means of levy on traders or dealers has also been tried on several occasions but not with very great success. Experience has shown that wheat levy on traders is tardy and does not work smoothly. Traders operate on a small margin and their main interest lies in quick turnover. Levy hinders this turnover. Since traders acquire stocks at prices which vary from day to day, levy which is necessarily to be delivered at a fixed price completely upsets the price mechanism in the market. Enforcement is also difficult because the number of traders is so large that effective supervision is not possible. The system creates such intractable distortions in the market that in the overall assessment it has been found to be not a very practicable mode.

The mode of procurement through levy on producers is a category in itself and lot of debate has taken place on the efficacy as well as wisdom of this system. Nevertheless it is a sure and tested method of procurement. The scheme generally is that small holdings—say up to 2 hectares—are exempted from the levy. For the remaining, a graded scale of levy is worked out, the quantity being little higher for irrigated areas and lower for the rain-fed areas and related to the size of the holdings. This system was adopted in a number of states during the scarcities of the sixties and the seventies and with a fair amount of success. But the farmers consider it a tyrannical method of procurement because in normal times, and more so in times of scarcities, the open market price generally rules higher than the procurement price and when the producers are forced to part with their produce—howsoever small the quantity may be—at a lower price, they think that they are being cheated of their labors.

An analysis of operational holdings according to size reveals that nearly 70 per cent of the total number are 2 hectares and below in size. But area-wise they account for only 20.8 per cent of the total cultivated area. If, therefore, holdings up to 2 hectares are exempted from the producers levy and a graded levy is imposed on the holdings above that limit, the operation would touch only 30 per cent holdings accounting for nearly 79 per cent of the cultivated area. As regards quantitative impact, broadly speaking, the levy works out to 12 to 15 per cent of the total produce.* It is a question of judgement whether it is tyrannical to force the producers to part with this much of their produce at the official support price ?

Justification for resorting to this form of procurement which is often characterized as tyrannical and exacting is that the state invests huge funds in irrigation works and other promotional and developmental activities in relation to agriculture and thus has a moral right to demand a minimum fraction of the production for the national buffer which serves a very basic and fundamental public purpose.

As explained in Chapter 11, with the distinction between the procurement price and support price having gradually disappeared, the operational mechanism of procurement has undergone a change. Under the price support policy, the government is committed to purchase all stocks of fair average quality offered at the support price. This commitment is not only confined to the developed and regulated markets but, in theory, holds good for all areas—distant and remote, wherever the stocks are being offered. This phenomenon is chiefly an offshoot of the times of plenty. As a result of successive bumper harvests after 1974, open market prices have tended to dip. Consequently, the government is always under pressure to enter the market everywhere to arrest the falling trend in prices by purchasing the stocks offered at the support price.

The emergence of the price support concept in conjunction with exceptionally favourable seasons continuously over a period of four years has changed the very complexion of the procurement operations. These factors have introduced an element of universality in these operations which are required to be undertaken in public interest. In this system all those constraints in the form of targets and levies have disappeared and these operations have now assumed the role of a very basic support to the market economy of the foodgrains,

*Derived from the scale levied in Madhya Pradesh during 1973 and 1974.

involving millions of producers. In fact, there is a general demand from the producers even in remote areas for purchase centres to be opened by the government or by its purchasing agents. Such a step is considered necessary to prevent exploitation of the producers by the trading community which tries to acquire their stocks at prices lower than the support price.

AGENCIES FOR PROCUREMENT

Let us now briefly deal with the agencies—both central and of the states—which operate in the foodgrain market and handle procurement. The Central Government, on its part, has set up a national agency, known as the Food Corporation of India, under the Food Corporations Act, 1964. Under this Act, the FCI, or for that matter a corporation set up in a state, is charged with the following responsibilities :

(1) to undertake purchase, storage, movement transport, distribution and sale of foodgrains and other foodstuffs ; and
(2) with the previous approval of the central government—
   (a) promote by such means as it thinks fit the production of foodgrains and other foodstuffs ;
   (b) set up, or assist in the setting up of rice mills, flour mills and other undertakings for the processing of foodgrains and other foodstuffs ; and
   (c) discharge such other function as may be prescribed or as are supplemental, incidental or consequential to any of the functions conferred on it under this Act.

The FCI has its subordinate offices in the states, down to the district. It has its own godowns and silos and has set up a number of processing plants. A number of states have also set up their own corporations which also perform such functions as price support purchases and procurement. Finally, the cooperatives play a very important part in carrying out the policy directives of the government.

Over the years a convention has developed that procurement of rice is done on the states' account while that of wheat and coarse grains is done on the central account. The rice stocks are procured by the states and quantities surplus to their requirements are surrendered to the central pool which is at the absolute disposal of the central government. As and when the states find stocks surplus to their requirements, as happened during the second half of the seventies when successful bumper crops were harvested, more quantities are surrendered to the central pool. But for monitoring the implementation of the buffer stocking policy the totality of stock position on central and states' account has to be taken into consideration.

COORDINATION BETWEEN THE CENTRE AND STATES

It would be necessary to take an integrated and unified view of the food economy of the country. While the food policy is laid down by the central government, it is implemented through the state governments. The entire mechanism of procurement operated through the system of Control Orders is regulated in overall parameters by the central government. However, the role of the state governments who enforce those orders is crucial. The procurement effort of the Food Corporation of India is supplemented to a very great extent by the state agencies, including the cooperative institutions. By and large the state agencies procure and hold the foodgrains on behalf of the Food Corporation of India for which they are paid necessary charges. There is thus a very intimate collaboration between the central agency and the state agencies so far as the procurement and storage of foodgrains are concerned.

Laws differ from state to state but are designed to achieve common objectives. Prior approval by the Government of India ensures uniformity in their fundamental outline. Quality specifications, cuts for deviations from them, and fixation of purchase prices—all are prescribed by the Government of India. The APC, a standing body of experts, reviews the crop prospects and other agricultural conditions pertaining to *kharif* and *rabi* crops and submits a report to the Department of Food setting forth its estimates of production and distribution, the estimates of cost of production, review of the price situation, and the support price or the procurement price, as the case may be, that should be fixed for a particular grain. This report is circulated to all the states and they are invited for a discussion which takes place at the Chief Ministers level. Thereafter the union government takes the final decision which naturally reflects the widest possible consensus. Detailed instructions are then drafted incorporating the decisions and the manner in which they are to be implemented. Supporting legislation, if required, is either initiated by the central government or the states are advised to submit drafts for approval as the case may be.

The procurement operations have to be planned jointly by the centre and the states. When so recommended by the central government to the Reserve Bank, credit for procuring foodgrains for the public distribution system is made available at a concessional rate of interest. How much grain should be procured, what are the credit requirements, costing and pricing of the stocks and their disposal through public distribution or otherwise and finally reimbursement of losses to the agencies concerned—all these matters require detailed planning to be done jointly by the centre and the states. Where, as in the case of pulses (gram) and oil-seeds, price support operations have to be undertaken as a promotional measure from which states stand to gain, the centre will have to prescribe the whole exercise to be carried out by the states. States are not free to dispose of the stocks acquired in price support operations ; their disposal will always be in accordance with the directions of the central government, which means mutual consultations.

Nevertheless, in some states, foodgrains are held by the state agencies on their own account for supplies through the public distribution system. Experience has brought to light a number of operational difficulties in integrating the state stocks with those in the central pool so far as management of the total stocks is concerned. Certain states sometimes enter into bilateral transactions and sell the procured stocks on commercial basis thereby making profit on them, whereas for supplies to the public distribution system within the state, they depend on the central government. This does not conduce to smooth and proper management of the food economy, and the central government has to intervene. Thus the system is operated by the centre and the states acting in a conjunctive manner, making it meaningful for each other. No other approach would work.

COSTS

Since costs are a very important factor which influence the market and determine the price for the consumers, the central as well as the state governments keep a close watch on the expenses connected with the procurement, distribution and maintenance of buffer stocks. These have been explained in an earlier chapter.

It was noticed in 1976 that the obligatory charges were continually increasing. The states were free to impose taxes on foodgrains and there were wide variations from state to state as can be seen from Table 13.1.

TABLE 13.1 : **Statement showing rate of Sales Tax on paddy and rice in various states**

States	1970-71	1971-72	1972-73	1973-74	1974-75	1975-76
1	2	3	4	5	6	7
Punjab	3%	3%	Rs. 2 per qtl	Rs. 2/- per qtl	7%	7%
Haryana	—	3%	3%	3%	7%	7%
Madhya Pradesh	—	—	—	2%	2%	2% on paddy 2% on rice
Andhra Pradesh	3¼%	3¼%	3¼%	—	3¼%	3¼%
Uttar Pradesh	1.5%	1.5%	1.5%	1.5%	1.5%	7% on superior Basmati (rest nil)

There was a noticeable tendency on the part of the states to progressively increase this tax, treating it as a source of revenue. This led to wide variations from state to state making it difficult to work out the economic cost of the stocks. The problems created by high prices in the lean years of 1973, 1974 and 1975 highlighted this tendency in an aggravated form, compelling the central government to intervene.

In September, 1976, the Central Sales Tax Act, 1956, was amended by inserting a provision which empowered the central government to declare particular goods of special importance in inter-state trade or commerce (foodgrains were so declared) whereafter the Sales Tax thereon would be limited to the extent prescribed under the Central Act. By this measure, the central government controlled the runaway tendency on the part of the states to go on increasing the tax on foodgrains.

Other expenses like market fee, commission to the various intermediaries and incidental expenses that a state proposes to pay while procuring foodgrains are also scrutinised by the central government minutely and kept to the minimum. The reimbursement to the state agencies by the FCI is done on the basis of the rates approved by the Food Department, and thus a measure of control is exercised on the pricing/costing.

The element of subsidy from the Central exchequer in the implementation of this policy is a vital factor integrating the centre and the states in the management of the food economy. Purchase, storage, maintenance and movement of stocks involve very substantial costs which the states find difficult to meet from their resources. So far, these subsidies are being met, almost totally, by the central government, excepting in the case of those stocks of rice which were till lately being retained by the states for their internal consumption. But from the 1978-79 *kharif* season (October-September) states which were retaining the rice stocks, notably Andhra Pradesh and West Bengal have informed the central government that they would be surrendering the entire procurement to the central pool in the first instance and drawing their monthly requirements therefrom subsequently. This has obviously been done to avoid the burden on the state exchequer and to take advantage of the central subsidy. Control of the central government in the management of the food economy, therefore, is very substantial. Nevertheless, it is the constant endeavour of the central government that the initiative of the states is not curbed and that they assume responsibility in this joint venture which is appropriately theirs.

14

Alternatives to the Present System

PART A

STRUCTURAL MODIFICATION TO THE EXISTING ARRANGEMENTS

PRESENT SYSTEM ANALYSED

UNDER the present arrangement the entire buffer stock is physically held by the FCI on the central account. Operational stocks are partly held by the FCI and partly by the states, though the bulk is held by the FCI. In the states where the FCI has been authorized to procure foodgrains as an agent of the state government, the stocks are held by this agency on state account. This is particularly so in the case of rice which, by convention, is procured on state account. From 1969-70 onwards, the states have held rice stocks for their consumption ranging from half a million to one million tonnes. Of late, because of the central subsidy element in the issue price of rice, states which were retaining rice stocks for their internal requirements are now making-over all the stocks to the central pool and drawing their requirements from it subsequently. This has resulted in the shifting of the entire subsidy burden on the central government. All in all, during the past three years, (1977-78-79) the FCI has handled foodgrain stocks varying within a range of 20 to 22 million tonnes annually.

It should be obvious that acquiring such huge quantities of foodgrains from all over the country and moving them to areas where they are needed, are operations of such huge magnitude that it is difficult for one agency to achieve optimum results. In consequence, there is considerable avoidable duplication and overlapping of operations. The existing arrangements suffer from a number of shortcomings, some of which are listed below :

(a) food being a subject in the concurrent list and being a commodity of vital need for the people, the operation of the buffer stocking policy has necessarily to be in a manner representing the highest degree of coordination with the state administrations. This ideal is yet to be achieved ;

(b) the state agencies are yet to play their full role in the procurement, storage, and distribution of foodgrains. The chief reason is that their financial position is weak and they have no resources to invest in undertaking these operations which, besides locking up substantial funds, also involve incurring of costs as well. Since these costs cannot be recovered from the consumers in full, substantial funds are required to be provided by the states by way of subsidy from general revenues, which is not always possible for them ;

(c) the food business entails numerous costs and risk, viz., deterioration in quality, losses due to theft and pilferage, fluctuations in open market prices, maintenance costs, etc. Each one of these elements is a potential cause of loss. The state agencies do not have the capacity to bear these losses with the result that they are most reluctant to undertake the procurement operations. Even the deficit states which ought to be quite concerned about making the supplies available to their consumers prefer to lean on the centre without fully inducting their agencies in this essential function ;

(d) the operational costs and carrying costs of stocks are heavy burdens. If they were to be realized from the consumers, the issue price would be so high that the very purpose of undertaking these operations would be defeated. The states feel that, with their limited resources, they cannot afford to bear the element of subsidy ;

(e) the dichotomy between the central and state agencies leads to friction in day-to-day operations. The most contentious disputes centre round the quality cuts. The extent to which the FCI is permitted to operate in the markets for purchasing stocks varies from state to state ; and within state, from grain to grain. In Andhra Pradesh, Madhya Pradesh, and Rajasthan, procurement of rice, as well as price support purchases of paddy, are almost entirely handled by the FCI. In Punjab and Haryana, the state agencies handle 65 and 80 per cent of wheat respectively, the balance being left to the FCI. In Uttar Pradesh practically all the rice procurement is done in the first instance by the state agencies. In the case of wheat, the FCI handles all the purchases in Rajasthan and Madhya Pradesh, while in Punjab, Haryana, and Uttar Pradesh it handles between one-fifth to one-fourth of the total procurement, the rest being purchased by the state agencies. State agencies first procure the stocks and then hand them over to the FCI. Three things happen in this process. First, the state agencies impose cuts and pay the farmers accordingly. But when they hand over the stocks to the FCI, they try to standardize and try to pass on the stocks as grade one. The FCI's grouse is that the state agencies retain the difference for which there is no justification. In the second place, the FCI is not able to lift all the stocks immediately after procurement. This is particularly true of Punjab, Haryana, Uttar Pradesh and Andhra Pradesh, where surpluses are very considerable, with the result the state agencies have to hold them for longer periods of time. The FCI no doubt pays the carrying charges, but in the meanwhile the stocks have deteriorated by sheer passage of time and have become liable for quality cuts. In this situation, and this is the third dimension of the problem, the state agencies complain that they are saddled with cuts for no fault of their's. And thus disputes are raised which remain unresolved for long, giving rise to a lot of resentment and infructuous work all round;

(f) in arranging storage and movement also, difficulties are encountered in the present working arrangement. The FCI cannot always act without the active help and cooperation of the states. This help and cooperation is not best secured in this arrangement, because responsibility for procurement, storage, and movement does not fully go with the authority at the local level. The states escape a very large measure of responsibility which, curiously enough, does not get pinpointed anywhere but gets diffused. The result is escalation in costs and waste of effort. This is not a happy state of affairs and leads to many complications;

(g) at the time of distribution, the states have to obtain the supplies from the FCI depots and again there are disputes about quality. The states complain that sub-standard stocks are being passed on to them while the explanation given by the FCI generally is that the stocks conform to the prescribed specifications. In a couple of instances it so happened that when the stocks were put on sale through the fair price shops, the consumers refused to accept them with the result that the capital of the shopkeepers as well as of the state agencies which had lifted the stock in bulk, got locked up with many complications all-round. Such a situation happens only when the identity of the two agencies engaged in the same work are separate and distinct with accountability resting at different points; and

(h) there is a trifle irrationality in the present working insofar as the storage and movement planning is done by the FCI almost in isolation. These operations ought to be planned in minute details in close consultation with the states all over the country. Generally speaking, this does not happen with the result that often stocks are not available where they are wanted and considerable wastage takes place in cross movement.

PRIVATE TRADE

The question of associating private trade with the procurement operations was raised in February 1978 by the Federation of All India Foodgrain Dealers Associations. In its memorandum it offered to take over the responsibility of holding national buffer as well as operational stocks.[4] It demanded two important facilities for taking over this responsibility; liberalization of bank credit for foodgrain trading, and extension of facilities for the construction of a chain of godowns. The scheme suggested by the Federation envisaged a kind of supplemental functioning by private trade alongside the public agencies in the matter of procurement and holding of stocks. It suggested that, to the extent assisted by the government, they will procure stocks and hold them for a period up to nine months after which they shall be taken over by the FCI. The Federation contended that procurement and holding costs of stocks would be lower than those at present incurred by the FCI.

Upon the submission of this memorandum, the feasibility of using selected private traders for procurement and storage of foodgrains on behalf of the government was examined at considerable length. A comparison of costs showed that the procurement costs of private trade would not only not work out cheaper but that they would be more (see Table 14.1). Secondly, the modification of the credit policy as demanded by the Federation would have meant involvement of substantial funds which it would not be possible for the government to provide. Thirdly, it would have been totally indefensible for the government to take upon itself the responsibility for making provision of land and other facilities for construction of storage godowns by private parties.

TABLE 14.1 : **Comparative statement showing charges allowed to the procurement agencies in Punjab & Haryana for various items in the procurement of wheat and those claimed/ payable to private trade as per the letter of the All India Foodgrains Dealers Federation.**

(Rate in Rs. per quintal)
(purchase price of Rs. 110 per quintal)

Items	Allowed to procurement agencies in Punjab & Haryana (Provisional)	As claimed or payable to private trade	Remarks
1.	2.	3	4
1. *Mandi* charges	3.85	3.85	(Actual claimed by the Federation)
2. *Mandi* labour	1.00	1.02	(As claimed by the Federation)
3. Storage charges	0.61	0.42	(As claimed by the Federation)
4. Forwarding charges	0.80	0.80	(Actual payable also to private traders)
5. Internal movement/unforeseen charges.	1.11	1.11	-do-
6. Gunny Cost	4.64	4.64	-do-
7. Interest charges	2.08	2.08	-do-

TABLE 14.1—(*Contd.*)

1	2	3	4
8. Sales/Purchase Tax	5.23	5.23	-do-
9. Establishment charges	1.00 (Irrespective of the period of storage)	—	(included under Commission charges).
10. Commission	—	3.30	3% of purchase price for storage up to 3 months.
		(4.95)	(4.5% of purchase price for storage up to 6 months.)
		(6.60)	(6% of purchase price for storage up to 9 months)
Total	20.32	22.45	For storage up to 3 months.
		24.10	For storage up to 6 months.
		25.75	For storage up to 9 months.

Notes

(*i*) Commission charges indicated against item No. 10 in respect of private traders would be applicable for taking over of stocks within three months.

(*ii*) Commission charges payable to private traders for storage from 3 to 6 months and from 6 to 9 months will be as follows :

Storage Period	*Amount* (*Rs. per quintal*)
3—6 months	4.95
6—9 months	6.60

There is no change in the Establishment charges paid to the State procuring agencies irrespective of the period of storage.

The total incidental charges payable for deliveries up to 6 months and 9 months by private traders will be Rs. 24.10 per quintal and Rs. 25.75 per quintal respectively against Rs. 20.32 per quintal for state procuring agencies.

(*iii*) In addition to the incidentals indicated, for deliveries beyond 31st July carrying charges comprising storage and interest charges would be payable both in the case of state procuring agencies as well as private traders.

The government came to the conclusion that the suggestion would be impracticable. The additional disadvantage—and a vital disadvantage—would be that in times of emergency, deployment of stocks would be rendered extremely difficult. Movement of the surplus stocks acquired in the northern states to all states in the country and tying up the movement schedule with the requirements of the states are operations which would be totally beyond the competence of private trade. The problem of turning over of the stocks, maintaining at the same time the prescribed levels with the help of fresh stocks, is of such great complexity that it cannot be accomplished when the buffer is held by thousands of wholesalers all over the country. Such an arrangement would render effective implementation of the policy almost totally impossible.

NEGLECT OF COARSE GRAINS ECONOMY

This study of the buffer stocking policy has also revealed that the price support policy has remained confined, by and large, to wheat and rice only. Coarse grains (maize, sorghum, *ragi*, *bajra*, etc.) which account for nearly 25 per cent of the total cultivated area and contribute roughly one-third to the total foodgrain production of the country, have not received the same attention and care as these two cereals have. Partly because these grains are subject to speedy decay and partly for the reason that they do not command an all-India market and demand for them is limited to the areas where they are grown, coarse grains have not been procured in substantial quantities over the years. There is yet another reason why government agencies have not resorted to a large scale procurement of these grains. Coarse grains are the staple food of the poorer sections of the community and any large scale withdrawal of supplies from the market will push up their prices, thereby causing hardship to the consumers. The coarse grains economy has, therefore, not been subjected to the full impact of the price support operations by the public agencies. There are, however, a few exceptions. In Maharashtra, Markfed undertakes extensive price support purchases every year in respect of sorghum (*jowar*). Karnataka also undertakes these operations for procuring *ragi*. Tamil Nadu and West Bengal also do a lot of procurement on state account, but they too confine themselves to rice only. In states like Haryana, Rajasthan, Madhya Pradesh,

Gujarat and Andhra Pradesh where coarse grains production is substantial, hardly any procurement is done.

The buffer stocking policy of the central government has crucial relevance to the coarse grains economy of the country. Extensive areas in the western belt of the country running from north to south and comprising, wholly or partially, Haryana, Rajasthan, western Madhya Pradesh, Gujarat, Maharashtra and Karnataka as well as the uplands on the Deccan Plateau in Andhra Pradesh grow substantial quantities of coarse grains. Except to a limited extent in maize and *jowar*, no technological breakthrough has taken place in other grains, with the result that over the years the overall production has not increased in any substantial measure. From the experience of the price support policy in relation to wheat and rice, it can be said with a degree of certainty that the time has come when the coarse grains economy needs a shot in the arm if it has to be pulled out of its stagnant condition. On the other hand, if the procured stocks are not disposed of quickly, there is every likelihood of deterioration in quality thereby causing loss to the public exchequer. As a matter of fact, procurement has to be planned to arrest the falling trend in prices in the peak marketing season and in areas where surplus of these crops is located. The authorities in charge of procurement must keep a very careful watch on the market trends and bring their best judgement to bear on the supply situations in those areas so that they know when to stop acquiring stocks.

On the distribution side, it is obvious that these grains will not command an all-India market ; the consumer acceptance is limited in respect of these grains and the stocks will, therefore, have to be kept in areas where they are the staple food of the people. Their disposal should be first in priority and if the use of these stocks is planned judiciously in combination with the National Rural Employment Programme, the disposal will be quick and the chances of losses will be minimal.

PROCUREMENT AND NREP

The need for intensifying price support operations with respect to coarse grains and the decision that the NREP need not be financed only out of the central stocks having been taken, have brought about a situation where a policy frame for linking the two must be urgently devised. Happily, the aims and objectives of these two vital state activities are complementary and mutually reinforcing. To tie up the NREP (to the extent possible) with procurement by states would not only give a boost to the coarse grains economy but would also put NREP on a sound and enduring base.

These arrangements are doubly necessary now so as to compel the state governments to take upon themselves a certain measure of responsibility in regard to procurement and storage of foodgrains. It has been the lesson of every scarcity, reinforced by the crisis created by the 1979 and 1982 drought, that the states must shoulder responsibility in regard to procurement and stocking of foodgrains. It is, therefore, necessary that all these three elements, namely the necessity of organizing price support operations in respect of coarse grains, requirements of the NREP and activating the states to get involved in the procurement operations, are fully integrated and woven into a definite pattern to be adopted throughout the country.

All these considerations suggest that the price support operations and distribution of coarse grains would best be done by the state agencies with the necessary support of the central government insofar as provision of finance, storage, and movement is concerned. Such an integrated and harmonious management of food economy should be the ideal which the administrators of food in this country should strive to achieve.

ACTION PLAN

The starting point in designing this policy frame is the states' commitment to organize procurement of coarse grains. Haryana, Punjab, Rajasthan, Madhya Pradesh, Gujarat, Maharashtra, Karnataka and Andhra Pradesh would be the principal states in this common striving. They must chart out the areas which have surplus of these grains and where, in the peak season, prices tend to fall below the support level. The state civil supplies corporations and the cooperative institutions must enter the market and undertake price support operations.

Storage of the grains will have to be carefully planned. The stocks should be moved to areas which, after the season is over, become deficient and would need the supplies. Also, certain centrally located places in areas where the NREP is under way may also be stocked with these foodgrains. Because of their poor keeping quality, it would be necessary to dispose of the stocks within 10 to 12 months of their acquisition. If, to begin with, the states set a target roughly equivalent to the allocations under the NREP, it would be a good commencement. In order that the state agencies do not run into losses at the very outset of these operations, it may be prudent to tailor the procurement operations to the annual requirements of the public distribution system and the NREP. If, for reasons of bumper harvests, larger quantities have necessarily to be procured, the question of take over of surplus quantities in the central pool will have to be considered.

It is not being suggested that the NREP be hinged entirely to the states' stocks. The core of the model suggested herein is, that to the extent states can procure foodgrains locally and consume them, they should become self-reliant ; for the rest, the stocks will be supplied from the central pool. It must be remembered that the basic objective of the NREP is to combine the food component with the work programmes of the various departments, using them as channels for reaching foodgrains to the interior areas and to make them available to the rural poor. This strategy is being suggested not only to improve the distribution aspect of the policy, but also to broadbase the present system of procurement. In this manner alone, can the coarse grains economy be linked with the buffer stocking policy of the central government in a constructive manner.

SCHEME OF LAW

Before putting forth suggestions for modifying the system, its legal framework may briefly be explained.

In 1964, the central government enacted the Food Corporations Act. The FCI was constituted under Section 3 of this Act as a statutory corporation. Section 17 contains a provision to the effect that the central government may, by notification in the official Gazette and after consultations with the government of a state, establish a Food Corporation for that state.

Section 18 deals with the capital structure of the State Food Corporations and is reproduced below :

"(1) The capital of a State Food Corporation shall be such sum not exceeding ten crores of rupees as the central government may, after consultation with the Food Corporation of India, fix.

"(2) The central government may, after such consultation from time to time increase the capital of the State Food Corporation to such extent and in such manner as that government may determine.

"(3) Such capital shall be provided—

"(a) by the central government after due appropriation made by Parliament by law for the purpose ; and

"(b) by the Food Corporation of India, in such proportion and subject to such terms and conditions as may be determined by the central government."

From a plain reading of this Section, it appears that States Food Corporations are envisaged as subsidiaries of the FCI. The power to constitute the board of directors of these corporations, the appointment of the chairman and general manager, their terms and conditions and their removal or disqualification—all these powers vest in the FCI. This scheme at first sight would appear to be somewhat akin to the one suggested earlier but in fact is materially different in one respect, namely it envisages a kind of vertical integration of the Food Corporation at the centre and those in the states—the latter being a kind of regional organization of the former. In such an arrangement, in the opinion of the present writer, the sense of participation and involvement of the states is completely absent. No system in which the active participation and involvement of the states is not secured would work in the field of food administration.

STATE CORPORATIONS

The events as they developed after the passing of this Act, vindicate this point. The state governments of U.P., West Bengal, Tamil Nadu, Punjab, Madhya Pradesh, Kerala, Andhra Pradesh, Karnataka and Bihar have established civil supplies corporations, not under the aforesaid Act but under the Companies Act of 1956. They have all been set up as government companies and are beyond the purview of the Food Corporations Act. Understandably, the state governments would not approve of a system in which a corporation operating within their boundaries and handling a vital commodity like foodgrains passes under complete control of the Central Food Corporation and the only role they have to play in the constitution or running of that Corporation is routine consultation by the Central Food Corporation in matters relating to the appointment of the chairman, the general manager, and other members of the board of directors. It must at all times be borne in mind that, in a federal system such as ours, the states would resent any move which they feel would inhibit their authority within their own sphere. Only that system would work which commands the largest area of common consent and which has been devised after adjusting all the contending claims and interests and whose foundations are laid on understanding, goodwill, and give and take. The model that is being suggested in this chapter is most likely to answer the requirements of the system needed to implement the present food policy.

THE NEW ARRANGEMENT AND ITS ADVANTAGES

The administrative structure required to give effect to the modified system would be that the FCI which is a statutory Corporation should convert itself into a holding company within the meaning of section 4 of the Companies Act, 1956. The State Civil Supplies Corporations which are also government companies set up by the state governments should be the subsidiaries of this company. The subsidiaries should fully integrate with the holding company and since these would be government companies at the centre and the states, it would be possible to achieve the requisite degree of coordination in the matter of day-to-day operations. The board of directors of the State Corporations should be headed by the State Food Minister, with representatives of the food, finance, and cooperation departments at the official level. Distinguished and reputed non-officials, having the background and experience of trade and commerce may also be nominated on the board, as indeed would be the nominees of the holding company. The broad policy to be followed by the subsidiaries in the matter of purchases and sales, securing finances and important matters relating to their functioning within the policy guidelines of the central government - all these shall be prescribed by the Central government and the national level company. Thus it will be possible to achieve a harmonious and integrated working of the corporation at the Central and State levels.

The advantages of such a system would be as follows :

(a) a greater degree of cohesion and coordination would be achieved between the centre and the states in the management of the food economy ;

(b) a greater control in the financial and administrative matters would pass on to the centre which would naturally be anxious to ensure proper functioning of the state corporations and their financial viability. The stakes of the state governments, at the same time, would also be there because the state minister would be the chairman of the board of directors and the state governments would be holding shares in them. The day to day control and management would be under the direct supervision of the state governments, which will then feel fully responsible for the success of the operations undertaken. In other words, the involvement of the state governments would be total ;

(c) The Government of India and the central agency would be relieved of the bothersome responsibility of command and control over the staff spread throughout the country and engaged in an operation which ought to be of direct concern to the states ;

(d) the effectiveness of the FCI would be greater and its impact on the market as well as on private trade would be very considerable. Food administration will then move as one machinery well oiled and well directed ;

(e) the decision taken by the Board would, truly speaking, be the decisions of both the central as well as the state governments imbued with realism ;

(f) both vertical as well as horizontal integration would be achieved resulting in all round saving of expenditure and effort. Financial discipline would also be enforced inasmuch as funds would flow through one artery from top to bottom, with one integrated organisation to account for them ; and

(g) procurement and distribution of foodgrains and regulation of the market would be done better.

DISTRIBUTION NETWORK

This structural integration would surely result in a rationalized and harmonized purchase arrangement. On the distribution side such an integration is all the more necessary. Where supply of an essential commodity is involved, prudence demands that the entire responsibility should not be entrusted to only one agency. Alternative channels should be available so that in case one fails, supplies can be maintained through others. The State civil supplies corporations and the cooperative network should, in the like manner, as in procurement, be pressed into the distribution function as well. At present, this system is being worked through certain practices which have been evolved over the years. Many decades ago, when large stocks of foodgrains started moving on government account, a number of storage depots came up at important junctions as well as at terminal rail points. These came to be known as central storage depots where bulk of the stocks are kept. From here the stocks are moved to slightly smaller depots in different parts of the states, the location of these being again chiefly determined by convenience of rail-road connections. Up to these points, movement takes place on central account. Movement beyond these points is treated as distribution and is accordingly charged to the states. In the case of West Bengal the position is somewhat different inasmuch as the grain is stocked even at third level points, which are generally at *tehsil* and block levels. Ever since the 1943 famine which ravaged this state most disastrously, and the deficit character of the state having persisted all through, a wide ranging network of storage/distribution points has been laid which, as the convention goes, is fed by the central agency. Such an extensive network run by the national agency does not exist in any other state and this is one question which comes up frequently in policy discussions and reviews.

In course of time, the problem of hill areas also came to notice and a system has been evolved under which the local administration is reimbursed the transport costs from the nearest central storage point to the pre-determined distribution point(s) in these states. This system is prevalent in the north-eastern region and Himachal Pradesh. Likewise there is the case of vast and sprawling states like Rajasthan and Madhya Pradesh where large expanse of desert, extensive forests and uninhabited areas, separate human habitations. Reaching foodgrains to these areas involve long leads entailing transportation costs. The problem is akin to that of hill areas though the complexion is somewhat different. Yet the principles applied to the latter are not applied to the former for which there does not seem to be any justification.

The time has come when it is necessary to put this area of food administration on a proper footing. The areas of responsibility between the centre and the states should be clearly defined. The national buffer is, at all times, to be held by the central agency, namely the FCI and all costs connected with it are to be borne by the central government. However, in regard to the operational stocks, which represent the quantities needed by the states from month to month, it should be possible to work out a system in which the states, after procuring them locally, hold them and feed their public distribution system in accordance with the allocations made by the central government. To begin with, an attempt should be made to pass on these stocks to the states at least on quarterly basis, though the ideal would be that six months operational stocks should be held by the states. Physical movement of stocks should not always be necessary to give effect to this scheme ; appropriate book adjustments may be carried out and the stock position reflected accordingly. In this way the states will feel responsible for managing the food economy. The financial burden will also get distributed between the centre and the states in an equitable manner.

It should be obvious that movement of stocks to the storage depots throughout the country is a continuous process and stocking of foodgrains cannot be done on any artificial basis treating them as the central buffer or as operational stocks meant for the needs of the states. The debate as to which and how many points should be designated as the central storage depots and which ones should be declared as points for retail distribution will be interminable. The only workable formula is that the transportation, distribution, and handling costs relative to the stocks sold within the state should be debited to the state account, and the rest to the central account. As stated earlier, the only rational arrangement would be that the states assume responsibility for the storage, transportation, and distribution of the stocks representing operational stocks. Where central agencies like the FCI, Central Warehousing Corporation, etc. are already handling the stocks, it may not be necessary to physically transfer them to the states ; only the appropriate debits may be raised.

INTEGRATED WORKING

The operational requirements of the management of the food economy and those of the NREP are inexorably creating compulsions necessitating a thoroughly integrated system of procurement and distribution. Where in pursuance of the central policy, the states undertake price support operations and procure stocks, the central government cannot disown its responsibility when it comes to a question of their disposal. Only through an integrated working of the centre and the states, would the costs incurred on procurement, storage, and disposal of foodgrains be kept to the minimum. In a lean year when large scale relief operations are organised such an integration of the central and the State operations would be inevitable.

Thus, in all conceivable situations, the administration of the food economy—both procurement as well as distribution—has to be vertically and horizontally integrated. Vertical integration would mean integration between the centre and the states as explained in the foregoing paragraphs. Horizontal coordination would mean parity between the prices and procurement of different kinds of foodgrains and maintaining equitable supplies to all areas, deficit and surplus. This point may be illustrated by citing the example of operations conducted in Madhya Pradesh in the lean years of 1973 and 1974. In both the years the paddy crop in the entire eastern region—traditionally known as the rice bowl of the state—suffered severe damage from drought. But by that curious yet merciful dispensation of nature in the trials and tribulations of human beings, the *jowar* (sorghum) and maize crops in the western belt matured very well and a normal crop was harvested. While procurement yielded meagre stocks in the east, it was enforced vigorously in the west, and the *jowar* and maize stocks were rushed to the scarcity areas of the east and thus the calamity was averted. This approach proved a boon in every respect : while on the one hand, the procurement of coarse grains gave the much needed buoyancy to their prices, it, on the other, yielded precious and sorely needed foodgrains for a region inhabited by nearly 12 million human beings.

PART B

U.S. SYSTEM OF FARMERS HELD RESERVE

THE SYSTEM EXPLAINED

The United States has evolved a new system under which grain reserves are largely held by the farmers themselves. A set of economic stimuli are designed to work in a manner that govern and regulate the offloading of stocks onto the market. Through the Food and Agriculture Act of 1977, the accumulation and release of buffer stock of grain has been given a legal sanction that shifts the emphasis from publicly-held to privately-held stocks. Mr. Gary L. Benjamin,* has estimated that from 1950 to 1976, privately-held carry over stocks in the United States varied from 19 million to 55 million tonnes (average 35 million tonnes) while the stocks held by the government touched the peak level of 85 million tonnes in 1961 (average 32 million tonnes).

For many decades the United States has been working through the loan programme administered by the Commodity Credit Corporation, an agency under the U.S. Department of Agriculture. Stated briefly, a farmer in the United States has the option to obtain a loan from this Corporation against his stocks. The loan rate and the period for which it can be had by the farmer are prescribed by the government. Depending on the market prices, the farmer can repay the loan plus interest at any point of time within the maturity period and retain ownership as well as control on his stocks, or on maturity default in the repayment of loan and surrender the stocks to the corporation.

During the fifties loan rates were generally higher than the average market prices. Further, there was no mechanism by which the production could be controlled. The net result was that the stocks with the commodity corporation swelled to a record figure of 85 million tonnes in 1961.

In the sixties, the US government introduced certain measures, the chief among them being the "set-aside", with a view to rationalizing land utilization for growing foodgrains and feedgrains. The

'Economic Perspectives' Volume 2, Issue 6—Nov. Dec. 1978 published by the Federal Reserve Bank of Chicago.

loan rate was also slightly scaled down. Simultaneously, exports under the "Food for Peace" programme were stepped up. The cumulative effect of all these measures was that the stocks with the government at the end of the decade came down substantially. Finally, the three-year scarcity spell in the first-half of the seventies depleted the US stocks almost completely by 1974.

THE 1977 ACT

The commodity loan mechanism has been defined in the 1977 Act which regulates the reserve programme and encourages the farmers to hold the grain stocks through a set of economic stimuli. The farmers-held grain reserve programme is basically different from the resale programme practised in the earlier years. The basic idea behind the former is to isolate grain from the market when supplies are large and prices are low, until prices rise to a more profitable level. The farmers retain ownership of their grain but if they release it before its value reaches a certain higher price level, they have to pay a penalty. The old resale programme, on the other hand, was designed as a stop-gap measure to avoid taking large quantities of grains into CCC inventories when prices were at or near the price support loan level. In this arrangement, grain was not isolated from the market, since farmers could offer it for sale at any time.

The basic objectives of the farmers-held reserve programme are:

(a) to strengthen farm prices when the supplies are excessive;
(b) to contain fluctuations in the prices of foodgrains and combat inflation;
(c) to protect the growers of foodgrains from increase in feed costs;
(d) to ensure greater continuity in foreign food aid ; and
(e) to maintain the position of the US as a pre-eminent exporter of foodgrains by assuring dependable sources of supplies and thereby securing further growth of overseas market for U.S. farm produce.

This system of farmers-held reserve is, in terms of historical evolution, a logical development flowing from the system of set-aside introduced more than a decade ago. In fact the former has come as a complementary mechanism for realizing the aims of the latter. A brief description of this system is given below.

Set-Aside

Means that the participating farmers agree to withhold from production an area equal to a percentage of the acres planted for harvest, including areas harvested on voluntary basis. This is a key requirement because eligibility for loans and payments is contingent on compliance with set-aside provisions.

Approved cover

The farmers agree to comply with the criteria set by the State Agricultural Stabilization and Conservation Committee in regard to the type of vegetation or conservation practice approved for set-aside areas. This programme is designed to control erosion of land by wind and water. Plantings of soyabeans and sweet sorghum are excluded under this practice.

Normal crop acreage (NCA)

This is determined by taking into consideration the total number of acres normally planted with the following crops, namely barley, corn, dry edible beans, flax, oats, rice, rye, sorghum, soyabeans, sugarbeets, sugarcane, sunflowers, upland cotton, and wheat. Other crops may be included as recommended by the State ASC Committee with the approval of the ASCS Deputy Administrator for State and County Operations (DASCO). In any set-aside programme, the total acreage of these crops planted on a farm plus that set-aside cannot exceed a farm's normal crop acreage.

Cross compliance

This requires a farmer to comply with both set-aside and the normal crop acreage requirements in order to become eligible for loans and payments on other crops included in his farm's normal crop acreage.

Offsetting compliance

This provision requires that the farmers participating in a set-aside programme shall not offset the reduction in production on the farms listed in the programme by increasing production on farms not listed under this programme.

Coming back to the farmers-held system, the following are the significant provisions of the 1977 Act. First, under section 101 limitations for all payments received on wheat, feedgrains, and upland cotton have been laid down. These are $45,000 in 1978, $45,000 in 1979 and $50,000 for 1980 and 1981. Next, section 401 lays down the loans and purchase rates at which the farmers can obtain loans against their stocks from the CCC or at which their stocks shall be purchased by the CCC. These rates are determined so as to maintain the parity and competitive relationship to other grains in domestic and export markets. Target prices which are supposed to represent remunerative levels which, in the judgement of the Secretary of Agriculture, the farmers should get in the open market, have also been prescribed. Farmers who participate in the set-aside programme agree to store their grain for a specific period of time until the price reaches this predetermined higher market level. In return the farmers receive a price support loan on their grain plus annual storage payments. In addition, if the grain has been in store for one year, interest is also waived or adjusted. Computation of payments under this programme is done by multiplying (i) the payment rate, and (ii) the farm programme acreage for the crop, by (iii) the farm programme payment yield for the crop. Thirdly, Sec. 402 deals with the programme acreages, payment yields, and set-aside programmes. The Secretary of Agriculture has the power to require, as a condition of loans, purchases and payments, that the acreage normally planted to the crops designated by the Secretary must be reduced by the amount of the set-aside or diversion. The Secretary is authorized to offer wheat and feedgrain producers an extended loan programme of 3 to 5 years duration. Finally, the quantity of wheat held under the farmer-held reserve shall not be less than three hundred million nor more than seven hundred million bushels.

TRIGGER POINTS

There are three trigger points in this mechanism tied to two prevailing loan support rates. The first being the accumulation point, which starts with the farmers signifying their willingness to participate in the reserve programme, when the market conditions are such that the farmer is encouraged to hold the stocks against commodity loans and withhold them from being offered in the market. Besides the loan, CCC also pays the farmer storage charges for holding the stocks. In addition, if the stocks continue to be in reserve for a year, interest on the loan is remitted. There is a further incentive in the shape of giving loans to the farmers for building or repairing storage capacity for holding grain production of two years.

The second trigger is the release price which is determined when the national average market price reaches 125 per cent of the then current national average loan rate for feedgrains or 140 per cent of the then current national average loan rate for wheat. At this stage, a farmer has three options:

(i) Pay off the reserve loan and sell the grain;
(ii) leave it in the reserve ; or
(iii) pay off the loan and hold the grain.

If the market price remains above the release price for more than a month, storage payments to the farmers are stopped. Early redemption before the release level is reached invites penalty. In that eventuality the farmers have to repay all storage payments plus interest, in addition to the original loan payment and interest. Above all these, there is a condition that minimum repayment must equal a price level of the per bushel release price of the grain multiplied with the quantity redeemed.

The third point is the call price trigger. At the 'call' level—when the national average market price reaches 140 per cent of the then current national average loan rate for feedgrain or 175 per cent of the then current national average loan rate for wheat—reserve loans are called by CCC. This means the farmers have 30 days after the call either to redeem the reserve loan or forfeit their grain to CCC. However, even after the farmers satisfy their loans at call, they are under no obligation to sell their grain. They can continue to hold the grain in storage for still higher prices.

At the inception of the reserve, the Secretary of Agriculture declared it his policy not to allow grain held in government inventories to be sold unless prices exceeded the call levels. This was an assurance to the farmers that government stocks would not be sold at a price which might affect the market to their detriment. The various rates in 1979 were as follows :

($ *per bushel*)

	Wheat	*Corn*
Loan rates	2.33	2.00
Release levels	3.29	2.50
Call levels	4.11	2.80

The minimum CCC sales prices for reserve commodities were 180 and 150 per cent of loan for wheat and feedgrains.

There is a further provision to take care of transportation problems. Prior to the repayment dateline, the employees of the county offices of the Department's Agricultural Stabilization and Conservation Service (ASCS) make an assessment to determine if it is physically possible for individual farmers to deliver their farm stored commodities. In areas where there is no commercial storage or adequate transportation, county agricultural stabilization and conservation committees are authorized to grant additional 30-day periods for farmers to repay their reserve loans for farm-stored crops. If transportation and storage problems persist, the department employees will make additional assessments at 30-day intervals to determine if a further 30-day extension should be offered.

REORGANIZATION OF THE SYSTEM

On January 7, 1980, following the suspension of grain shipments to the Soviet Union, changes were made in the 'call' and 'release' levels. In October, 1980, in order to identify major policy changes that require farmers to sign new reserve agreements with ASCS, the reserve was labeled Reserve I, Reserve II and Reserve III. Major changes were introduced in the release and call levels, loan rates, storage payments and in the redemption time. Reserve I consisted of the commodities entered before January 7, 1980. Reserve II came into effect from 7th January and Reserve III from August 25, 1980. The position about the loan rates and the release and call levels as revised is summarised in Table A.

The Agriculture and Food Act of 1981 (P.L. 97-98) brought about major changes in the system inasmuch as minimum target prices to serve as 'protection price' for each of the crop years from 1982 through 1985 were prescribed as shown in Table B.

Table A

(price in $ per bushel)

Rates/Levels		Reserve I		Reserve II		Reserve III	
		Percent	Price	Percent	Price	Percent	Price
Loan	Wheat				2.50		3.00*
	Corn			—	2.10		2.25*
Release	Wheat	140	4.20	150	4.50	140	4.20
	Corn	125	2.81	125	2.81	125	2.81
Call	Wheat	175	5.25	185	5.55	175	5.25
	Corn	140	3.15	145	3.26	145	3.26

*revised to 3.55 and 2.55 w.e.f. 22nd December, 1981.

Table B

($ per bushel)

	1982	1983	1984	1985
Wheat	4.05	4.30	4.45	4.65
Corn	2.70	2.86	3.03	3.18

Minimum loan rates for the four year period have also been laid down. The Act provides three options for adjusting production : (1) a set-aside programme for wheat and feedgrains, (2) crop-specific, reduced acreage programmes for these crops as well as for cotton and rice, and (3) a paid acreage diversion programme for wheat, feedgrains, cotton and rice. Participation in the set-aside or reduced acreage programmes is a condition of eligibility for price support. This Act gives the Secretary flexibility to determine when farmers can withdraw their grain from the farmer-owned grain reserve, and when withdrawals should be encouraged by ending storage payments or increasing interest rates. The Secretary has the authority to waive or adjust interest payments on reserve loans. Reserve loan rates are also at the Secretary's discretion, except that they cannot be lower than rates for regular commodity loans. The Secretary can set a limit on the quantum of grain in the reserve, but not less than 700 million bushels of wheat and one billion bushels of feedgrains which limits are much higher than those fixed under the 1977 Act. The law bars sales of government-owned grain at less than 110 per cent of the reserve trigger price.*

*Farm Program Fact Sheet, January 1982. United States Department of Agriculture—Agricultural Stabilization and Conservation Service.

RELEVANCE TO INDIA

This system of holding the grain reserves is another model for consideration in the context of the domestic or international food security system. But before any views are expressed on its applicability to India, comments made by Benjamin may briefly be quoted here. He thinks that this new system is designed "partly to constrain the volatility in grain prices." In other words, the depression in the foodgrain prices by ever-increasing production in the United States is an important problem that the US government seeks to tackle by means of this system. But according to him the government costs in running this system could be very substantial. Excluding the international wheat reserve which the government has to directly purchase and store, the farmers-held reserve of 28 to 30 million tonnes would involve an outlay of \$ 275 million in storage payments alone, after the stocks have been in reserve for a year, waiver of the interest charges would add another \$ 150 million. These would be the net annual government costs, besides the loan funds advanced by CCC. He has also pointed out that studies show that on-farm storage which the system definitely encourages, will be less economical than commerical storage, thus multiplying the social costs.

There are fundamental differences between the US and Indian systems in approach and mechanics. Whereas in the United States the main problem is to regulate production in a manner that will not upset the market prices and supplies, in India the policy of building up a buffer stock has been adopted in the light of the experience of scarcities. The approach in the United States is basically producer-oriented, while in India the objective is to make minimum quantities of foodgrain available to consumers at all times.

The aim in US is not only to maintain the price level in the domestic market but also to sustain her export market of both the foodgrains and feedgrains. India has not yet become an exporting country on a sustained basis, though in the past few years some commodity loans have been given to Vietnam, Bangladesh, Afghanistan, Pakistan, Nepal and Mauritius. The most significant transaction, in the export of grain has been the return of 2.0 million tonnes of wheat loan given to us by USSR in 1973-74. Nevertheless these exports represent one time transactions.

The US mechanism is highly complicated and sophisticated and is incapable of being adopted in India. The heart of the mechanism lies in the set-aside programme by which food grains production is regulated. The producers in the United States are well organized and have the economic capability of regulating their production in the manner determined by the Secretary of Agriculture, which is chiefly guided by an assessment as to how the market is going to behave in future. Planting of crops is increased or decreased accordingly and the administration undertakes to compensate the farmers in case they are induced to reduce the area under food crops. Commodity loans on a massive scale are also made available to the farmers. In India, on the other hand, agriculture is practised as an industry by an infinitesimally small proportion of farmers ; for almost 95 per cent of the farmers it is a means of subsistance. It is, therefore, totally impracticable to think that the Indian farmers could be persuaded to adopt the system of set-aside which is an integral part of the U.S. mechanism. Nor, in the circumstances of this country's agriculture, would it be feasible to think of introducing such a system.

The US system is workable because of the efficient storage and the supporting infrastructure that exists in that country. It is because of this infrastructure that the US farmers can store and withhold stocks for two to three years. These facilities are woefully lacking in India. The farmers, by and large, store the grain in the traditional manner which does not promise the health of grain for more than a few months. This is particularly true of wheat and coarse grains which are susceptible to infestation very fast. The farmers who have the marketable surplus, therefore, are inclined to dispose of the stocks as soon as they can. The storage facilities even with government agencies and arrangements for prophylactic treatment of stocks are quite inadequate and the attempt is always to turnover the stocks as quickly as possible.

To make commodity loans available to the farmers for the stocks produced by them would be totally beyond the resources of the government. In our system whatever is offered for sale in the market at the support price is purchased by the public agencies. During the agricultural years 1978-79 and 1982-83, the price support purchases of both rice and wheat were record ones, yet they accounted for only 12-14 and 20-25 per cent of the total production. For procuring these quantities the public agencies were financed to the extent of over Rs. 2032 and 3033 crores* by the commercial banks on the guarantee of the central government. The remaining produce still finds its financing through private trade channels. Clearly, the type of financing CCC does in the United States is unthinkable in India.

In the past when the stocks with public agencies had gone above the twenty million tonnes mark, a section of public opinion argued that not an insignificant part of the inflation was owing to these stocks. Purely on narrow considerations, there is substance in this argument. If the government were to finance even a small proportion of the stocks left with the producers, the money requirements would be so staggering that the inflationary spiral would soar very high. In fact, the government has not relaxed the curbs on credit availability for financing the foodgain trade despite powerful and persistent lobbying from the interested quarters. The type and magnitude of financing operations CCC does in U.S. are obviously impracticable in India at the present juncture.

*Ten million make a crore.

PART C

INSURANCE CONCEPT

THE CONCEPT EXPLAINED

Yet one more system of domestic food security is conceivable which could operate with the support of the international food security system. The first World Food Conference held in Rome in 1974 adopted, among others, a resolution requiring the governments to adopt an International Undertaking on World Food Security and invited the governments to enter into discussions to study the feasibility of establishing grain reserves at strategic points.

Collective effort—the core of the insurance philosophy—to safeguard against anticipated calamities is the central point of this system. In other words, the system is supported by a world financing institution like the International Monetary Fund by providing monetary reserves to be drawn upon when imports are to be resorted to. This is an important innovative approach and was enlarged in 1981. In a recent review it was found that under this mechanism credits of SDRs 300 million had been made available to five developing countries. Drawing on this facility, however, is restricted by the country's credit standing with IMF, and there are obvious limitations in borrowing money to finance current consumption.*

Another arrangement could be where a number of countries pledge a specified quantity of grain reserve for the use of deficit countries in times of need. The new international wheat agreement with substantive economic provisions and trigger mechanism that has been under negotiation for the past few years is the broad framework of such a system. However, it has not yet found favour with the exporting countries.

STUDY BY I.F.P.R.I.

The International Food Policy Research Institute, Washington, has published a study** on the insurance approach to the problem of food security. This study makes a reference to Gale Johnson's proposal

---

*FAO Document CFS : 83/4, December 1982.

**Research Report 4—Food Security : An Insurance Approach by Panos Konandreas, Barbara Huddleston and Virabongsa Ramangkura International Food Policy Rasearch Institute, Washington, USA. September 1978.

of a food insurance scheme under which the developed and developing exporting countries would undertake to provide cover for the developing importing countries in the case of shortfall in production "below a given percentage of their production trends." The International Monetary Fund would arrange to make the requisite foreign exchange available to the country(s) when needed to import foodgrains, above a certain quantity. But this concept was considered insufficient in a situation where shortfall in production may not be occurring but foodgrain prices in the world market may be reaching such high levels that the import bills of the deficit countries go on mounting and which these countries may not be able to afford. During 1978 and 1979 despite comfortable levels of food production in the world, prices were continuously going up and the market did not seem to stabilize. Even if the scarce foreign exchange resources were made available to the importing countries for expending them on import of foodgrains, it has been pointed out by the study, their economic development would be so considerably retarded that the remedy may prove worse than the malady.

The study follows the approach adopted by Shlomo Reutlinger who has redefined food insecurity in the developing countries in terms of foreign exchange requirements for import of foodgrains to sustain consumption at the given level. The study adopts some further refinements to this, viz., a five-year time frame, focusing attention on individual countries instead of studying a group of countries and specific operating rules to be observed at the country level. Of this approach, two variants have been formulated (i) a compensatory financing mechanism and (ii) a combined foodgrain reserve and compensatory financing mechanism. Under the former mechanism the system provides a member-country with funds necessary to cover overruns in its cereal import bill. Recipient countries use these funds to import food to meet their consumption targets. Briefly stated, the system operates thus—if in a year food production in a country falls short of the adjusted demand compelling it to import foodgrains, and if the import bill is less than a certain percentage of the trend import bill, the country would receive no compensation or assistance. But in a year when the domestic production is low and the world prices are high resulting in a substantially higher import bill which is more than the trend import bill by a specified percentage, the country would receive the compensation from the system equivalent to the difference between the actual import bill and the trend import bill.

COMPENSATORY FINANCING MECHANISM

The study has prepared simulated models of the variants for estimating the cost and distribution of benefits. Sixty-five developing importing countries have been listed and their aggregate projected demand, trend production, trend import, and import variability of food deficit have been worked out. From these the probability distributions of the total cost of the scheme operating purely as a compensatory financing mechanism for the five-year period (1978-1982) and for the middle year (1980) have been computed. The study concludes, "The striking finding from this analysis is that the total costs of operating the system at various grain levels are not significantly different. Thus, criteria other than expected costs should determine the choice of the appropriate size of the grain reserve, if any. One such criterion is how well the presence of grain in the system raises the physical availability of grain in every member country to 95 per cent of trend production during very high price years." The study comes to a finding that while an eight million tonnes reserve achieves 77.5 per cent probability of every member country receiving the supplies in the first year, a reserve level of 20 million tonnes provides as high a guarantee as 98.5 per cent probability of satisfying the objective in the first year and 62.5 per cent in 1982. It has been found that the larger the grain reserve, the lower cost of compensatory financing components. The study also analyses the costs of the scheme under alternative rules of operation with different sets of assumptions.

The study has compiled estimates of cereal production trends and variability from the trend in respect of India for the period 1960-1975 and after applying the annual growth rate, the income elasticity of demands, the per capita trend consumption (163 kg. per person per year) and projecting the population for the period 1975-85, came to the conclusion that in a combined grain reserve of 20 million tonnes and the compensatory financing mechanism, India would get 16.88 per cent share in compensatory financing and 32.81 per cent share in the grain reserve. The study came to the conclusion that the share of India in this scheme is so substantial that it makes the whole scheme somewhat skewed. In fact it has observed that the trend of the world market prices of foodgrains is largely influenced by the level of production in India and the quantities that may be imported by it for meeting its consumption requirements. This study is based on the world price situation as it obtained in 1977 and 1978.

In the case of a combined grain reserve and compensatory finance mechanism, the system operates on the basis of the trigger price at which the international finance would be available for acquiring stocks, subject to the general condition that the world grain market is not interfered with materially. The study comes to the conclusion that the compensatory mechanism simplicitor might ultimately mean a greater strain on the commodity market, pushing up the prices and entailing greater cost-burdens on the importing countries. A combined grain reserve system backed by the compensatory financing mechanism would, in the opinion of the authors, provide a more cost effective way of achieving the same objective.

At this point both this approach and the draft of the new international wheat agreement meet in their essentials. The central idea incorporated in the Draft Wheat Trade Convention is that the exporting and importing countries shall hold a certain quantity of grain reserves which in their totality would be called the World Foodgrain Reserve to be deployed when the foodgrain supplies fall short of the demand. The operational mechanism of this reserve is tied to a set of price levels which are supposed to act as triggers, bringing the mechanism into operation at the appropriate time. The draft agreement prepared by a drafting committee for the Negotiating Conference set up by UNCTAD provided that, within a specified band of prices which are called lower and upper points, the international wheat trade shall operate freely and through normal market channels. Then there is the first falling point and the first rising point, on reaching which the representatives of the World Community on the executive committee of the International Wheat Council will meet and review the situation and decide upon the measures to be taken in the event of the price on the indicator scale rising or falling further. Upon the price touching the second point on the rising side, release of some stocks on the market should take place. On the falling side the accumulation of stocks by the governments shall normally come into operation. Finally, there is the third falling and the third rising point when the world foodgrain reserve should completely become operational.

COMPARISON WITH INDIAN SYSTEM

Speaking purely from the conceptual standpoint, India's buffer stocking policy is basically an insurance approach. The buffer stock is kept as an insurance against diminution in supplies in times of falling production. The compensatory financing mechanism simplicitor would not suit a country like India. In times of scarcities the situation will surely be aggravated by rising price phenomenon. Availability of funds whether on bilateral basis or from the world financial institutions, would not enable the deficit countries to procure food supplies. Assurance of funds does not necessarily mean certainty of obtaining supplies and therefore this mechanism cannot be trusted to achieve the objectives which the buffer stocking policy of a country like India serves. The inevitable conclusion, therefore, is that a combined system in which a grain reserve is buttressed by the compensatory finance mechanism is the ideal solution for both domestic and international food security.

No system of food security can work without the back up of foodgrain reserves. But the question of choosing wise and judicious price triggers is of such crucial relevance to this system that its very success depends on them. The purpose of this system is to protect the humanity—particularly in the most seriously affected countries—from the harmful effects of fluctuations in supplies and prices. When one talks of rising or falling price points, one is unconsciously thinking of certain quantitative levels which are considered necessary or desirable for accumulating or releasing stocks onto the market to achieve the desired objectives. A true votary of the market system may find such an approach irrational or even unacceptable. But the fact remains that food price is one subject about which the world community is seriously concerned and is trying to lay down a mechanism which may insure it against abnormal fluctuations. This, as stated earlier, is the objective of the Indian policy as well and therefore, the efforts that are being made in the various fora such as FAO, UNCTAD and the International Wheat Council have our support. As a matter of fact the objective of the Indian system goes farther than the purely insurance approach. It aims at protecting the vulnerable sections of society from abnormal fluctuations in the food supply as well as market prices at all times. With a high degree of underemployment and unemployment and with a sizable population below the poverty line, the necessity of a public distribution system as is being run in this country is both an urgent social necessity as well as an economic need. This system which subserves larger social objectives, has been evolved and perfected over a number of years and has come to stay.

PART THREE

WORLD DIMENSIONS OF FOOD SECURITY

15

World Dimensions of Food Security : Evolution of the International Buffer Policy

EARLY BEGINNINGS

In this chapter an attempt will be made briefly to trace the relationship of the Indian policy on buffer stocking with the evolution of a comparable model on the international scene. It is indeed remarkable that the final stage in the development of the Indian policy was reached almost at the same time and in similar circumstances when the FAO initiated action for evolving a world food security system. This phenomenon represents Tolstoy's 'contemporaneous connection' in the development of human institutions.

The alarming depletion of cereal stocks of the major exporting countries since 1972 focussed attention of the world community on the important question of maintaining an adequate stock of foodgrains throughout the year. Earlier these countries had bumper harvests leading to accumulation of stocks and consequent depression in prices. This necessitated a re-examination on the part of the member nations of their stockholding policies. We have already discussed how the United States—the biggest exporter of foodgrains—modified the CCC operations and devised the farmers-held reserve system in the wake of mounting surpluses. At the same time, the FAO stressed the urgency of an assurance of adequate availability of food as the common responsibility of the international community.

D.G.'S PROPOSALS ON INTERNATIONAL UNDERTAKING

While putting forth his proposal for a world system of food security, the Director General of the FAO had observed in June 1973 that it was "a common responsibility of the entire international community to assure an adequate availability of basic food stuffs not only on humanitarian grounds, but also for the economic and social stability of the world." To translate this responsibility, he suggested that the countries :

(a) undertake to adopt national stock holding policies;
(b) undertake to review or establish national stock policies for cereals and to set targets for national stocks and maintain them at those levels;
(c) hold consultations on the adequacy of the stock levels and on short-term action; and
(d) undertake an international programme to extend and coordinate assistance to developing countries.

The seventeenth session of the FAO conference held in November 1973 supported the Director General's initiative and referred the draft international undertaking to a working party on world food security which met in May 1974 and finalized the draft. The Council of FAO at its 63rd session (July 1974) endorsed the undertaking and authorized the Director General to make it available to the World Food Conference. (See the Appendix).

WORLD FOOD CONFERENCE OF 1974

In pursuance of the United Nations General Assembly Resolution, the FAO convened a World Food Conference in November, 1974. This conference endorsed the objectives, policies and guidelines set out in the undertaking and urged upon the member-countries to cooperate in bringing it into operation.

INDIA'S STAND

While India supported the objectives, she believed that the operational mechanics of the undertaking needed further consideration. It was pointed out that the undertaking aimed at complementary arrangements for the management of national reserves with a view to meeting the emergency needs of the developing countries. The Indian representative made a strong plea that governments of major cereal producing, consuming and trading countries be invited to participate in negotiations to establish international grain reserves, to be located on strategic points that would bring about a greater degree of stability in the market for grains.

This suggestion received wide support and finally the following paragraph was included :

> "Invites governments of all major food, primarily cereals, producing, consuming, and trading countries to enter as soon as possible into discussion in appropriate international fora, with a view to accelerating the implementation of the principles contained in the proposed International Undertaking on World Food Security, and also with a view to studying the feasibility of establishing grain reserves to be located at strategic points."

The reference to "grain reserves" is to national reserves. At the instance of several developing countries the resolution provided for technical, financial, and food assistance to develop and implement appropriate national food stock policies in developing countries, including extension of storage and transport facilities.

COMMITTEE ON WORLD FOOD SECURITY

A Committee on World Food Security was set up towards the close of 1975. It has a special relationship with the World Food Council which is the decision-making body on matters concerning World Food Security. This Committee is required to—

(a) keep the current and prospective demand, supply and stock position for basic foodstuffs under continuous review ;
(b) make periodic evaluation of the adequacy of current and prospective stock levels, in aggregate, in exporting and importing countries ;
(c) review the steps taken by governments to implement the International Undertaking on World Food Security ; and
(d) recommend such short-term and long-term policy action as may be considered necessary.

At its first meeting in April 1976, India suggested the following measures :

(a) the concept of minimum safe level of carry over stocks should be accepted at 17-18 per cent of annual world consumption ;
(b) national stock policies of developed countries should be formulated and production permitting, implemented by the end of 1977 ;
(c) the international grain arrangements should *inter alia* contain provisions of reasonable range of minimum and maximum prices and there should be an obligation on the developed exporting countries to sell minimum quantities of foodgrains to developing countries when prices move towards the agreed maximum ;
(d) a world reserve stock at a level of 5-6 per cent of consumption should be maintained with a possible mechanism for international management and supervision ;
(e) the target of food aid should be enhanced ; and
(f) provisions for financial/food assistance for developing countries be made to build up their stocks.

ASSESSMENT OF THE SITUATION

The World Food Council had at the same time made an assessment of the total food requirements in the coming decades, based on the projected trends of production and population. For the developing countries the increase in the demand for foodgrains was estimated at 3.3 per cent per annum over a thirty-year period stretching from 1970 to the end of the century. Against this projected increase, the disturbing fact highlighted by the council was that the best growth rate in agricultural production was 2.8 per cent achieved during the decade 1960-70, while during 1970-75 this rate came down to 2.5 per cent. Even if these countries somehow succeed in maintaining the average general growth of 2.8 per cent, food gap of developing countries will increase to 85 million tonnes by 1985 because of growth in population and incomes. This projection was based on the assumption of normal conditions ; the gap would be much larger in years of short crops.

The FAO Council had already suggested a minimum safe level of world carry over stocks for cereals within a range of 17-18 per cent of world consumption. Of this total, the reserve element was suggested at 5-6 per cent, the rest working or pipeline stock. India pointed out that the estimates were on the low side as they provided for meeting the risks of only one major production shortfall and not of two successive shortfalls. It further assumed complete accessibility to the reserve wherever held which more often than not would not be the case.

NEGOTIATING CONFERENCE OF THE UNCTAD

Since this new approach to the question of World Food Security, having multifarious facets, impinged on policy questions relating to production policies, trade on government and private account and problems relating to transportation, it was felt that the overall consideration of these matters should appropriately be done in the United Nations Conference on Trade and Development. Accordingly a Negotiating Conference of the UNCTAD was set up which, in its first meeting in February 1978, considered the draft International Agreement. Differences on many important points continued to persist and the Negotiating Conference could not finalize the draft. At the suggestion of the Chairman of the Conference, it was decided that an Interim Committee consisting of Argentina, Australia, Brazil, Canada, Egypt, the EEC, Finland, India, Japan, Kenya, the USSR and the USA should be set up to continue the discussions and attempt reconciliation of the different points of view on the outstanding issues.

The Committee on World Food Security held its third session in April 1978 and applied itself to the outstanding matters pertaining to the world food security. Being assailed by the distress and suffering caused by the famine in the Sahelian zone and other parts of Africa it made an urgent appeal to provide aid to the famine stricken areas. The committee observed that the only basis of food security in the long run could be increasing food production and from this basic hypothesis, it recommended :

(a) the developing countries should adopt and strengthen policies calculated to provide incentive to the producers to increase the food production ;
(b) the aid-giving countries should support the above policies and programmes of the developing countries ;
(c) all countries who are in a position to do so should take steps to achieve the target of 10 million tonnes of food aid in

cereals and 50 million tonnes under the International Emergency Food Reserve so as to make these two important instruments of World Food Security operational ;

(d) member-countries should by the end of 1978 define and adopt national stock policies and targets ; and

(e) member-countries should endeavour to implement the policies referred to above by the end of 1979.

The committee made recommendations relating to mutual consultations, exchange of information, and support to vital programmes with common objectives. The committee also reviewed the pending issues pertaining to the International Grains Arrangement and recommended :

(a) the size of the reserve stocks should be determined at an adequate level so as to ensure that requirements in times of shortages owing to widespread crop failures or natural disasters are met ;

(b) suitable provisions for giving international assistance to developing countries for building up the reserves and creating infrastructure, therefore, should be included in the agreement ;

(c) the price range should be examined in such a manner that the developing countries are in a position to satisfy their import requirements without adverse effects on their economic development ; and

(d) the interests of the producers should also be borne in mind while determining the price range.

The Interim Committee met four times during the period May to October 1978 to resolve the differences which had come to persist at the Negotiating Conference. The basic issues on which the differences persisted were the supply and purchase commitments, whether or not there should be maximum/minimum prices and their range, the size of reserve stock and its distribution among the countries and assistance to developing countries for discharging their stockholding obligations. Nothing came out of these discussions except that the member countries stated their respective positions on the outstanding issues and decided to remit them to the Negotiating Conference. The Interim Committee prepared drafts of the Wheat Trade

Convention, the Coarse Grains Trade Convention and the Food Aid Convention containing alternative draft provisions reflecting the respective position of the importing and exporting countries and forwarded them to the Negotiating Conference. The Conference met in Geneva in November 1978 for nearly three weeks in which the differences were narrowed down to three subjects, (a) size of the reserve stock, (b) price range and (c) assistance to developing countries.

On the first point, India advocated a reserve stock of 30 million tonnes which was tacitly supported by one or two exporting countries also. But the EEC was vociferous in opposing it and suggested that the size should be around 15-17 million tonnes. As regards the last point there was a general consensus of opinion that assistance should be given to developing countries to build up their infrastructure for implementing national stockholding policies and discharging their obligations under the international system. The developed countries, however, took the line that such assistance should be channelized on bilateral or even multilateral basis and there was no need to incorporate formal provisions in the agreement. They vehemently opposed India's suggestion to create a fund under the international agreement to which contributions were to be made by the member countries and out of which the assistance was to be given to the developing countries.

Price range with a trigger mechanism constituted by far the most controversial subject. India took the initiative in proposing a price range to govern the various action points and suggested $80 per tonne as the lower price signifying the accumulation point and $160 per tonne as the upper level when release operations from the international reserve should commence. The exporting countries did not accept this range and suggested a range of $140-200. The differences were quite basic and continued to persist and the Conference finally adjourned without reaching any agreement on these issues. While adjourning, the Conference authorized the Chairman to reconvene the Interim Committee to further discuss the matters and work out agreed solutions of the outstanding issues whereafter the Negotiating Conference could meet again.

The Interim Committee met in December 1978 and after further narrowing down the differences, recommended to the Secretary General of UNCTAD to reconvene the Negotiating Conference. The Conference met for the third time in January-February 1979 without achieving any success in resolving the differences on the above mentioned three subjects. There was a general feeling that further bilateral and multilateral consultations were needed among major wheat exporting and importing countries to create a suitable climate for reaching an agreement on price mechanism. The Conference accordingly adjourned and the International Wheat Council was asked to take steps for extending the 1971 Agreement beyond June 1979 and at the same time continue exploring possibilities on resolving the outstanding issues and come up with a proposal for reconvening the Negotiating Conference at the appropriate time.

D.G.'S ACTION PLAN

The Committee on World Food Security continued with its deliberations and held its fourth session in Rome from April 5 to 11, 1979. Besides examining the pending questions, it took up for consideration the following five point 'plan of action' suggested by Dr. Edouard Saouma, Director General of the FAO :

(a) adoption of reserve stock policies by the member countries ;
(b) prescribing criteria for management and release of national stocks held in pursuance of the undertaking ;
(c) devising special measures to assist low income deficit countries to meet current import requirements and emergency needs ;
(d) suggesting special arrangements for food security assistance ; and
(e) collective self-reliance of developing countries.

Dr. Saouma made it clear that the plan of action was no substitute for the new international grains agreement with substantive provisions relating to stock levels, prices, and food aid provisions as well as special provisions for developing countries. It was only intended to channelize the efforts of the world community in the desired direction pending conclusion of the international agreement.

The Committee approved and recommended the five-point action plan of the Director General for adoption by the member-countries. The Committee laid considerable emphasis on the information system which should be built up by the FAO Secretariat with the cooperation of all countries, particularly the centrally planned economies. It said that, to improve the flow of data specially from regions vulnerable to crop failure, governments of developing countries should set up or strengthen national early warning and crop forecasting systems using whatever information was readily available.

The Committee agreed that in order to improve the assessment of world food security and the adequacy of stocks, the long term trends and prospects regarding production, consumption and trade in basic foods should be analysed. Attention should be paid to the underlying causes of the sharp rise in the cereal imports of the developing countries. The committee also suggested that a closer study of the role of non-cereal foods in world food security should be made and the estimates of stock movements in the USSR and China should be studied for improving the analysis of world food security.

INTERNATIONAL WHEAT AGREEMENT

The efforts of the various world bodies to design an international grains agreement represent a process to capture and reintroduce a historical development that preceded them. The first International Wheat Agreement was drawn up in 1949. This was revised and renewed in 1953, 1956, 1959 and 1962. Upto this time, the agreement was in respect of wheat alone and the objectives in general terms were :

(a) to assure supplies of wheat and wheat-flour to importing countries and markets for wheat and wheat-flour to exporting countries at equitable and stable prices;
(b) to promote the expansion of the international trade in wheat and wheat-flour and to secure the freest possible flow of this trade in the interests of both exporting and importing countries ;
(c) to overcome the serious hardship caused to producers and consumers by burdensome surpluses and critical shortages of wheat ;
(d) to encourage the use and consumption of wheat and wheat-flour generally, in particular in developing countries, so as to improve health and nutrition in those countries and thus to assist in their development ; and

(e) in general to further international cooperation in connection with world wheat problems, recognizing the relationship of the trade in wheat to the economic stability of markets for other agricultural products.

SPECIAL FEATURES OF 1962 AGREEMENT

The International Wheat Agreement of 1962 for the first time made a distinction between commercial purchases and special transactions. The former was defined as a purchase both on government as well as private trade account conforming to the usual commercial practices in international trade while the latter was defined as a transaction not conforming with the usual commercial practices, such as:

(a) sales on credit in which as a result of government intervention the interest rate, period of payment or other terms do not conform with the commercial rates, periods or terms prevailing in the world market ;
(b) sales for which funds have been obtained from the exporting countries specifically earmarked for the transaction ;
(c) sales for currency of the importing country which is not convertible or transferable into the currency or goods of the exporting country ;
(d) sales under trade agreements with special payment arrangements ;
(e) barter transactions ;
(f) a gift of wheat or purchase out of a grant made by the exporting country for that special purpose ; and
(g) any other categories of transaction which deviate from the normal commercial practices as may be determined by the International Wheat Council.

This agreement further introduced a new system of regulating the sale within certain price ranges. Article 6 laid down the basic minimum and maximum prices for the duration of the agreement with all the necessary clarifications and Article 4 required each importing country to purchase not less than the percentage specified for that country in Annexure A to the Agreement of its total commercial purchases in any crop year from exporting countries at prices within the price range. Exporting countries were also obliged to make wheat available for purchase by importing countries in quantities sufficient to satisfy their commercial requirements within the price range. If the Council made a 'maximum price declaration' in respect of an exporting country under Article 13, that country shall make available for purchase by importing countries at not greater than the maximum price, its balance of commitment towards the importing countries with the safeguard that the balance of entitlement of any single importing country with respect to all exporting countries was not exceeded. Similar provisions were enacted in case the maximum price declaration was made in respect of all or some of the exporting countries, regulating the purchases by the importing countries in the aforesaid manner.

Part III of the Agreement (Articles 9 to 12) contained important provisions relating to adjustments to be made in situations of short crops, balance of payment or monetary difficulties and additional purchases in times of critical needs. In case of short crops, and upon an intimation being given by the exporting country to the Council, the adjustment was, in the first instance, to be made by reducing the obligation of the country concerned. Simultaneously, the Council would increase the commitments of other exporting countries as represented by the datum quantities determined under Article 15 to the extent agreed to by each of them. If such increases did not offset the relief given to the country who reported short crop, the import entitlements were next to be reduced, again with reference to the datum quantities and to the extent agreed by the countries concerned. If these measures failed to offset the relief given to the exporting countries, the Council could, as a final measure, reduce *pro rata* the entitlements of all the importing countries as represented by the datum quantities.

Similarly when an importing country faced a critical situation of food shortage, it could send an appeal to the Council for assistance in obtaining supplies and upon the receipt of such an appeal the Council would give urgent consideration to it and make appropriate recommendations to the exporting countries regarding action to be taken by them.

The Agreement contained detailed provisions for consultations and convening of the Council meeting in situations when maximum price declarations had been made or when the minimum price came to prevail. In brief, the 1962 agreement provided as comprehensive a mechanism for regulating wheat trade amongst member countries as was practicable at that time, taking care of all conceivable situations having a bearing on wheat trade. The system of reporting the transactions, their evaluation and studies in the growth of wheat trade and consumption and the annual review of the world wheat situation were all provided for in the Agreement, as indeed they were in the earlier agreements. Thus the entire conspectus of wheat economy was covered by the International Wheat Agreement of 1962.

1967 AGREEMENT

In June 1967, the principal exporting countries, namely, Argentina, Australia, Canada, Denmark, Finland, Japan, Norway, Sweden, Switzerland, the U.K., the U.S.A. and the EEC agreed to negotiate an agreement on grains on as wide a basis as possible. It was decided for the first time that the agreement should be in two parts—one, containing the convention relating to the wheat trade and the other relating to food aid. These two parts were to constitute two legal instruments which should be ratified by the member countries separately. The article defining the objectives was materially altered, in that, clauses (c) and (d) of the 1962 agreement were dropped. These clauses related to the disposal of surpluses, tackling of hardships in times of critical shortages of wheat, and encouraging consumption of wheat particularly in developing countries for improving nutritional standards. But the basic mechanism of the minimum and maximum prices and the obligations under the maximum price declaration or the prices approaching the minimum as also adjustments to be made in times of short crop or balance of payment difficulties or in case of purchases in critical times were, by and large, retained as in the previous agreement. However, certain new features were introduced. Supply commitments of the exporting countries on commercial account were set out in clear terms, while in the event of maximum price declaration the importing countries were given the liberty of purchasing wheat from any other source without this being regarded as any breach of the agreement. In regard to the minimum and maximum price, a number of varieties of wheat grown and exported by the principal exporting countries namely Canada, the USA, Argentina, Australia, theEEC, Sweden, Greece and Spain and their prices were set out, whereas in the 1962 agreement only one minimum and one maximum price was mentioned on a global basis. This was a distinct improvement over the earlier agreement inasmuch as it introduced a considerable degree of flexibility. Other provisions related to the establishment of datum quantities, recording and reporting, consultations, annual review of wheat availability, etc. were retained. A new article entitled "Guide-lines Relating to Concessional Transactions" was incorporated stipulating that the member coun'ries should ensure that concessional transactions were additional to commercial sale and that mutual consultation with exporting countries whose commercial sales might be affected by such concessional transactions shall be done.

FOOD AID CONVENTION

In the Food Aid Convention a total of 4.2 million tonnes of grain was committed by the following countries :

	percentage	*'000 M.T.*
United States	42.0	1,890
Canada	11.0	495
Australia	5.0	225
Argentina	0.5	23
E.E.C.	23.0	1.035
United Kingdom	5.0	225
Switzerland	0.7	32
Sweden	1.2	54
Denmark	0.6	27
Norway	0.3	14
Finland	0.3	14
Japan	5.0	225

A country wishing to make the whole or a part of its contribution in terms of cash could do so and its share was to be calculated by evaluating the quantity determined for that country at the prescribed rate. This aid could be supplied on the following terms :

(a) sales for the currency of the importing country which is not transferable and is not convertible into currency or goods and services for use by the contributing country ; and/or

(b) a gift of grain or a monetary grant used to purchase grain for the importing country.

Grain purchases under the aid convention were to be only from the participating countries. The Convention took steps to facilitate the grain exports of developing member countries—the countries being the members of the International Grains Arrangement of 1967. However a ceiling was imposed on this method of obtaining aid by inserting a provision to the effect that not less than 25 per cent of the cash contribution to purchase grain for food aid or that part of such contribution required to purchase 0.2 million metric tons of grain shall be used to purchase grain produced in developing countries. It was also prescribed that contributions in the form of grains shall be placed in f.o.b. forward position by the donor countries. The donor countries could, in respect of their contribution, specify a recipient country or countries.

1971 AGREEMENT

The International Grains Arrangement of 1967 was enacted for a period of five years ending June 1971. While drafting the 1971 Agreement a basic change was introduced in the system. Almost the entire Part II (Commercial) of the 1967 Arrangement containing the minimum/maximum prices and their role, adjustments in case of short crop or balance of payment difficulties, etc., was deleted. The substantive provisions incorporated in the 1962 Agreement and further refined in 1967, were dropped. The 1971 Agreement, which is in force, is really left with only routine provisions such as recording and reporting of transactions, estimates of requirements and availability of wheat, mutual consultations, disputes and complaints, and annual review of the world wheat situation. Only future historians will tell whether deletion of these provisions was a step backwards at a time when the world is desperately searching for a mechanism of food security.

PRESENT DIFFICULTIES

If a new international grains agreement has not yet been concluded and if a food security system still eludes the world community, it is perhaps indicative of the complex and diverse interests of the exporting and importing (or of the developed and developing) countries and of the supremacy of commerce over the concept of security. During the informal consultations among the members of the Interim

Committee in June 1979 when the annual meeting of the International Wheat Council took place, new problems were pointed out by the exporting countries. It was not enough, they said, that there should be adequate stocks with the surplus countries, but what was crucially important was that the means should be easily available for transporting these stocks to the places where they were needed. They argued that the transport bottlenecks were so considerable that serious attention was required to be paid to solve them. Apart from physical constraints, freight rates have also gone up substantially in recent times because of the energy crisis. These costs are indeed so high that transporting foodgrains to deficit areas makes them altogether costly.

Further argument of the exporting countries was that there was a complete change in the relativity of demand and supply of foodgrains in the world. While an overall fall in the production of foodgrains to the extent of 30 to 35 million tonnes was expected over the 1978 level production, there were large demands from USSR and China which were impinging on the market. The result was that the prices were going up sharply and speculative conditions continued to prevail in the market. In a situation like this when prices were showing an upward trend, they said, it would not be realistic to expect the exporting countries to bind themselves to a price range according to which international trade in wheat should take place. The exporting countries were successful in finally persuading the Council to adopt a resolution asking the Executive Secretary to prepare a detailed paper on the transport problems. The importing countries felt that the focus of attention had been shifted from the basic questions besetting the conclusion of the new international grains agreement.

On the food aid issue, the present convention has fixed a minimum of 4.2 million tonnes whereas the World Food Conference had fixed it at 10 million tonnes. This target was endorsed and adopted by all international bodies. In subsequent discussions in 1980 amongst the member countries on the International Wheat Agreement, additional commitments were made taking the total to 7.6 million tonnes. But a number of contributing countries revised their commitments to the previous lower figures as the Negotiating Conference did not succeed in establishing a new wheat trade convention. The United States and Sweden, however, announced that they would honour their commitments for enhanced quantities as from

1979. Today what appears to be a fairly certain minimum of the food aid level is slightly less than 6.8 million tonnes.

EMERGENCY RESERVE

The World Food Council has been endeavouring to perfect two mechanisms for dealing with emergencies. One is the international emergency reserve which is already in existence and whose target is currently fixed at 0.5 million tonnes. Annual allocations, however, are still below this level. The World Food Council and the Committee on Food Security of the FAO have considered this level to be insufficient for the magnitude of the problem facing the world community. The Council proposed before the Fifth Ministerial Conference at Ottawa in September 1979 that the target be enhanced to 0.75 million tonnes, to be effective from 1981. This proposal, however, did not materialize.

The other mechanism is of a financial nature to be operated with the help of the International Monetary Fund. The idea is to provide some kind of food security insurance scheme for low income food deficit countries under which it would be possible for countries facing balance of payment difficulties to draw foreign exchange to finance their import of cereals in excess of value. The World Bank and the IMF gave their concurrence to this scheme, and the IMF's financing facility for cereal imports was set up in May 1981 for an initial four years period. Experience of the past two years has revealed certain limitations. For one, this facility covers only loans for the financing of reserves under international agreements which explicitly include the main world exporters and importers. Secondly, once a member country has used its quota under the compensatory financing facility to cover shortfalls in its export earnings, its drawings, for cereal imports are limited to merely 25 per cent of the quota. Obviously, there is need for some flexibility in this scheme.

WORLD FOOD PROGRAMME

The WFP have developed an innovative approach whereby a group of donors and agencies are supporting a five-year programme in Mali to restructure her foodgrain marketing and support production incentives. Funds generated from the sale of commodities are being used to subsidize procurement and distribution of grain, combined with technical assistance—the final goal being food security.

D.G.'S INITIATIVE

The most significant development in this evolutionary process of world food security has been a comprehensive review by the D.G. FAO, Dr. Saouma, of the concept of world food security and the framework of the various international institutions dealing with food issues. In a major policy paper* prepared for the eighth session of the Committee on World Food Security held in April 1983, the Director General, Dr. Edouard Saouma redefined the components of food security and proposed a new approach for the 1980s. In this review it was stated that the trends of the past eight years indicate that the growth has been on a cyclic pattern of surpluses and shortages. The food self-sufficiency of the developing countries has fallen and the basic causes of insecurity remain. Food reserve programmes have been initiated in 72 countries—including 60 developing countries. The United States has set up a wheat reserve of 4 million tonnes to meet emergency needs the world over, and large national buffer stocks built by major food deficit countries, viz., China, India, Indonesia and Japan, have contributed to world food security. Taking an overall view, the review concludes, the concept of world food security has established itself as a permanent landscape of our times.

A new dimension has been added to the concept—elimination of chronic malnutrition as the ultimate goal of the strategy for food security. The conceptual frame should accordingly include board policy issues relating to agricultural and rural development, food production, improved access to stocks and international trade. Dr. Saouma has therefore, proposed a new concept so as to cover the various dimensions and components of food security thus :

(i) the ultimate objective of world food security should be to ensure that all people at all times have both physical and economic access to the basic food they need ;

(ii) food security should have three specific aims, namely ensuring production of adequate food supplies ; maximizing stability in the flow of supplies ; and securing access to

*CFS: 83/4 December, 1982, Food and Agriculture Organisation of the United Nations, Rome. (Para. 112)

available supplies on the part of those who need them ; and

(iii) action will be needed on a wide front including all factors that have a bearing on the capacity of both countries and people to produce or purchase food. While cereals will continue to be the main focus of attention, the action should cover all basic foodstuffs necessary for health. Agricultural and rural development, food production, food reserves, the functioning of national and international cereal markets, the foreign exchange needs of importing countries, trade liberalization and export earnings, the purchasing power of the poorest strata of the population, financial resources and technical assistance, the flow of food aid and arrangements to meet emergency needs; these are some, but by no means all, of the specific areas where action is needed to enhance food security.

In designing and executing national food security programmes, many developing countries will need multilateral and/or bilateral aid. Such assistance should be well matched as between its three main components (financial aid, food aid, and technical expertise) and fully integrated with the resources available locally.

This according to Dr. Saouma should be the strategy for the 1980s and specific measures at national, regional and international levels should be undertaken to realize the goal of world food security.

SUMMING UP

We have reached the end of this brief review of developments in the global dimensions of food security. To a casual observer it would appear that the efforts to lay down a dependable and universally acceptable model of food security have failed. It cannot, however, be denied that these efforts have succeeded in creating an awareness, a sensitivity towards the global need of food security. The World Food Conference had suggested a growth ratio of food production in the developing countries if the basic tenets of food security were to be realized. This target is yet to be achieved. In Africa, food production is not increasing as fast as the population and hence per capita production today is less than what it was 10 years ago.

According to a review of world food production, investment and trade presented to the Fifth Ministerial Session of the World

Food Council held at Ottawa in September 1979, it was stated that dependence on food imports by the developing countries has increased from 32 million tonnes annually in 1962-64 to 77 million tonnes in 1977-78. The trends show that this figure will reach 145 million tonnes by 1990. The outlook for poor countries would almost certainly get worse unless their own food production increases sharply ; there are more hungry people today, than in 1974 when the World Food Conference was held for the first time. One billion people are affected by hunger and malnutrition; nearly half of them are victims of serious malnutrition. The world must produce enough foodgrains to feed an additional 72 million people every year. These are some of the stark and appalling facts highlighted by the review.

In a world comprising sovereign states and governed by dominant national interests, international systems grow gradually and with apparent lack of swift executive action. But they have the seeds of future growth ; they have potential of developing into systems of universal application. International bodies work through a system of consensus, composing differences and trying to achieve the widest area of agreement. A world system designed to serve a definite purpose emerges slowly but definitely. This has been the history of the United Nations and its allied organizations. So it is with the evolution of the world food security system. Humanity has to live on hope and survive through mutual help and cooperation. The first basic principle of world food security has been firmly established that in matters of food, commerce and enlightened sense of mutual help have to go together ; in grave emergencies, the former has to be subordinated to the latter. This is a great achievement of the FAO and other international bodies dealing with these and kindred issues.

The quest for world food security as well as for a mechanism that will ensure it goes on.

APPENDIX

INTERNATIONAL UNDERTAKING ON WORLD FOOD SECURITY

COMMON PURPOSE AND RESPONSIBILITY

GOVERNMENTS adhering to this Undertaking, taking account of Resolution 3/73 adopted by the seventeenth session of the FAO conference, recognize that that assurance of world food security is a common responsibility of the entire international community. They therefore, undertake to cooperate in doing their utmost to ensure the availability at all times of adequate world supplies of basic foodstuffs, primarily cereals, so as to avoid acute food shortages in the event of widespread crop failures or natural disasters, sustain a steady expansion of production and reduce fluctuations in production and prices.

Recognizing that food security needs to be tackled from several sides, especially through strengthening the food production base of developing countries, appropriate national stock policies, food aid programmes, and other measures including long term trade agreements, governments undertake to adopt national and international measures to ensure an accelerated growth of food production, as appropriate, and in particular to assist the developing countries which are highly vulnerable to crop fluctuations and where there are increasing consumption requirements.

As regards stockholding policies, all governments, in conformity with their institutional and constitutional requirements should :

(a) adopt policies concerning cereal stocks* which take into account the policies of other countries and would result in maintaining a minimum safe level of basic cereal stocks for the world as a whole ;

(b) review or establish, or take measures aimed at establishing, stock targets or objectives which have the purpose of maintaining stocks of cereals in the country or in the

*The term 'stocks' means the supply of cereals carried over in stock at the end of the marketing year of the country concerned.

interested groups of countries concerned at least at the levels regarded as necessary for ensuring continuity of supplies including provision for emergency situations in case of crop failure of natural disaster ;*

(c) take measures aimed at ensuring stocks are replenished as soon as feasible, whenever they have been drawn down below such minimum levels to meet food shortages.

In periods of acute food shortages, nations holding stocks in excess of minimum safe levels for meeting domestic needs and emergencies undertake to make such supplies available for export at reasonable terms.

GUIDELINES FOR ESTABLISHING AND HOLDING STOCKS

In establishing, reviewing and/or adjusting national stock policies and desirable minimum stock levels, governments should give consideration to the following guidelines, which are understood as a framework within which each country would develop its own stock policies according to its circumstances :

(a) vulnerability to crop failure owing to drought, floods or other natural hazards, and extent of resulting shortfalls in national cereals output ;
(b) the size of normal annual requirements for domestic consumption and where applicable for export ;
(c) the degree of dependence in normal conditions on imports of cereals and the scale of possible emergency import requirements in relation to the average level of world trade of the product concerned ;
(d) the period of time required for imports to be arranged and delivered to the country in periods of emergency or sudden domestic shortage, and for internal transportation to centres of consumption ;
(e) the period of time likely to be required to expand cereal production sufficiently to replenish stocks if these are drawn down to meet food shortages ;

---

*It is recognized that some of the major exporting countries of grains and specially rice are developing countries which lack the capital resources required to maintain stocks beyond current requirements.

(f) the proportion of national supplies entering commercial market channels ;

(g) the requirements of any government distribution programme of foodgrains to vulnerable sections of the population ;

(h) the desirability of locating stocks in a manner and place which ensure that the cereals are available for delivery when and where they are most likely to be required; and which with the available storage and transport facilities minimise the financial costs involved and also, where appropriate, facilitate urgent shipments to recipient countries in the shortest possible time ;

(i) pledge to World Food Programme and other international food aid programmes and allocations for bilateral food aid programmes, including specific pledges for national and regional stock building ;

(j) maintaining a regular flow of supplies at reasonable prices to meet foreseeable variations in demand from importing countries ;

(k) the possibility of an interruption in the flow of imported supplies by events outside the government's control (dock strike in exporting country, shipping difficulties, etc.) ; and

(l) the special position of developing countries as set out in Part IV below.

The special difficulties of a number of developing countries in maintaining national stocks at desirable minimum levels place an added responsibility on the rest of the international community for ensuring world food security. Governments should take this into account in fixing their stock targets or objectives, and should where possible earmark stocks or funds for meeting international emergency requirements.

NECESSARY SAFEGUARDS

Bearing in mind the serious problems which have arisen in the past owing to the accumulation and disposal of large agriculture surpluses, full consideration should be given by governments to the possible repercussions on the structure of production and trade which might arise from implementing the world food security policy. Governments should continue in this respect to observe the principles and consultative obligations as developed within the FAO and the consultative sub-committee on Surplus Disposal which may be amended and extended as necessary. To this end :

(a) all countries should endeavour to arrange their national food stock policies in ways which avoid adverse effects on the structure of production or international trade, paying particular attention to the interests of developing countries heavily dependent on food exports ; and
(b) governments should recognize the need to promote the efficient use of world agricultural resources and consider measures designed to afford producers adequate protection against the effects on world prices of accumulation, retention and release of stocks held as a result of this Undertaking.

SPECIAL ASSISTANCE TO DEVELOPING COUNTRIES

To promote the effective participation of developing countries in this Undertaking, in order to achieve the objectives of world food security, it is imperative to ensure the adequate availability of cereals and accordingly an acceleration of the rate of growth of their agricultural production. Such an increase requires a constant review by the developing countries of their overall agricultural production policies and the various alternative courses they may follow as well as the active support of the international community in the development programmes of the developing countries within the context of their national development priorities. The concerned international financial and technical organizations, the developed and other potential contributor countries should urgently take the necessary measures to enable the developing countries to obtain the required financial, technical and material assistance and in particular fertilizers and other inputs needed to increase their agricultural production.

Continued reliance would also need to be placed on bilateral food aid programmes and the World Food Programme for meeting shortages which cannot be covered through normal commercial trade, as well as unforeseen shortages and emergency situations.

International assistance also has an important role in providing food aid and financial assistance on soft terms or in grant form for meeting the minimum requirements of cereals and the maintenance of stocks, and particularly emergency stocks, in the developing countries for research on the development of storage facilities suited to conditions in these countries, and in furnishing advice on stock and related policies within the context of national development programmes. Developed countries and other potential contributors as well as the international and regional development agencies concerned should give additional assistance in identifying and mobilizing the resources required by developing countries for these purposes.

As regards the WFP in particular, the degree to which it can assist developing countries by providing food aid for national reserves is severely restricted by its resource position and its priorities. Governments should, therefore, consider making additional resources available to the WFP, to enable the programme to play its role to the fullest possible extent in assisting developing countries to achieve food security as well as in emergency operations.

INFORMATION SYSTEM

The effective functioning of the world food security system will depend greatly on the availability of timely and adequate information. Government members of FAO should furnish to the Director General on a regular basis all the available information on national stock levels, government stockholding programmes and policies, current and prospective export availabilities and import requirements for cereals, and relevant aspects of the supply and demand situation, as well as on assistance provided to the food production programmes in developing countries. Other governments should be invited to provide similar information. In order to avoid unfavourable market repercussions in particular, the Director General of FAO should ensure, where so requested by a government, that the data supplied by that government to the Information System are made available on a restricted basis only to the governments adhering to the Undertaking.

To keep all governments directly informed of current developments in the international cereal position during periods when world supplies are scarce the Director General of FAO should prepare, on a quarterly basis or more frequently, concise factual appraisals of the situation and outlook which should be circulated promptly to governments.

In the assembly and analysis of information and statistics, the Director General of FAO should seek the assistance of the

International Wheat Council and other inter-governmental organisations concerned.

INTER-GOVERNMENTAL CONSULTATION

The adequacy of world cereal production and stocks should be kept under continuing review, so that timely action can be taken to maintain world food security. For this purpose, the governments adhering to this Undertaking should, with the assistance of FAO and other concerned inter-governmental organizations consult together to :

(a) review the progress in accelerating cereals productions in developing countries and the assistance provided to them for this purpose, particularly in regard to the supply of essential agricultural inputs;
(b) make periodic evaluations of the adequacy of current and prospective stock levels, in aggregate in exporting and importing countries, for assuring a regular flow of supplies of cereals to meet requirements in domestic and world markets, including food aid requirements, in times of short crops and serious crop failure; account should be taken of the considerations set out in the guidelines; and
(c) examine such short term and longer term policy action as considered necessary to remedy any difficulty foreseen in assuring adequate cereal supplies for minimum world food security.

PROVISION FOR REVIEW OF THE UNDERTAKING

This Undertaking, including arrangements and guidelines, may have to be revised, particularly if future international negotiations lead to the assumption by governments of specific commitments substantially affecting the Undertaking.

Index